The GNU Emacs Lisp Reference Manual: Volume 2

The
GNU Emacs Lisp
Reference Manual

GNU Emacs Version 19.29
for Unix Users

Edition 2.4, June 1995

Volume 2

by Bil Lewis, Dan LaLiberte,
and the GNU Manual Group

Edition 2.4
Revised for Emacs Version 19.29,
June, 1995.

ISBN 1-882114-71-X

Published by the Free Software Foundation
59 Temple Place, Suite 330
Boston, MA 02111-1307 USA

Cover art by Etienne Suvasa.

Short Contents

Volume 1

Volume 2

Table of Contents

Volume 1

Volume 2

21 Documentation

GNU Emacs Lisp has convenient on-line help facilities, most of which derive their information from the documentation strings associated with functions and variables. This chapter describes how to write good documentation strings for your Lisp programs, as well as how to write programs to access documentation.

Note that the documentation strings for Emacs are not the same thing as the Emacs manual. Manuals have their own source files, written in the Texinfo language; documentation strings are specified in the definitions of the functions and variables they apply to. A collection of documentation strings is not sufficient as a manual because a good manual is not organized in that fashion; it is organized in terms of topics of discussion.

21.1 Documentation Basics

A documentation string is written using the Lisp syntax for strings, with double-quote characters surrounding the text of the string. This is because it really is a Lisp string object. The string serves as documentation when it is written in the proper place in the definition of a function or variable. In a function definition, the documentation string follows the argument list. In a variable definition, the documentation string follows the initial value of the variable.

When you write a documentation string, make the first line a complete sentence (or two complete sentences) since some commands, such as `apropos`, show only the first line of a multi-line documentation string. Also, you should not indent the second line of a documentation string, if you have one, because that looks odd when you use C-h f (`describe-function`) or C-h v (`describe-variable`). See Section A.3 [Documentation Tips], page 317.

Documentation strings may contain several special substrings, which stand for key bindings to be looked up in the current keymaps when the documentation is displayed. This allows documentation strings to refer to the keys for related commands and be accurate even when a user rearranges the key bindings. (See Section 21.2 [Accessing Documentation], page 2.)

Within the Lisp world, a documentation string accessible through the function or variable that it describes:

- The documentation for a function is stored in the function definition itself (see Section 11.2 [Lambda Expressions], page 158, vol. 1). The function `documentation` knows how to extract it.

- The documentation for a variable is stored in the variable's property list under the property name `variable-documentation`. The function `documentation-property` knows how to extract it.

To save space, the documentation for preloaded functions and variables (including primitive functions and autoloaded functions) is stored in the file 'emacs/etc/DOC-*version*'. The documentation for functions and variables loaded during the Emacs session from byte-compiled files is stored in those files (see Section 14.3 [Docs and Compilation], page 196, vol. 1).

The data structure inside Emacs has an integer offset into the file, or a list containing a string and an integer, in place of the documentation string. The functions documentation and documentation-property use that information to read the documentation from the appropriate file; this is transparent to the user.

For information on the uses of documentation strings, see section "Help" in *The GNU Emacs Manual*.

The 'emacs/lib-src' directory contains two utilities that you can use to print nice-looking hardcopy for the file 'emacs/etc/DOC-*version*'. These are 'sorted-doc.c' and 'digest-doc.c'.

21.2 Access to Documentation Strings

documentation-property *symbol property* &optional   Function
         verbatim
   This function returns the documentation string that is recorded *symbol*'s property list under property *property*. It retrieves the text from a file if necessary, and runs substitute-command-keys to substitute actual key bindings. (This substitution is not done if *verbatim* is non-nil; the *verbatim* argument exists only as of Emacs 19.)

```
(documentation-property 'command-line-processed
    'variable-documentation)
     ⇒ "t once command line has been processed"
(symbol-plist 'command-line-processed)
     ⇒ (variable-documentation 188902)
```

documentation *function* &optional *verbatim*   Function
   This function returns the documentation string of *function*. It reads the text from a file if necessary. Then (unless *verbatim* is non-nil) it calls substitute-command-keys, to return a value containing the actual (current) key bindings.

   The function documentation signals a void-function error if *function* has no function definition. However, it is ok if the function definition has no documentation string. In that case, documentation returns nil.

   Here is an example of using the two functions, documentation and documentation-property, to display the documentation strings for several symbols in a '*Help*' buffer.

```
(defun describe-symbols (pattern)
  "Describe the Emacs Lisp symbols matching PATTERN.
All symbols that have PATTERN in their name are described
in the '*Help*' buffer."
  (interactive "sDescribe symbols matching: ")
  (let ((describe-func
          (function
           (lambda (s)
             ;; Print description of symbol.
             (if (fboundp s)                    ; It is a function.
                 (princ
                  (format "%s\t%s\n%s\n\n" s
                    (if (commandp s)
                        (let ((keys (where-is-internal s)))
                          (if keys
                              (concat
                               "Keys: "
                               (mapconcat 'key-description
                                          keys " "))
                            "Keys: none"))
                      "Function")
                    (or (documentation s)
                        "not documented"))))

             (if (boundp s)                    ; It is a variable.
                 (princ
                  (format "%s\t%s\n%s\n\n" s
                    (if (user-variable-p s)
                        "Option " "Variable")
                    (or (documentation-property
                         s 'variable-documentation)
                        "not documented")))))))
         sym-list)
    ;; Build a list of symbols that match pattern.
    (mapatoms (function
               (lambda (sym)
                 (if (string-match pattern (symbol-name sym))
                     (setq sym-list (cons sym sym-list))))))
    ;; Display the data.
    (with-output-to-temp-buffer "*Help*"
      (mapcar describe-func (sort sym-list 'string<))
      (print-help-return-message))))
```

The `describe-symbols` function works like `apropos`, but provides more
information.

```
(describe-symbols "goal")

---------- Buffer: *Help* ----------
goal-column      Option
*Semipermanent goal column for vertical motion, as set by C-x C-n, or nil.

set-goal-column Command: C-x C-n
Set the current horizontal position as a goal for C-n and C-p.
```

```
Those commands will move to this position in the line moved to
rather than trying to keep the same horizontal position.
With a non-nil argument, clears out the goal column
so that C-n and C-p resume vertical motion.
The goal column is stored in the variable 'goal-column'.

temporary-goal-column    Variable
Current goal column for vertical motion.
It is the column where point was
at the start of current run of vertical motion commands.
When the 'track-eol' feature is doing its job, the value is 9999.
---------- Buffer: *Help* ----------
```

Snarf-documentation *filename*   Function

This function is used only during Emacs initialization, just before the
runnable Emacs is dumped. It finds the file offsets of the documentation strings stored in the file *filename*, and records them in the in-core
function definitions and variable property lists in place of the actual
strings. See Section B.1 [Building Emacs], page 323.

Emacs finds the file *filename* in the 'emacs/etc' directory. When the
dumped Emacs is later executed, the same file is found in the directory
doc-directory. Usually *filename* is "DOC-*version*".

doc-directory   Variable

This variable holds the name of the directory which should contion
the file "DOC-*version*" that contains documentation strings for built-in
and preloaded functions and variables.

In most cases, this is the same as data-directory. They may be
different when you run Emacs from the directory where you built it,
without actually installing it. See data-directory in Section 21.5
[Help Functions], page 6.

In older Emacs versions, exec-directory was used for this.

21.3 Substituting Key Bindings in Documentation

When documentation strings refer to key sequences, they should use the
current, actual key bindings. They can do so using certain special text
sequences described below. Accessing documentation strings in the usual
way substitutes current key binding information for these special sequences.
This works by calling substitute-command-keys. You can also call that
function yourself.

Here is a list of the special sequences and what they mean:

\[*command*]

> stands for a key sequence that will invoke *command*, or 'M-x
> *command*' if *command* has no key bindings.

\{*mapvar*}

        stands for a summary of the value of *mapvar*, which should be a keymap. The summary is made by `describe-bindings`.

\<*mapvar*>

        stands for no text itself. It is used for a side effect: it specifies *mapvar* as the keymap for any following '\[*command*]' sequences in this documentation string.

Please note: Each '\' must be doubled when written in a string in Emacs Lisp.

substitute-command-keys *string*   Function

    This function scans *string* for the above special sequences and replaces them by what they stand for, returning the result as a string. This permits display of documentation that refers accurately to the user's own customized key bindings.

    Here are examples of the special sequences:

```
(substitute-command-keys
    "To abort recursive edit, type: \\[abort-recursive-edit]")
⇒ "To abort recursive edit, type: C-]"

(substitute-command-keys
    "The keys that are defined for the minibuffer here are:
  \\{minibuffer-local-must-match-map}")
⇒ "The keys that are defined for the minibuffer here are:

?               minibuffer-completion-help
SPC             minibuffer-complete-word
TAB             minibuffer-complete
LFD             minibuffer-complete-and-exit
RET             minibuffer-complete-and-exit
C-g             abort-recursive-edit
"

(substitute-command-keys
    "To abort a recursive edit from the minibuffer, type\
\\<minibuffer-local-must-match-map>\\[abort-recursive-edit].")
⇒ "To abort a recursive edit from the minibuffer, type C-g."
```

21.4 Describing Characters for Help Messages

    These functions convert events, key sequences or characters to textual descriptions. These descriptions are useful for including arbitrary text characters or key sequences in messages, because they convert non-printing and whitespace characters to sequences of printing characters. The description of a non-whitespace printing character is the character itself.

key-description *sequence*   Function
> This function returns a string containing the Emacs standard notation
> for the input events in *sequence*. The argument *sequence* may be a
> string, vector or list. See Section 18.5 [Input Events], page 285, vol. 1,
> for more information about valid events. See also the examples for
> `single-key-description`, below.

single-key-description *event*   Function
> This function returns a string describing *event* in the standard Emacs
> notation for keyboard input. A normal printing character appears as
> itself, but a control character turns into a string starting with 'C-',
> a meta character turns into a string starting with 'M-', and space,
> linefeed, etc. appear as 'SPC', 'LFD', etc. A function key symbol appears
> as itself. An event that is a list appears as the name of the symbol in
> the CAR of the list.
>
> ```
> (single-key-description ?\C-x)
>      ⇒ "C-x"
> (key-description "\C-x \M-y \n \t \r \f123")
>      ⇒ "C-x SPC M-y SPC LFD SPC TAB SPC RET SPC C-l 1 2 3"
> (single-key-description 'C-mouse-1)
>      ⇒ "C-mouse-1"
> ```

text-char-description *character*   Function
> This function returns a string describing *character* in the standard
> Emacs notation for characters that appear in text—like `single-key-
> description`, except that control characters are represented with a
> leading caret (which is how control characters in Emacs buffers are
> usually displayed).
>
> ```
> (text-char-description ?\C-c)
>      ⇒ "^C"
> (text-char-description ?\M-m)
>      ⇒ "M-m"
> (text-char-description ?\C-\M-m)
>      ⇒ "M-^M"
> ```

21.5 Help Functions

Emacs provides a variety of on-line help functions, all accessible to the
user as subcommands of the prefix C-h. For more information about them,
see section "Help" in *The GNU Emacs Manual*. Here we describe some
program-level interfaces to the same information.

apropos *regexp* &optional *do-all predicate*   Command
> This function finds all symbols whose names contain a match for the
> regular expression *regexp*, and returns a list of them (see Section 30.2

[Regular Expressions], page 193). It also displays the symbols in a buffer named '*Help*', each with a one-line description.

If *do-all* is non-`nil`, then `apropos` also shows key bindings for the functions that are found.

If *predicate* is non-`nil`, it should be a function to be called on each symbol that has matched *regexp*. Only symbols for which *predicate* returns a non-`nil` value are listed or displayed.

In the first of the following examples, `apropos` finds all the symbols with names containing 'exec'. In the second example, it finds and returns only those symbols that are also commands. (We don't show the output that results in the '*Help*' buffer.)

```
(apropos "exec")
    ⇒ (Buffer-menu-execute command-execute exec-directory
    exec-path execute-extended-command execute-kbd-macro
    executing-kbd-macro executing-macro)
(apropos "exec" nil 'commandp)
    ⇒ (Buffer-menu-execute execute-extended-command)
```

The command `C-h a` (`command-apropos`) calls `apropos`, but specifies a *predicate* to restrict the output to symbols that are commands. The call to `apropos` looks like this:

```
(apropos string t 'commandp)
```

super-apropos *regexp* &optional *do-all*   Command
    This function differs from `apropos` in that it searches documentation strings as well as symbol names for matches for *regexp*. By default, it searches the documentation strings only for preloaded functions and variables. If *do-all* is non-`nil`, it scans the names and documentation strings of all functions and variables.

help-map   Variable
    The value of this variable is a local keymap for characters following the Help key, `C-h`.

help-command   Prefix Command
    This symbol is not a function; its function definition is actually the keymap known as `help-map`. It is defined in 'help.el' as follows:

```
(define-key global-map "\C-h" 'help-command)
(fset 'help-command help-map)
```

print-help-return-message &optional *function*   Function
    This function builds a string that explains how to restore the previous state of the windows after a help command. After building the message, it applies *function* to it if *function* is non-`nil`. Otherwise it calls `message` to display it in the echo area.

This function expects to be called inside a `with-output-to-temp-buffer` special form, and expects `standard-output` to have the value bound by that special form. For an example of its use, see the long example in Section 21.2 [Accessing Documentation], page 2.

help-char   *Variable*

The value of this variable is the help character—the character that Emacs recognizes as meaning Help. By default, it is 8, which is `C-h`. When Emacs reads this character, if `help-form` is non-`nil` Lisp expression, it evaluates that expression, and displays the result in a window if it is a string.

Usually the value of `help-form`'s value is `nil`. Then the help character has no special meaning at the level of command input, and it becomes part of a key sequence in the normal way. The standard key binding of `C-h` is a prefix key for several general-purpose help features.

The help character is special after prefix keys, too. If it has no binding as a subcommand of the prefix key, it runs `describe-prefix-bindings`, which displays a list of all the subcommands of the prefix key.

help-form   *Variable*

If this variable is non-`nil`, its value is a form to evaluate whenever the character `help-char` is read. If evaluating the form produces a string, that string is displayed.

A command that calls `read-event` or `read-char` probably should bind `help-form` to a non-`nil` expression while it does input. (The exception is when `C-h` is meaningful input.) Evaluating this expression should result in a string that explains what the input is for and how to enter it properly.

Entry to the minibuffer binds this variable to the value of `minibuffer-help-form` (see Section 17.8 [Minibuffer Misc], page 272, vol. 1).

prefix-help-command   *Variable*

This variable holds a function to print help for a prefix character. The function is called when the user types a prefix key followed by the help character, and the help character has no binding after that prefix. The variable's default value is `describe-prefix-bindings`.

describe-prefix-bindings   *Function*

This function calls `describe-bindings` to display a list of all the subcommands of the prefix key of the most recent key sequence. The prefix described consists of all but the last event of that key sequence. (The last event is, presumably, the help character.)

The following two functions are found in the library 'helper'. They are
for modes that want to provide help without relinquishing control, such as
the "electric" modes. You must load that library with (require 'helper)
in order to use them. Their names begin with 'Helper' to distinguish them
from the ordinary help functions.

Helper-describe-bindings   Command
This command pops up a window displaying a help buffer containing
a listing of all of the key bindings from both the local and global
keymaps. It works by calling describe-bindings.

Helper-help   Command
This command provides help for the current mode. It prompts the
user in the minibuffer with the message 'Help (Type ? for further
options)', and then provides assistance in finding out what the key
bindings are, and what the mode is intended for. It returns nil.

This can be customized by changing the map Helper-help-map.

data-directory   Variable
This variable holds the name of the directory in which Emacs finds
certain documentation and text files that come with Emacs. In older
Emacs versions, exec-directory was used for this.

make-help-screen *fname help-line help-text help-map*   Macro
This macro defines a help command named *fname* that acts like a
prefix key that shows a list of the subcommands it offers.

When invoked, *fname* displays *help-text* in a window, then reads and
executes a key sequence according to *help-map*. The string *help-text*
should describe the bindings available in *help-map*.

The command *fname* is defined to handle a few events itself, by
scrolling the display of *help-text*. When *fname* reads one of those special events, it does the scrolling and then reads another event. When
it reads an event that is not one of those few, and which has a binding
in *help-map*, it executes that key's binding and then returns.

The argument *help-line* should be a single-line summary of the alternatives in *help-map*. In the current version of Emacs, this argument
is used only if you set the option three-step-help to t.

three-step-help   User Option
If this variable is non-nil, commands defined with make-help-screen
display their *help-line* strings in the echo area at first, and display the
longer *help-text* strings only if the user types the help character again.

22 Files

In Emacs, you can find, create, view, save, and otherwise work with files and file directories. This chapter describes most of the file-related functions of Emacs Lisp, but a few others are described in Chapter 24 [Buffers], page 55, and those related to backups and auto-saving are described in Chapter 23 [Backups and Auto-Saving], page 45.

Many of the file functions take one or more arguments that are file names. A file name is actually a string. Most of these functions expand file name arguments using `expand-file-name`, so that '~' is handled correctly, as are relative file names (including '../'). These functions don't recognize environment variable substitutions such as '$HOME'. See Section 22.8.4 [File Name Expansion], page 32.

22.1 Visiting Files

Visiting a file means reading a file into a buffer. Once this is done, we say that the buffer is *visiting* that file, and call the file "the visited file" of the buffer.

A file and a buffer are two different things. A file is information recorded permanently in the computer (unless you delete it). A buffer, on the other hand, is information inside of Emacs that will vanish at the end of the editing session (or when you kill the buffer). Usually, a buffer contains information that you have copied from a file; then we say the buffer is visiting that file. The copy in the buffer is what you modify with editing commands. Such changes to the buffer do not change the file; therefore, to make the changes permanent, you must *save* the buffer, which means copying the altered buffer contents back into the file.

In spite of the distinction between files and buffers, people often refer to a file when they mean a buffer and vice-versa. Indeed, we say, "I am editing a file," rather than, "I am editing a buffer that I will soon save as a file of the same name." Humans do not usually need to make the distinction explicit. When dealing with a computer program, however, it is good to keep the distinction in mind.

22.1.1 Functions for Visiting Files

This section describes the functions normally used to visit files. For historical reasons, these functions have names starting with 'find-' rather than 'visit-'. See Section 24.4 [Buffer File Name], page 59, for functions and variables that access the visited file name of a buffer or that find an existing buffer by its visited file name.

In a Lisp program, if you want to look at the contents of a file but not alter it, the fastest way is to use `insert-file-contents` in a temporary buffer. Visiting the file is not necessary and takes longer. See Section 22.3 [Reading from Files], page 17.

find-file *filename*   Command
    This command selects a buffer visiting the file *filename*, using an existing buffer if there is one, and otherwise creating a new buffer and reading the file into it. It also returns that buffer.

    The body of the `find-file` function is very simple and looks like this:

```
(switch-to-buffer (find-file-noselect filename))
```

    (See `switch-to-buffer` in Section 25.7 [Displaying Buffers], page 78.)

    When `find-file` is called interactively, it prompts for *filename* in the minibuffer.

find-file-noselect *filename*   Function
    This function is the guts of all the file-visiting functions. It finds or creates a buffer visiting the file *filename*, and returns it. It uses an existing buffer if there is one, and otherwise creates a new buffer and reads the file into it. You may make the buffer current or display it in a window if you wish, but this function does not do so.

    When `find-file-noselect` uses an existing buffer, it first verifies that the file has not changed since it was last visited or saved in that buffer. If the file has changed, then this function asks the user whether to reread the changed file. If the user says 'yes', any changes previously made in the buffer are lost.

    If `find-file-noselect` needs to create a buffer, and there is no file named *filename*, it displays the message 'New file' in the echo area, and leaves the buffer empty.

    The `find-file-noselect` function calls `after-find-file` after reading the file (see Section 22.1.2 [Subroutines of Visiting], page 13). That function sets the buffer major mode, parses local variables, warns the user if there exists an auto-save file more recent than the file just visited, and finishes by running the functions in `find-file-hooks`.

    The `find-file-noselect` function returns the buffer that is visiting the file *filename*.

```
(find-file-noselect "/etc/fstab")
     ⇒ #<buffer fstab>
```

find-file-other-window *filename*   Command
    This command selects a buffer visiting the file *filename*, but does so in a window other than the selected window. It may use another ex-

isting window or split a window; see Section 25.7 [Displaying Buffers], page 78.

When this command is called interactively, it prompts for *filename*.

find-file-read-only *filename*   Command
This command selects a buffer visiting the file *filename*, like `find-file`, but it marks the buffer as read-only. See Section 24.7 [Read Only Buffers], page 63, for related functions and variables.

When this command is called interactively, it prompts for *filename*.

view-file *filename*   Command
This command visits *filename* in View mode, and displays it in a recursive edit, returning to the previous buffer when done. View mode is a mode that allows you to skim rapidly through the file but does not let you modify it. Entering View mode runs the normal hook `view-mode-hook`. See Section 20.4 [Hooks], page 360, vol. 1.

When `view-file` is called interactively, it prompts for *filename*.

find-file-hooks   Variable
The value of this variable is a list of functions to be called after a file is visited. The file's local-variables specification (if any) will have been processed before the hooks are run. The buffer visiting the file is current when the hook functions are run.

This variable works just like a normal hook, but we think that renaming it would not be advisable.

find-file-not-found-hooks   Variable
The value of this variable is a list of functions to be called when `find-file` or `find-file-noselect` is passed a nonexistent file name. `find-file-noselect` calls these functions as soon as it detects a nonexistent file. It calls them in the order of the list, until one of them returns non-nil. `buffer-file-name` is already set up.

This is not a normal hook because the values of the functions are used and they may not all be called.

22.1.2 Subroutines of Visiting

The `find-file-noselect` function uses the `create-file-buffer` and `after-find-file` functions as subroutines. Sometimes it is useful to call them directly.

create-file-buffer *filename*   Function
This function creates a suitably named buffer for visiting *filename*, and returns it. It uses *filename* (sans directory) as the name if that name

is free; otherwise, it appends a string such as '`<2>`' to get an unused name. See also Section 24.9 [Creating Buffers], page 65.

Please note: `create-file-buffer` does *not* associate the new buffer with a file and does not select the buffer. It also does not use the default major mode.

```
(create-file-buffer "foo")
     ⇒ #<buffer foo>
(create-file-buffer "foo")
     ⇒ #<buffer foo<2>>
(create-file-buffer "foo")
     ⇒ #<buffer foo<3>>
```

This function is used by `find-file-noselect`. It uses `generate-new-buffer` (see Section 24.9 [Creating Buffers], page 65).

after-find-file &optional *error warn*   Function
This function sets the buffer major mode, and parses local variables (see Section 20.1.3 [Auto Major Mode], page 347, vol. 1). It is called by `find-file-noselect` and by the default revert function (see Section 23.3 [Reverting], page 53).

If reading the file got an error because the file does not exist, but its directory does exist, the caller should pass a non-`nil` value for *error*. In that case, `after-find-file` issues a warning: '`(New File)`'. For more serious errors, the caller should usually not call `after-find-file`.

If *warn* is non-`nil`, then this function issues a warning if an auto-save file exists and is more recent than the visited file.

The last thing `after-find-file` does is call all the functions in `find-file-hooks`.

22.2 Saving Buffers

When you edit a file in Emacs, you are actually working on a buffer that is visiting that file—that is, the contents of the file are copied into the buffer and the copy is what you edit. Changes to the buffer do not change the file until you *save* the buffer, which means copying the contents of the buffer into the file.

save-buffer &optional *backup-option*   Command
This function saves the contents of the current buffer in its visited file if the buffer has been modified since it was last visited or saved. Otherwise it does nothing.

`save-buffer` is responsible for making backup files. Normally, *backup-option* is `nil`, and `save-buffer` makes a backup file only if this is the first save since visiting the file. Other values for *backup-option* request the making of backup files in other circumstances:

- With an argument of 4 or 64, reflecting 1 or 3 C-u's, the `save-buffer` function marks this version of the file to be backed up when the buffer is next saved.
- With an argument of 16 or 64, reflecting 2 or 3 C-u's, the `save-buffer` function unconditionally backs up the previous version of the file before saving it.

save-some-buffers &optional *save-silently-p exiting*   Command
> This command saves some modified file-visiting buffers. Normally it asks the user about each buffer. But if *save-silently-p* is non-`nil`, it saves all the file-visiting buffers without querying the user.
>
> The optional *exiting* argument, if non-`nil`, requests this function to offer also to save certain other buffers that are not visiting files. These are buffers that have a non-`nil` local value of `buffer-offer-save`. (A user who says yes to saving one of these is asked to specify a file name to use.) The `save-buffers-kill-emacs` function passes a non-`nil` value for this argument.

buffer-offer-save   Variable
> When this variable is non-`nil` in a buffer, Emacs offers to save the buffer on exit even if the buffer is not visiting a file. The variable is automatically local in all buffers. Normally, Mail mode (used for editing outgoing mail) sets this to `t`.

write-file *filename*   Command
> This function writes the current buffer into file *filename*, makes the buffer visit that file, and marks it not modified. Then it renames the buffer based on *filename*, appending a string like '`<2>`' if necessary to make a unique buffer name. It does most of this work by calling `set-visited-file-name` and `save-buffer`.

write-file-hooks   Variable
> The value of this variable is a list of functions to be called before writing out a buffer to its visited file. If one of them returns non-`nil`, the file is considered already written and the rest of the functions are not called, nor is the usual code for writing the file executed.
>
> If a function in `write-file-hooks` returns non-`nil`, it is responsible for making a backup file (if that is appropriate). To do so, execute the following code:
>
> ```
> (or buffer-backed-up (backup-buffer))
> ```
>
> You might wish to save the file modes value returned by `backup-buffer` and use that to set the mode bits of the file that you write. This is what `save-buffer` normally does.

Even though this is not a normal hook, you can use `add-hook` and `remove-hook` to manipulate the list. See Section 20.4 [Hooks], page 360, vol. 1.

local-write-file-hooks   Variable
> This works just like `write-file-hooks`, but it is intended to be made local to particular buffers. It's not a good idea to make `write-file-hooks` local to a buffer—use this variable instead.
>
> The variable is marked as a permanent local, so that changing the major mode does not alter a buffer-local value. This is convenient for packages that read "file" contents in special ways, and set up hooks to save the data in a corresponding way.

write-contents-hooks   Variable
> This works just like `write-file-hooks`, but it is intended for hooks that pertain to the contents of the file, as opposed to hooks that pertain to where the file came from. Such hooks are usually set up by major modes, as buffer-local bindings for this variable. Switching to a new major mode always resets this variable.

after-save-hook   Variable
> This normal hook runs after a buffer has been saved in its visited file.

file-precious-flag   Variable
> If this variable is non-`nil`, then `save-buffer` protects against I/O errors while saving by writing the new file to a temporary name instead of the name it is supposed to have, and then renaming it to the intended name after it is clear there are no errors. This procedure prevents problems such as a lack of disk space from resulting in an invalid file.
>
> As a side effect, backups are necessarily made by copying. See Section 23.1.2 [Rename or Copy], page 46. Yet, at the same time, saving a precious file always breaks all hard links between the file you save and other file names.
>
> Some modes set this variable non-`nil` locally in particular buffers.

require-final-newline   User Option
> This variable determines whether files may be written out that do *not* end with a newline. If the value of the variable is `t`, then `save-buffer` silently adds a newline at the end of the file whenever the buffer being saved does not already end in one. If the value of the variable is non-`nil`, but not `t`, then `save-buffer` asks the user whether to add a newline each time the case arises.

If the value of the variable is `nil`, then `save-buffer` doesn't add newlines at all. `nil` is the default value, but a few major modes set it to `t` in particular buffers.

22.3 Reading from Files

You can copy a file from the disk and insert it into a buffer using the `insert-file-contents` function. Don't use the user-level command `insert-file` in a Lisp program, as that sets the mark.

insert-file-contents *filename* &optional *visit beg end*   Function
         replace
This function inserts the contents of file *filename* into the current buffer after point. It returns a list of the absolute file name and the length of the data inserted. An error is signaled if *filename* is not the name of a file that can be read.

The function `insert-file-contents` checks the file contents against the defined file formats, and converts the file contents if appropriate. See Section 22.12 [Format Conversion], page 40. It also calls the functions in the list `after-insert-file-functions`; see Section 29.18.7 [Saving Properties], page 185.

If *visit* is non-`nil`, this function additionally marks the buffer as unmodified and sets up various fields in the buffer so that it is visiting the file *filename*: these include the buffer's visited file name and its last save file modtime. This feature is used by `find-file-noselect` and you probably should not use it yourself.

If *beg* and *end* are non-`nil`, they should be integers specifying the portion of the file to insert. In this case, *visit* must be `nil`. For example,

```
(insert-file-contents filename nil 0 500)
```

inserts the first 500 characters of a file.

If the argument *replace* is non-`nil`, it means to replace the contents of the buffer (actually, just the accessible portion) with the contents of the file. This is better than simply deleting the buffer contents and inserting the whole file, because (1) it preserves some marker positions and (2) it puts less data in the undo list.

If you want to pass a file name to another process so that another program can read the file, use the function `file-local-copy`; see Section 22.11 [Magic File Names], page 37.

22.4 Writing to Files

You can write the contents of a buffer, or part of a buffer, directly to a file on disk using the `append-to-file` and `write-region` functions. Don't use these functions to write to files that are being visited; that could cause confusion in the mechanisms for visiting.

append-to-file *start end filename*   Command
  This function appends the contents of the region delimited by *start* and *end* in the current buffer to the end of file *filename*. If that file does not exist, it is created. This function returns `nil`.

  An error is signaled if *filename* specifies a nonwritable file, or a nonexistent file in a directory where files cannot be created.

write-region *start end filename &optional append visit*   Command
  This function writes the region delimited by *start* and *end* in the current buffer into the file specified by *filename*.

  If *start* is a string, then `write-region` writes or appends that string, rather than text from the buffer.

  If *append* is non-`nil`, then the specified text is appended to the existing file contents (if any).

  If *visit* is `t`, then Emacs establishes an association between the buffer and the file: the buffer is then visiting that file. It also sets the last file modification time for the current buffer to *filename*'s modtime, and marks the buffer as not modified. This feature is used by `save-buffer`, but you probably should not use it yourself.

  If *visit* is a string, it specifies the file name to visit. This way, you can write the data to one file (*filename*) while recording the buffer as visiting another file (*visit*). The argument *visit* is used in the echo area message and also for file locking; *visit* is stored in `buffer-file-name`. This feature is used to implement `file-precious-flag`; don't use it yourself unless you really know what you're doing.

  The function `write-region` converts the data which it writes to the appropriate file formats specified by `buffer-file-format`. See Section 22.12 [Format Conversion], page 40. It also calls the functions in the list `write-region-annotate-functions`; see Section 29.18.7 [Saving Properties], page 185.

  Normally, `write-region` displays a message 'Wrote file *filename*' in the echo area. If *visit* is neither `t` nor `nil` nor a string, then this message is inhibited. This feature is useful for programs that use files for internal purposes, files that the user does not need to know about.

22.5 File Locks

When two users edit the same file at the same time, they are likely to interfere with each other. Emacs tries to prevent this situation from arising by recording a *file lock* when a file is being modified. Emacs can then detect the first attempt to modify a buffer visiting a file that is locked by another Emacs job, and ask the user what to do.

File locks do not work properly when multiple machines can share file systems, such as with NFS. Perhaps a better file locking system will be implemented in the future. When file locks do not work, it is possible for two users to make changes simultaneously, but Emacs can still warn the user who saves second. Also, the detection of modification of a buffer visiting a file changed on disk catches some cases of simultaneous editing; see Section 24.6 [Modification Time], page 61.

file-locked-p *filename*   Function
This function returns `nil` if the file *filename* is not locked by this Emacs process. It returns `t` if it is locked by this Emacs, and it returns the name of the user who has locked it if it is locked by someone else.

```
(file-locked-p "foo")
     ⇒ nil
```

lock-buffer &optional *filename*   Function
This function locks the file *filename*, if the current buffer is modified. The argument *filename* defaults to the current buffer's visited file. Nothing is done if the current buffer is not visiting a file, or is not modified.

unlock-buffer   Function
This function unlocks the file being visited in the current buffer, if the buffer is modified. If the buffer is not modified, then the file should not be locked, so this function does nothing. It also does nothing if the current buffer is not visiting a file.

ask-user-about-lock *file other-user*   Function
This function is called when the user tries to modify *file*, but it is locked by another user named *other-user*. The value it returns determines what happens next:

- A value of `t` says to grab the lock on the file. Then this user may edit the file and *other-user* loses the lock.
- A value of `nil` says to ignore the lock and let this user edit the file anyway.
- This function may instead signal a `file-locked` error, in which case the change that the user was about to make does not take place.

The error message for this error looks like this:

> ⎹error⎸ `File is locked:` *file* *other-user*

where `file` is the name of the file and *other-user* is the name of the user who has locked the file.

The default definition of this function asks the user to choose what to do. If you wish, you can replace the `ask-user-about-lock` function with your own version that decides in another way. The code for its usual definition is in 'userlock.el'.

22.6 Information about Files

The functions described in this section all operate on strings that designate file names. All the functions have names that begin with the word 'file'. These functions all return information about actual files or directories, so their arguments must all exist as actual files or directories unless otherwise noted.

22.6.1 Testing Accessibility

These functions test for permission to access a file in specific ways.

file-exists-p *filename*   Function
   This function returns t if a file named *filename* appears to exist. This does not mean you can necessarily read the file, only that you can find out its attributes. (On Unix, this is true if the file exists and you have execute permission on the containing directories, regardless of the protection of the file itself.)

   If the file does not exist, or if fascist access control policies prevent you from finding the attributes of the file, this function returns nil.

file-readable-p *filename*   Function
   This function returns t if a file named *filename* exists and you can read it. It returns nil otherwise.

```
(file-readable-p "files.texi")
    ⇒ t
(file-exists-p "/usr/spool/mqueue")
    ⇒ t
(file-readable-p "/usr/spool/mqueue")
    ⇒ nil
```

file-executable-p *filename*   Function
   This function returns t if a file named *filename* exists and you can execute it. It returns nil otherwise. If the file is a directory, execute

permission means you can check the existence and attributes of files
inside the directory, and open those files if their modes permit.

file-writable-p *filename*   Function
    This function returns t if the file *filename* can be written or created by
you, and nil otherwise. A file is writable if the file exists and you can
write it. It is creatable if it does not exist, but the specified directory
does exist and you can write in that directory.

    In the third example below, 'foo' is not writable because the parent
directory does not exist, even though the user could create such a
directory.

```
(file-writable-p "~/foo")
     ⇒ t
(file-writable-p "/foo")
     ⇒ nil
(file-writable-p "~/no-such-dir/foo")
     ⇒ nil
```

file-accessible-directory-p *dirname*   Function
    This function returns t if you have permission to open existing files in
the directory whose name as a file is *dirname*; otherwise (or if there
is no such directory), it returns nil. The value of *dirname* may be
either a directory name or the file name of a directory.

    Example: after the following,

```
(file-accessible-directory-p "/foo")
     ⇒ nil
```

we can deduce that any attempt to read a file in '/foo/' will give an
error.

file-ownership-preserved-p *filename*   Function
    This function returns t if deleting the file *filename* and then creating
it anew would keep the file's owner unchanged.

file-newer-than-file-p *filename1* *filename2*   Function
    This function returns t if the file *filename1* is newer than file *filename2*.
If *filename1* does not exist, it returns nil. If *filename2* does not exist,
it returns t.

    In the following example, assume that the file 'aug-19' was written
on the 19th, 'aug-20' was written on the 20th, and the file 'no-file'
doesn't exist at all.

```
(file-newer-than-file-p "aug-19" "aug-20")
     ⇒ nil
```

```
(file-newer-than-file-p "aug-20" "aug-19")
     ⇒ t
(file-newer-than-file-p "aug-19" "no-file")
     ⇒ t
(file-newer-than-file-p "no-file" "aug-19")
     ⇒ nil
```

You can use `file-attributes` to get a file's last modification time as a list of two numbers. See Section 22.6.4 [File Attributes], page 23.

22.6.2 Distinguishing Kinds of Files

This section describes how to distinguish various kinds of files, such as directories, symbolic links, and ordinary files.

file-symlink-p *filename*   Function
If the file *filename* is a symbolic link, the `file-symlink-p` function returns the file name to which it is linked. This may be the name of a text file, a directory, or even another symbolic link, or it may be a nonexistent file name.

If the file *filename* is not a symbolic link (or there is no such file), `file-symlink-p` returns `nil`.

```
(file-symlink-p "foo")
     ⇒ nil
(file-symlink-p "sym-link")
     ⇒ "foo"
(file-symlink-p "sym-link2")
     ⇒ "sym-link"
(file-symlink-p "/bin")
     ⇒ "/pub/bin"
```

file-directory-p *filename*   Function
This function returns `t` if *filename* is the name of an existing directory, `nil` otherwise.

```
(file-directory-p "~rms")
     ⇒ t
(file-directory-p "~rms/lewis/files.texi")
     ⇒ nil
(file-directory-p "~rms/lewis/no-such-file")
     ⇒ nil
(file-directory-p "$HOME")
     ⇒ nil
```

```
(file-directory-p
 (substitute-in-file-name "$HOME"))
     ⇒ t
```

file-regular-p *filename*   Function

This function returns t if the file *filename* exists and is a regular file (not a directory, symbolic link, named pipe, terminal, or other I/O device).

22.6.3 Truenames

The *truename* of a file is the name that you get by following symbolic links until none remain, then expanding to get rid of '.' and '..' as components. Strictly speaking, a file need not have a unique truename; the number of distinct truenames a file has is equal to the number of hard links to the file. However, truenames are useful because they eliminate symbolic links as a cause of name variation.

file-truename *filename*   Function

The function `file-truename` returns the true name of the file *filename*. This is the name that you get by following symbolic links until none remain. The argument must be an absolute file name.

See Section 24.4 [Buffer File Name], page 59, for related information.

22.6.4 Other Information about Files

This section describes the functions for getting detailed information about a file, other than its contents. This information includes the mode bits that control access permission, the owner and group numbers, the number of names, the inode number, the size, and the times of access and modification.

file-modes *filename*   Function

This function returns the mode bits of *filename*, as an integer. The mode bits are also called the file permissions, and they specify access control in the usual Unix fashion. If the low-order bit is 1, then the file is executable by all users, if the second-lowest-order bit is 1, then the file is writable by all users, etc.

The highest value returnable is 4095 (7777 octal), meaning that everyone has read, write, and execute permission, that the SUID bit is set for both others and group, and that the sticky bit is set.

```
(file-modes "~/junk/diffs")
     ⇒ 492                    ; Decimal integer.
(format "%o" 492)
     ⇒ "754"                  ; Convert to octal.
```

```
(set-file-modes "~/junk/diffs" 438)
     ⇒ nil

(format "%o" 438)
     ⇒ "666"                    ; Convert to octal.

% ls -l diffs
  -rw-rw-rw-  1 lewis 0 3063 Oct 30 16:00 diffs
```

file-nlinks *filename*   Function
    This functions returns the number of names (i.e., hard links) that file
filename has. If the file does not exist, then this function returns nil.
Note that symbolic links have no effect on this function, because they
are not considered to be names of the files they link to.

```
% ls -l foo*
-rw-rw-rw-  2 rms        4 Aug 19 01:27 foo
-rw-rw-rw-  2 rms        4 Aug 19 01:27 foo1

(file-nlinks "foo")
     ⇒ 2
(file-nlinks "doesnt-exist")
     ⇒ nil
```

file-attributes *filename*   Function
    This function returns a list of attributes of file *filename*. If the specified
file cannot be opened, it returns nil.

    The elements of the list, in order, are:

0. t for a directory, a string for a symbolic link (the name linked to),
   or nil for a text file.

1. The number of names the file has. Alternate names, also known
   as hard links, can be created by using the add-name-to-file
   function (see Section 22.7 [Changing File Attributes], page 26).

2. The file's UID.

3. The file's GID.

4. The time of last access, as a list of two integers. The first integer
   has the high-order 16 bits of time, the second has the low 16 bits.
   (This is similar to the value of current-time; see Section 34.5
   [Time of Day], page 260.)

5. The time of last modification as a list of two integers (as above).

6. The time of last status change as a list of two integers (as above).

7. The size of the file in bytes.

8. The file's modes, as a string of ten letters or dashes, as in 'ls -l'.

9. t if the file's GID would change if file were deleted and recreated; nil otherwise.

10. The file's inode number.

11. The file system number of the file system that the file is in. This element and the file's inode number together give enough information to distinguish any two files on the system—no two files can have the same values for both of these numbers.

For example, here are the file attributes for 'files.texi':

```
(file-attributes "files.texi")
     ⇒  (nil
         1
         2235
         75
         (8489 20284)
         (8489 20284)
         (8489 20285)
         14906
         "-rw-rw-rw-"
         nil
         129500
         -32252)
```

and here is how the result is interpreted:

nil   is neither a directory nor a symbolic link.

1   has only one name (the name 'files.texi' in the current default directory).

2235   is owned by the user with UID 2235.

75   is in the group with GID 75.

(8489 20284)
            was last accessed on Aug 19 00:09. Unfortunately, you cannot convert this number into a time string in Emacs.

(8489 20284)
            was last modified on Aug 19 00:09.

(8489 20285)
            last had its inode changed on Aug 19 00:09.

14906   is 14906 characters long.

"-rw-rw-rw-"
            has a mode of read and write access for the owner, group, and world.

nil   would retain the same GID if it were recreated.

129500   has an inode number of 129500.

-32252   is on file system number -32252.

22.7 Changing File Names and Attributes

The functions in this section rename, copy, delete, link, and set the modes
of files.

In the functions that have an argument *newname*, if a file by the name
of *newname* already exists, the actions taken depend on the value of the
argument *ok-if-already-exists*:

- Signal a `file-already-exists` error if *ok-if-already-exists* is `nil`.

- Request confirmation if *ok-if-already-exists* is a number.

- Replace the old file without confirmation if *ok-if-already-exists* is any
  other value.

add-name-to-file *oldname newname* &optional   Function
        ok-if-already-exists

This function gives the file named *oldname* the additional name *new-name*. This means that *newname* becomes a new "hard link" to *oldname*.

In the first part of the following example, we list two files, 'foo' and
'foo3'.

```
% ls -l fo*
-rw-rw-rw-  1 rms          29 Aug 18 20:32 foo
-rw-rw-rw-  1 rms          24 Aug 18 20:31 foo3
```

Then we evaluate the form (add-name-to-file "~/lewis/foo"
"~/lewis/foo2"). Again we list the files. This shows two names,
'foo' and 'foo2'.

```
(add-name-to-file "~/lewis/foo1" "~/lewis/foo2")
     ⇒ nil

% ls -l fo*
-rw-rw-rw-  2 rms          29 Aug 18 20:32 foo
-rw-rw-rw-  2 rms          29 Aug 18 20:32 foo2
-rw-rw-rw-  1 rms          24 Aug 18 20:31 foo3
```

Finally, we evaluate the following:

```
(add-name-to-file "~/lewis/foo" "~/lewis/foo3" t)
```

and list the files again. Now there are three names for one file: 'foo',
'foo2', and 'foo3'. The old contents of 'foo3' are lost.

```
(add-name-to-file "~/lewis/foo1" "~/lewis/foo3")
     ⇒ nil
% ls -l fo*
-rw-rw-rw-  3 rms         29 Aug 18 20:32 foo
-rw-rw-rw-  3 rms         29 Aug 18 20:32 foo2
-rw-rw-rw-  3 rms         29 Aug 18 20:32 foo3
```

This function is meaningless on VMS, where multiple names for one file are not allowed.

See also `file-nlinks` in Section 22.6.4 [File Attributes], page 23.

rename-file *filename newname* &optional   Command
     ok-if-already-exists
This command renames the file *filename* as *newname*.

If *filename* has additional names aside from *filename*, it continues to have those names. In fact, adding the name *newname* with `add-name-to-file` and then deleting *filename* has the same effect as renaming, aside from momentary intermediate states.

In an interactive call, this function prompts for *filename* and *newname* in the minibuffer; also, it requests confirmation if *newname* already exists.

copy-file *oldname newname* &optional *ok-if-exists time*   Command
This command copies the file *oldname* to *newname*. An error is signaled if *oldname* does not exist.

If *time* is non-`nil`, then this functions gives the new file the same last-modified time that the old one has. (This works on only some operating systems.)

In an interactive call, this function prompts for *filename* and *newname* in the minibuffer; also, it requests confirmation if *newname* already exists.

delete-file *filename*   Command
This command deletes the file *filename*, like the shell command 'rm *filename*'. If the file has multiple names, it continues to exist under the other names.

A suitable kind of `file-error` error is signaled if the file does not exist, or is not deletable. (On Unix, a file is deletable if its directory is writable.)

See also `delete-directory` in Section 22.10 [Create/Delete Dirs], page 37.

make-symbolic-link *filename newname* &optional   Command
        ok-if-exists

This command makes a symbolic link to *filename*, named *newname*.
This is like the shell command 'ln -s *filename newname*'.

In an interactive call, this function prompts for *filename* and *newname*
in the minibuffer; also, it requests confirmation if *newname* already
exists.

define-logical-name *varname string*   Function

This function defines the logical name *name* to have the value *string*.
It is available only on VMS.

set-file-modes *filename mode*   Function

This function sets mode bits of *filename* to *mode* (which must be an
integer). Only the low 12 bits of *mode* are used.

set-default-file-modes *mode*   Function

This function sets the default file protection for new files created by
Emacs and its subprocesses. Every file created with Emacs initially
has this protection. On Unix, the default protection is the bitwise
complement of the "umask" value.

The argument *mode* must be an integer. Only the low 9 bits of *mode*
are used.

Saving a modified version of an existing file does not count as creating
the file; it does not change the file's mode, and does not use the default
file protection.

default-file-modes   Function

This function returns the current default protection value.

On MS-DOS, there is no such thing as an "executable" file mode bit.
So Emacs considers a file executable if its name ends in '.com', '.bat' or
'.exe'. This is reflected in the values returned by `file-modes` and `file-attributes`.

22.8 File Names

Files are generally referred to by their names, in Emacs as elsewhere. File
names in Emacs are represented as strings. The functions that operate on a
file all expect a file name argument.

In addition to operating on files themselves, Emacs Lisp programs often
need to operate on the names; i.e., to take them apart and to use part
of a name to construct related file names. This section describes how to
manipulate file names.

The functions in this section do not actually access files, so they can operate on file names that do not refer to an existing file or directory.

On VMS, all these functions understand both VMS file-name syntax and Unix syntax. This is so that all the standard Lisp libraries can specify file names in Unix syntax and work properly on VMS without change. On MS-DOS, these functions understand MS-DOS file-name syntax as well as Unix syntax.

22.8.1 File Name Components

The operating system groups files into directories. To specify a file, you must specify the directory and the file's name within that directory. Therefore, Emacs considers a file name as having two main parts: the *directory name* part, and the *nondirectory* part (or *file name within the directory*). Either part may be empty. Concatenating these two parts reproduces the original file name.

On Unix, the directory part is everything up to and including the last slash; the nondirectory part is the rest. The rules in VMS syntax are complicated.

For some purposes, the nondirectory part is further subdivided into the name proper and the *version number*. On Unix, only backup files have version numbers in their names; on VMS, every file has a version number, but most of the time the file name actually used in Emacs omits the version number. Version numbers are found mostly in directory lists.

file-name-directory *filename*   Function
This function returns the directory part of *filename* (or `nil` if *filename* does not include a directory part). On Unix, the function returns a string ending in a slash. On VMS, it returns a string ending in one of the three characters ':', ']', or '>'.

```
(file-name-directory "lewis/foo")   ; Unix example
     ⇒ "lewis/"
(file-name-directory "foo")         ; Unix example
     ⇒ nil
(file-name-directory "[X]FOO.TMP")  ; VMS example
     ⇒ "[X]"
```

file-name-nondirectory *filename*   Function
This function returns the nondirectory part of *filename*.

```
(file-name-nondirectory "lewis/foo")
     ⇒ "foo"
(file-name-nondirectory "foo")
     ⇒ "foo"
```

```
;; The following example is accurate only on VMS.
(file-name-nondirectory "[X]FOO.TMP")
    ⇒ "FOO.TMP"
```

file-name-sans-versions *filename*   Function

This function returns *filename* without any file version numbers, backup version numbers, or trailing tildes.

```
(file-name-sans-versions "~rms/foo.~1~")
    ⇒ "~rms/foo"
(file-name-sans-versions "~rms/foo~")
    ⇒ "~rms/foo"
(file-name-sans-versions "~rms/foo")
    ⇒ "~rms/foo"
;; The following example applies to VMS only.
(file-name-sans-versions "foo;23")
    ⇒ "foo"
```

file-name-sans-extension *filename*   Function

This function returns *filename* minus its "extension," if any. The extension, in a file name, is the part that starts with the last '.' in the last name component. For example,

```
(file-name-sans-extension "foo.lose.c")
    ⇒ "foo.lose"
(file-name-sans-extension "big.hack/foo")
    ⇒ "big.hack/foo"
```

22.8.2 Directory Names

A *directory name* is the name of a directory. A directory is a kind of file, and it has a file name, which is related to the directory name but not identical to it. (This is not quite the same as the usual Unix terminology.) These two different names for the same entity are related by a syntactic transformation. On Unix, this is simple: a directory name ends in a slash, whereas the directory's name as a file lacks that slash. On VMS, the relationship is more complicated.

The difference between a directory name and its name as a file is subtle but crucial. When an Emacs variable or function argument is described as being a directory name, a file name of a directory is not acceptable.

The following two functions convert between directory names and file names. They do nothing special with environment variable substitutions such as '$HOME', and the constructs '~', and '..'.

file-name-as-directory *filename*   Function
  This function returns a string representing *filename* in a form that the operating system will interpret as the name of a directory. In Unix, this means appending a slash to the string. On VMS, the function converts a string of the form '[X]Y.DIR.1' to the form '[X.Y]'.

```
(file-name-as-directory "~rms/lewis")
     ⇒ "~rms/lewis/"
```

directory-file-name *dirname*   Function
  This function returns a string representing *dirname* in a form that the operating system will interpret as the name of a file. On Unix, this means removing a final slash from the string. On VMS, the function converts a string of the form '[X.Y]' to '[X]Y.DIR.1'.

```
(directory-file-name "~lewis/")
     ⇒ "~lewis"
```

Directory name abbreviations are useful for directories that are normally accessed through symbolic links. Sometimes the users recognize primarily the link's name as "the name" of the directory, and find it annoying to see the directory's "real" name. If you define the link name as an abbreviation for the "real" name, Emacs shows users the abbreviation instead.

directory-abbrev-alist   Variable
  The variable `directory-abbrev-alist` contains an alist of abbreviations to use for file directories. Each element has the form (*from . to*), and says to replace *from* with *to* when it appears in a directory name. The *from* string is actually a regular expression; it should always start with '^'. The function `abbreviate-file-name` performs these substitutions.

  You can set this variable in 'site-init.el' to describe the abbreviations appropriate for your site.

  Here's an example, from a system on which file system '/home/fsf' and so on are normally accessed through symbolic links named '/fsf' and so on.

```
(("^/home/fsf" . "/fsf")
 ("^/home/gp" . "/gp")
 ("^/home/gd" . "/gd"))
```

To convert a directory name to its abbreviation, use this function:

abbreviate-file-name *dirname*   Function
  This function applies abbreviations from `directory-abbrev-alist` to its argument, and substitutes '~' for the user's home directory.

22.8.3 Absolute and Relative File Names

All the directories in the file system form a tree starting at the root directory. A file name can specify all the directory names starting from the root of the tree; then it is called an *absolute* file name. Or it can specify the position of the file in the tree relative to a default directory; then it is called a *relative* file name. On Unix, an absolute file name starts with a slash or a tilde ('~'), and a relative one does not. The rules on VMS are complicated.

file-name-absolute-p *filename*   Function

This function returns t if file *filename* is an absolute file name, nil otherwise. On VMS, this function understands both Unix syntax and VMS syntax.

```
(file-name-absolute-p "~rms/foo")
    ⇒ t
(file-name-absolute-p "rms/foo")
    ⇒ nil
(file-name-absolute-p "/user/rms/foo")
    ⇒ t
```

22.8.4 Functions that Expand Filenames

Expansion of a file name means converting a relative file name to an absolute one. Since this is done relative to a default directory, you must specify the default directory name as well as the file name to be expanded. Expansion also simplifies file names by eliminating redundancies such as './' and 'name/../'.

expand-file-name *filename* &optional *directory*   Function

This function converts *filename* to an absolute file name. If *directory* is supplied, it is the directory to start with if *filename* is relative. (The value of *directory* should itself be an absolute directory name; it may start with '~'.) Otherwise, the current buffer's value of default-directory is used. For example:

```
(expand-file-name "foo")
    ⇒ "/xcssun/users/rms/lewis/foo"
(expand-file-name "../foo")
    ⇒ "/xcssun/users/rms/foo"
(expand-file-name "foo" "/usr/spool/")
    ⇒ "/usr/spool/foo"
(expand-file-name "$HOME/foo")
    ⇒ "/xcssun/users/rms/lewis/$HOME/foo"
```

Filenames containing '.' or '..' are simplified to their canonical form:

```
(expand-file-name "bar/../foo")
     ⇒ "/xcssun/users/rms/lewis/foo"
```

'`~/`' is expanded into the user's home directory. A '`/`' or '`~`' following a '`/`' is taken to be the start of an absolute file name that overrides what precedes it, so everything before that '`/`' or '`~`' is deleted. For example:

```
(expand-file-name
 "/a1/gnu//usr/local/lib/emacs/etc/MACHINES")
     ⇒ "/usr/local/lib/emacs/etc/MACHINES"
(expand-file-name "/a1/gnu/~/foo")
     ⇒ "/xcssun/users/rms/foo"
```

In both cases, '`/a1/gnu/`' is discarded because an absolute file name follows it.

Note that `expand-file-name` does *not* expand environment variables; only `substitute-in-file-name` does that.

file-relative-name *filename directory*   Function
This function does the inverse of expansion—it tries to return a relative name that is equivalent to *filename* when interpreted relative to *directory*. (If such a relative name would be longer than the absolute name, it returns the absolute name instead.)

```
(file-relative-name "/foo/bar" "/foo/")
     ⇒ "bar")
(file-relative-name "/foo/bar" "/hack/")
     ⇒ "/foo/bar")
```

default-directory   Variable
The value of this buffer-local variable is the default directory for the current buffer. It should be an absolute directory name; it may start with '`~`'. This variable is local in every buffer.

`expand-file-name` uses the default directory when its second argument is `nil`.

On Unix systems, the value is always a string ending with a slash.

```
default-directory
     ⇒ "/user/lewis/manual/"
```

substitute-in-file-name *filename*   Function
This function replaces environment variables references in *filename* with the environment variable values. Following standard Unix shell syntax, '`$`' is the prefix to substitute an environment variable value.

The environment variable name is the series of alphanumeric characters (including underscores) that follow the '`$`'. If the character following

the '$' is a '{', then the variable name is everything up to the matching
'}'.

Here we assume that the environment variable HOME, which holds the
user's home directory name, has value '/xcssun/users/rms'.

```
(substitute-in-file-name "$HOME/foo")
     ⇒ "/xcssun/users/rms/foo"
```

If a '~' or a '/' appears following a '/', after substitution, everything
before the following '/' is discarded:

```
(substitute-in-file-name "bar/~/foo")
     ⇒ "~/foo"
(substitute-in-file-name "/usr/local/$HOME/foo")
     ⇒ "/xcssun/users/rms/foo"
```

On VMS, '$' substitution is not done, so this function does nothing on
VMS except discard superfluous initial components as shown above.

22.8.5 Generating Unique File Names

Some programs need to write temporary files. Here is the usual way to
construct a name for such a file:

```
(make-temp-name (concat "/tmp/" name-of-application))
```

Here we use the directory '/tmp/' because that is the standard place on Unix
for temporary files. The job of make-temp-name is to prevent two different
users or two different jobs from trying to use the same name.

make-temp-name *string*   Function
     This function generates string that can be used as a unique name. The
     name starts with *string*, and ends with a number that is different in
     each Emacs job.

```
(make-temp-name "/tmp/foo")
     ⇒ "/tmp/foo021304"
```

To prevent conflicts among different libraries running in the same
Emacs, each Lisp program that uses make-temp-name should have its
own *string*. The number added to the end of the name distinguishes
between the same application running in different Emacs jobs.

22.8.6 File Name Completion

This section describes low-level subroutines for completing a file name.
For other completion functions, see Section 17.5 [Completion], page 258,
vol. 1.

file-name-all-completions *partial-filename directory*   Function
This function returns a list of all possible completions for a file whose
name starts with *partial-filename* in directory *directory*. The order
of the completions is the order of the files in the directory, which is
unpredictable and conveys no useful information.

The argument *partial-filename* must be a file name containing no directory part and no slash. The current buffer's default directory is
prepended to *directory*, if *directory* is not absolute.

In the following example, suppose that the current default directory,
'~rms/lewis', has five files whose names begin with 'f': 'foo', 'file~',
'file.c', 'file.c.~1~', and 'file.c.~2~'.

```
(file-name-all-completions "f" "")
     ⇒ ("foo" "file~" "file.c.~2~"
              "file.c.~1~" "file.c")

(file-name-all-completions "fo" "")
     ⇒ ("foo")
```

file-name-completion *filename directory*   Function
This function completes the file name *filename* in directory *directory*.
It returns the longest prefix common to all file names in directory
directory that start with *filename*.

If only one match exists and *filename* matches it exactly, the function
returns t. The function returns nil if directory *directory* contains no
name starting with *filename*.

In the following example, suppose that the current default directory
has five files whose names begin with 'f': 'foo', 'file~', 'file.c',
'file.c.~1~', and 'file.c.~2~'.

```
(file-name-completion "fi" "")
     ⇒ "file"

(file-name-completion "file.c.~1" "")
     ⇒ "file.c.~1~"

(file-name-completion "file.c.~1~" "")
     ⇒ t

(file-name-completion "file.c.~3" "")
     ⇒ nil
```

completion-ignored-extensions   User Option
file-name-completion usually ignores file names that end in any
string in this list. It does not ignore them when all the possible completions end in one of these suffixes or when a buffer showing all possible
completions is displayed.

A typical value might look like this:

```
completion-ignored-extensions
     ⇒ (".o" ".elc" "~" ".dvi")
```

22.9 Contents of Directories

A directory is a kind of file that contains other files entered under various names. Directories are a feature of the file system.

Emacs can list the names of the files in a directory as a Lisp list, or display the names in a buffer using the `ls` shell command. In the latter case, it can optionally display information about each file, depending on the options passed to the `ls` command.

directory-files *directory* &optional *full-name*   Function
      match-regexp nosort
This function returns a list of the names of the files in the directory *directory*. By default, the list is in alphabetical order.

If *full-name* is non-`nil`, the function returns the files' absolute file names. Otherwise, it returns the names relative to the specified directory.

If *match-regexp* is non-`nil`, this function returns only those file names that contain a match for that regular expression—the other file names are excluded from the list.

If *nosort* is non-`nil`, `directory-files` does not sort the list, so you get the file names in no particular order. Use this if you want the utmost possible speed and don't care what order the files are processed in. If the order of processing is visible to the user, then the user will probably be happier if you do sort the names.

```
(directory-files "~lewis")
     ⇒ ("#foo#" "#foo.el#" "." ".."
        "dired-mods.el" "files.texi"
        "files.texi.~1~")
```

An error is signaled if *directory* is not the name of a directory that can be read.

file-name-all-versions *file dirname*   Function
This function returns a list of all versions of the file named *file* in directory *dirname*.

insert-directory *file switches* &optional *wildcard*   Function
   full-directory-p
  This function inserts (in the current buffer) a directory listing for directory *file*, formatted with `ls` according to *switches*. It leaves point after the inserted text.

  The argument *file* may be either a directory name or a file specification including wildcard characters. If *wildcard* is non-`nil`, that means treat *file* as a file specification with wildcards.

  If *full-directory-p* is non-`nil`, that means *file* is a directory and switches do not contain '`-d`', so that the listing should show the full contents of the directory. (The '`-d`' option to `ls` says to describe a directory itself rather than its contents.)

  This function works by running a directory listing program whose name is in the variable `insert-directory-program`. If *wildcard* is non-`nil`, it also runs the shell specified by `shell-file-name`, to expand the wildcards.

insert-directory-program   Variable
  This variable's value is the program to run to generate a directory listing for the function `insert-directory`.

22.10 Creating and Deleting Directories

  Most Emacs Lisp file-manipulation functions get errors when used on files that are directories. For example, you cannot delete a directory with `delete-file`. These special functions exist to create and delete directories.

make-directory *dirname*   Function
  This function creates a directory named *dirname*.

delete-directory *dirname*   Function
  This function deletes the directory named *dirname*. The function `delete-file` does not work for files that are directories; you must use `delete-directory` for them. If the directory contains any files, `delete-directory` signals an error.

22.11 Making Certain File Names "Magic"

  You can implement special handling for certain file names. This is called making those names *magic*. You must supply a regular expression to define the class of names (all those that match the regular expression), plus a handler that implements all the primitive Emacs file operations for file names that do match.

The variable `file-name-handler-alist` holds a list of handlers, together with regular expressions that determine when to apply each handler. Each element has this form:

    (regexp . handler)

All the Emacs primitives for file access and file name transformation check the given file name against `file-name-handler-alist`. If the file name matches *regexp*, the primitives handle that file by calling *handler*.

The first argument given to *handler* is the name of the primitive; the remaining arguments are the arguments that were passed to that operation. (The first of these arguments is typically the file name itself.) For example, if you do this:

    (file-exists-p filename)

and *filename* has handler *handler*, then *handler* is called like this:

    (funcall handler 'file-exists-p filename)

Here are the operations that a magic file name handler gets to handle:

`add-name-to-file`, `copy-file`, `delete-directory`, `delete-file`, `diff-latest-backup-file`, `directory-file-name`, `directory-files`, `dired-compress-file`, `dired-uncache`, `expand-file-name`, `file-accessible-directory-p`, `file-attributes`, `file-directory-p`, `file-executable-p`, `file-exists-p`, `file-local-copy`, `file-modes`, `file-name-all-completions`, `file-name-as-directory`, `file-name-completion`, `file-name-directory`, `file-name-nondirectory`, `file-name-sans-versions`, `file-newer-than-file-p`, `file-readable-p`, `file-regular-p`, `file-symlink-p`, `file-truename`, `file-writable-p`, `get-file-buffer`, `insert-directory`, `insert-file-contents`, `load`, `make-directory`, `make-symbolic-link`, `rename-file`, `set-file-modes`, `set-visited-file-modtime`, `unhandled-file-name-directory`, `verify-visited-file-modtime`, `write-region`.

Handlers for `insert-file-contents` typically need to clear the buffer's modified flag, with `(set-buffer-modified-p nil)`, if the *visit* argument is non-`nil`. This also has the effect of unlocking the buffer if it is locked.

The handler function must handle all of the above operations, and possibly others to be added in the future. It need not implement all these operations itself—when it has nothing special to do for a certain operation, it can reinvoke the primitive, to handle the operation "in the usual way". It should always reinvoke the primitive for an operation it does not recognize. Here's one way to do this:

```
(defun my-file-handler (operation &rest args)
  ;; First check for the specific operations
  ;; that we have special handling for.
  (cond ((eq operation 'insert-file-contents) ...)
        ((eq operation 'write-region) ...)
```

```
      ...
;; Handle any operation we don't know about.
(t (let ((inhibit-file-name-handlers
            (cons 'my-file-handler
                    (and (eq inhibit-file-name-operation operation)
                          inhibit-file-name-handlers)))
          (inhibit-file-name-operation operation))
      (apply operation args)))))
```

When a handler function decides to call the ordinary Emacs primitive for the operation at hand, it needs to prevent the primitive from calling the same handler once again, thus leading to an infinite recursion. The example above shows how to do this, with the variables `inhibit-file-name-handlers` and `inhibit-file-name-operation`. Be careful to use them exactly as shown above; the details are crucial for proper behavior in the case of multiple handlers, and for operations that have two file names that may each have handlers.

inhibit-file-name-handlers   Variable
    This variable holds a list of handlers whose use is presently inhibited for a certain operation.

inhibit-file-name-operation   Variable
    The operation for which certain handlers are presently inhibited.

find-file-name-handler *file operation*   Function
    This function returns the handler function for file name *file*, or `nil` if there is none. The argument *operation* should be the operation to be performed on the file—the value you will pass to the handler as its first argument when you call it. The operation is needed for comparison with `inhibit-file-name-operation`.

file-local-copy *filename*   Function
    This function copies file *filename* to an ordinary non-magic file, if it isn't one already.

    If *filename* specifies a "magic" file name, which programs outside Emacs cannot directly read or write, this copies the contents to an ordinary file and returns that file's name.

    If *filename* is an ordinary file name, not magic, then this function does nothing and returns `nil`.

unhandled-file-name-directory *filename*   Function
    This function returns the name of a directory that is not magic. It uses the directory part of *filename* if that is not magic. Otherwise, it asks the handler what to do.

    This is useful for running a subprocess; every subprocess must have a non-magic directory to serve as its current directory, and this function is a good way to come up with one.

22.12 File Format Conversion

The variable `format-alist` defines a list of *file formats*, which describe textual representations used in files for the data (text, text-properties, and possibly other information) in an Emacs buffer. Emacs performs format conversion if appropriate when reading and writing files.

format-alist   *Variable*
 This list contains one format definition for each defined file format.

Each format definition is a list of this form:

(*name doc-string regexp from-fn to-fn modify mode-fn*)

Here is what the elements in a format definition mean:

name   The name of this format.

doc-string A documentation string for the format.

regexp   A regular expression which is used to recognize files represented in this format.

from-fn   A function to call to decode data in this format (to convert file data into the usual Emacs data representation).

              The *from-fn* is called with two args, *begin* and *end*, which specify the part of the buffer it should convert. It should convert the text by editing it in place. Since this can change the length of the text, *from-fn* should return the modified end position.

              One responsibility of *from-fn* is to make sure that the beginning of the file no longer matches *regexp*. Otherwise it is likely to get called again.

to-fn   A function to call to encode data in this format (to convert the usual Emacs data representation into this format).

              The *to-fn* is called with two args, *begin* and *end*, which specify the part of the buffer it should convert. There are two ways it can do the conversion:

              • By editing the buffer in place. In this case, *to-fn* should return the end-position of the range of text, as modified.

              • By returning a list of annotations. This is a list of elements of the form (*position . string*), where *position* is an integer specifying the relative position in the text to be written, and *string* is the annotation to add there. The list must be sorted in order of position when *to-fn* returns it.

                When `write-region` actually writes the text from the buffer to the file, it intermixes the specified annotations at the corresponding positions. All this takes place without modifying the buffer.

modify   A flag, t if the encoding function modifies the buffer, and nil if it works by returning a list of annotations.

mode   A mode function to call after visiting a file converted from this format.

The function insert-file-contents automatically recognizes file formats when it reads the specified file. It checks the text of the beginning of the file against the regular expressions of the format definitions, and if it finds a match, it calls the decoding function for that format. Then it checks all the known formats over again. It keeps checking them until none of them is applicable.

Visiting a file, with find-file-noselect or the commands that use it, performs conversion likewise (because it calls insert-file-contents); it also calls the mode function for each format that it decodes. It stores a list of the format names in the buffer-local variable buffer-file-format.

buffer-file-format   Variable

This variable states the format of the visited file. More precisely, this is a list of the file format names that were decoded in the course of visiting the current buffer's file. It is always local in all buffers.

When write-region writes data into a file, it first calls the encoding functions for the formats listed in buffer-file-format, in the order of appearance in the list.

format-write-file *file format*   Function

This command writes the current buffer contents into the file *file* in format *format*, and makes that format the default for future saves of the buffer. The argument *format* is a list of format names.

format-find-file *file format*   Function

This command finds the file *file*, converting it according to format *format*. It also makes *format* the default if the buffer is saved later.

The argument *format* is a list of format names. If *format* is nil, no conversion takes place. Interactively, typing just RET for *format* specifies nil.

format-insert-file *file format %optional beg end*   Function

This command inserts the contents of file *file*, converting it according to format *format*. If *beg* and *end* are non-nil, they specify which part of the file to read, as in insert-file-contents (see Section 22.3 [Reading from Files], page 17).

The return value is like what insert-file-contents returns: a list of the absolute file name and the length of the data inserted (after conversion).

The argument *format* is a list of format names. If *format* is `nil`, no conversion takes place. Interactively, typing just RET for *format* specifies `nil`.

auto-save-file-format   Variable
This variable specifies the format to use for auto-saving. Its value is a list of format names, just like the value of `buffer-file-format`; but it is used instead of `buffer-file-format` for writing auto-save files. This variable is always local in all buffers.

22.13 Files and MS-DOS

Emacs on MS-DOS makes a distinction between text files and binary files. This is necessary because ordinary text files on MS-DOS use a two character sequence between lines: carriage-return and linefeed (CRLF). Emacs expects just a newline character (a linefeed) between lines. When Emacs reads or writes a text file on MS-DOS, it needs to convert the line separators. This means it needs to know which files are text files and which are binary. It makes this decision when visiting a file, and records the decision in the variable `buffer-file-type` for use when the file is saved.

See Section 33.3 [MS-DOS Subprocesses], page 233, for a related feature for subprocesses.

buffer-file-type   Variable
This variable, automatically local in each buffer, records the file type of the buffer's visited file. The value is `nil` for text, `t` for binary.

find-buffer-file-type *filename*   Function
This function determines whether file *filename* is a text file or a binary file. It returns `nil` for text, `t` for binary.

file-name-buffer-file-type-alist   User Option
This variable holds an alist for distinguishing text files from binary files. Each element has the form (*regexp . type*), where *regexp* is matched against the file name, and *type* may be is `nil` for text, `t` for binary, or a function to call to compute which. If it is a function, then it is called with a single argument (the file name) and should return `t` or `nil`.

default-buffer-file-type   User Option
This variable specifies the default file type for files whose names don't indicate anything in particular. Its value should be `nil` for text, or `t` for binary.

find-file-text *filename*   Command
Like `find-file`, but treat the file as text regardless of its name.

find-file-binary *filename*   Command
    Like `find-file`, but treat the file as binary regardless of its name.

23 Backups and Auto-Saving

Backup files and auto-save files are two methods by which Emacs tries to protect the user from the consequences of crashes or of the user's own errors. Auto-saving preserves the text from earlier in the current editing session; backup files preserve file contents prior to the current session.

23.1 Backup Files

A *backup file* is a copy of the old contents of a file you are editing. Emacs makes a backup file the first time you save a buffer into its visited file. Normally, this means that the backup file contains the contents of the file as it was before the current editing session. The contents of the backup file normally remain unchanged once it exists.

Backups are usually made by renaming the visited file to a new name. Optionally, you can specify that backup files should be made by copying the visited file. This choice makes a difference for files with multiple names; it also can affect whether the edited file remains owned by the original owner or becomes owned by the user editing it.

By default, Emacs makes a single backup file for each file edited. You can alternatively request numbered backups; then each new backup file gets a new name. You can delete old numbered backups when you don't want them any more, or Emacs can delete them automatically.

23.1.1 Making Backup Files

backup-buffer   Function
This function makes a backup of the file visited by the current buffer, if appropriate. It is called by `save-buffer` before saving the buffer the first time.

buffer-backed-up   Variable
This buffer-local variable indicates whether this buffer's file has been backed up on account of this buffer. If it is non-`nil`, then the backup file has been written. Otherwise, the file should be backed up when it is next saved (if backups are enabled). This is a permanent local; `kill-local-variables` does not alter it.

make-backup-files   User Option
This variable determines whether or not to make backup files. If it is non-`nil`, then Emacs creates a backup of each file when it is saved for the first time—provided that `backup-inhibited` is `nil` (see below).

The following example shows how to change the `make-backup-files`
variable only in the 'RMAIL' buffer and not elsewhere. Setting it `nil`
stops Emacs from making backups of the 'RMAIL' file, which may save
disk space. (You would put this code in your '.emacs' file.)

```
(add-hook 'rmail-mode-hook
          (function (lambda ()
                      (make-local-variable
                       'make-backup-files)
                      (setq make-backup-files nil))))
```

backup-enable-predicate   Variable
This variable's value is a function to be called on certain occasions to
decide whether a file should have backup files. The function receives
one argument, a file name to consider. If the function returns `nil`,
backups are disabled for that file. Otherwise, the other variables in
this section say whether and how to make backups.

The default value is this:

```
(lambda (name)
  (or (< (length name) 5)
      (not (string-equal "/tmp/"
                         (substring name 0 5)))))
```

backup-inhibited   Variable
If this variable is non-`nil`, backups are inhibited. It records the result
of testing `backup-enable-predicate` on the visited file name. It can
also coherently be used by other mechanisms that inhibit backups
based on which file is visited. For example, VC sets this variable non-
`nil` to prevent making backups for files managed with a version control
system.

This is a permanent local, so that changing the major mode does not
lose its value. Major modes should not set this variable—they should
set `make-backup-files` instead.

23.1.2 Backup by Renaming or by Copying?

There are two ways that Emacs can make a backup file:

• Emacs can rename the original file so that it becomes a backup file, and
  then write the buffer being saved into a new file. After this procedure,
  any other names (i.e., hard links) of the original file now refer to the
  backup file. The new file is owned by the user doing the editing, and its
  group is the default for new files written by the user in that directory.

• Emacs can copy the original file into a backup file, and then overwrite
  the original file with new contents. After this procedure, any other

names (i.e., hard links) of the original file still refer to the current version of the file. The file's owner and group will be unchanged.

The first method, renaming, is the default.

The variable `backup-by-copying`, if non-`nil`, says to use the second method, which is to copy the original file and overwrite it with the new buffer contents. The variable `file-precious-flag`, if non-`nil`, also has this effect (as a sideline of its main significance). See Section 22.2 [Saving Buffers], page 14.

backup-by-copying   Variable
   If this variable is non-`nil`, Emacs always makes backup files by copying.

The following two variables, when non-`nil`, cause the second method to be used in certain special cases. They have no effect on the treatment of files that don't fall into the special cases.

backup-by-copying-when-linked   Variable
   If this variable is non-`nil`, Emacs makes backups by copying for files with multiple names (hard links).

   This variable is significant only if `backup-by-copying` is `nil`, since copying is always used when that variable is non-`nil`.

backup-by-copying-when-mismatch   Variable
   If this variable is non-`nil`, Emacs makes backups by copying in cases where renaming would change either the owner or the group of the file.

   The value has no effect when renaming would not alter the owner or group of the file; that is, for files which are owned by the user and whose group matches the default for a new file created there by the user.

   This variable is significant only if `backup-by-copying` is `nil`, since copying is always used when that variable is non-`nil`.

23.1.3 Making and Deleting Numbered Backup Files

If a file's name is 'foo', the names of its numbered backup versions are 'foo.~v~', for various integers v, like this: 'foo.~1~', 'foo.~2~', 'foo.~3~', ..., 'foo.~259~', and so on.

version-control   User Option
   This variable controls whether to make a single non-numbered backup file or multiple numbered backups.

   nil   Make numbered backups if the visited file already has numbered backups; otherwise, do not.

never   Do not make numbered backups.

anything else
          Make numbered backups.

The use of numbered backups ultimately leads to a large number of backup versions, which must then be deleted. Emacs can do this automatically or it can ask the user whether to delete them.

kept-new-versions   User Option
     The value of this variable is the number of newest versions to keep
     when a new numbered backup is made. The newly made backup is
     included in the count. The default value is 2.

kept-old-versions   User Option
     The value of this variable is the number of oldest versions to keep when
     a new numbered backup is made. The default value is 2.

If there are backups numbered 1, 2, 3, 5, and 7, and both of these variables have the value 2, then the backups numbered 1 and 2 are kept as old versions and those numbered 5 and 7 are kept as new versions; backup version 3 is excess. The function `find-backup-file-name` (see Section 23.1.4 [Backup Names], page 48) is responsible for determining which backup versions to delete, but does not delete them itself.

trim-versions-without-asking   User Option
     If this variable is non-`nil`, then saving a file deletes excess backup
     versions silently. Otherwise, it asks the user whether to delete them.

dired-kept-versions   User Option
     This variable specifies how many of the newest backup versions to keep
     in the Dired command . (`dired-clean-directory`). That's the same
     thing `kept-new-versions` specifies when you make a new backup file.
     The default value is 2.

23.1.4 Naming Backup Files

The functions in this section are documented mainly because you can customize the naming conventions for backup files by redefining them. If you change one, you probably need to change the rest.

backup-file-name-p *filename*   Function
     This function returns a non-`nil` value if *filename* is a possible name
     for a backup file. A file with the name *filename* need not exist; the
     function just checks the name.

```
(backup-file-name-p "foo")
    ⇒ nil
(backup-file-name-p "foo~")
    ⇒ 3
```

The standard definition of this function is as follows:

```
(defun backup-file-name-p (file)
  "Return non-nil if FILE is a backup file \
name (numeric or not)..."
  (string-match "~$" file))
```

Thus, the function returns a non-`nil` value if the file name ends with a '~'. (We use a backslash to split the documentation string's first line into two lines in the text, but produce just one line in the string itself.)

This simple expression is placed in a separate function to make it easy to redefine for customization.

make-backup-file-name *filename*   Function

This function returns a string that is the name to use for a non-numbered backup file for file *filename*. On Unix, this is just *filename* with a tilde appended.

The standard definition of this function is as follows:

```
(defun make-backup-file-name (file)
  "Create the non-numeric backup file name for FILE.
..."
  (concat file "~"))
```

You can change the backup-file naming convention by redefining this function. The following example redefines `make-backup-file-name` to prepend a '.' in addition to appending a tilde:

```
(defun make-backup-file-name (filename)
  (concat "." filename "~"))

(make-backup-file-name "backups.texi")
    ⇒ ".backups.texi~"
```

find-backup-file-name *filename*   Function

This function computes the file name for a new backup file for *filename*. It may also propose certain existing backup files for deletion. `find-backup-file-name` returns a list whose CAR is the name for the new backup file and whose CDR is a list of backup files whose deletion is proposed.

Two variables, `kept-old-versions` and `kept-new-versions`, determine which backup versions should be kept. This function keeps those versions by excluding them from the CDR of the value. See Section 23.1.3 [Numbered Backups], page 47.

In this example, the value says that '~rms/foo.~5~' is the name to use for the new backup file, and '~rms/foo.~3~' is an "excess" version that the caller should consider deleting now.

```
(find-backup-file-name "~rms/foo")
     ⇒ ("~rms/foo.~5~" "~rms/foo.~3~")
```

file-newest-backup *filename*   Function
　　This function returns the name of the most recent backup file for
　　filename, or `nil` if that file has no backup files.

　　Some file comparison commands use this function so that they can
　　automatically compare a file with its most recent backup.

23.2 Auto-Saving

　　Emacs periodically saves all files that you are visiting; this is called *auto-
saving*. Auto-saving prevents you from losing more than a limited amount
of work if the system crashes. By default, auto-saves happen every 300
keystrokes, or after around 30 seconds of idle time. See section "Auto-Saving:
Protection Against Disasters" in *The GNU Emacs Manual*, for information
on auto-save for users. Here we describe the functions used to implement
auto-saving and the variables that control them.

buffer-auto-save-file-name   Variable
　　This buffer-local variable is the name of the file used for auto-saving
　　the current buffer. It is `nil` if the buffer should not be auto-saved.

```
buffer-auto-save-file-name
=> "/xcssun/users/rms/lewis/#files.texi#"
```

auto-save-mode *arg*   Command
　　When used interactively without an argument, this command is a tog-
　　gle switch: it turns on auto-saving of the current buffer if it is off, and
　　vice-versa. With an argument *arg*, the command turns auto-saving on
　　if the value of *arg* is `t`, a nonempty list, or a positive integer. Other-
　　wise, it turns auto-saving off.

auto-save-file-name-p *filename*   Function
　　This function returns a non-`nil` value if *filename* is a string that could
　　be the name of an auto-save file. It works based on knowledge of the
　　naming convention for auto-save files: a name that begins and ends
　　with hash marks ('#') is a possible auto-save file name. The argument
　　filename should not contain a directory part.

```
(make-auto-save-file-name)
     ⇒ "/xcssun/users/rms/lewis/#files.texi#"
(auto-save-file-name-p "#files.texi#")
     ⇒ 0
(auto-save-file-name-p "files.texi")
     ⇒ nil
```

The standard definition of this function is as follows:

```
(defun auto-save-file-name-p (filename)
  "Return non-nil if FILENAME can be yielded by..."
  (string-match "^#.*#$" filename))
```

This function exists so that you can customize it if you wish to change
the naming convention for auto-save files. If you redefine it, be sure to
redefine the function `make-auto-save-file-name` correspondingly.

make-auto-save-file-name   Function

This function returns the file name to use for auto-saving the current
buffer. This is just the file name with hash marks ('#') appended and
prepended to it. This function does not look at the variable `auto-save-visited-file-name` (described below); you should check that
before calling this function.

```
(make-auto-save-file-name)
    ⇒ "/xcssun/users/rms/lewis/#backup.texi#"
```

The standard definition of this function is as follows:

```
(defun make-auto-save-file-name ()
  "Return file name to use for auto-saves \
of current buffer.
..."
  (if buffer-file-name
      (concat
       (file-name-directory buffer-file-name)
       "#"
       (file-name-nondirectory buffer-file-name)
       "#")
    (expand-file-name
     (concat "#%" (buffer-name) "#"))))
```

This exists as a separate function so that you can redefine it to customize the naming convention for auto-save files. Be sure to change
`auto-save-file-name-p` in a corresponding way.

auto-save-visited-file-name   Variable

If this variable is non-`nil`, Emacs auto-saves buffers in the files they
are visiting. That is, the auto-save is done in the same file that you are
editing. Normally, this variable is `nil`, so auto-save files have distinct
names that are created by `make-auto-save-file-name`.

When you change the value of this variable, the value does not take
effect until the next time auto-save mode is reenabled in any given
buffer. If auto-save mode is already enabled, auto-saves continue to
go in the same file name until `auto-save-mode` is called again.

recent-auto-save-p   Function
> This function returns t if the current buffer has been auto-saved since
> the last time it was read in or saved.

set-buffer-auto-saved   Function
> This function marks the current buffer as auto-saved. The buffer will
> not be auto-saved again until the buffer text is changed again. The
> function returns nil.

auto-save-interval   User Option
> The value of this variable is the number of characters that Emacs
> reads from the keyboard between auto-saves. Each time this many
> more characters are read, auto-saving is done for all buffers in which
> it is enabled.

auto-save-timeout   User Option
> The value of this variable is the number of seconds of idle time that
> should cause auto-saving. Each time the user pauses for this long,
> Emacs auto-saves any buffers that need it. (Actually, the specified
> timeout is multiplied by a factor depending on the size of the current
> buffer.)

auto-save-hook   Variable
> This normal hook is run whenever an auto-save is about to happen.

auto-save-default   User Option
> If this variable is non-nil, buffers that are visiting files have auto-
> saving enabled by default. Otherwise, they do not.

do-auto-save &optional *no-message current-only*   Command
> This function auto-saves all buffers that need to be auto-saved. It
> saves all buffers for which auto-saving is enabled and that have been
> changed since the previous auto-save.
>
> Normally, if any buffers are auto-saved, a message that says
> 'Auto-saving...' is displayed in the echo area while auto-saving is
> going on. However, if *no-message* is non-nil, the message is inhibited.
>
> If *current-only* is non-nil, only the current buffer is auto-saved.

delete-auto-save-file-if-necessary   Function
> This function deletes the current buffer's auto-save file if delete-
> auto-save-files is non-nil. It is called every time a buffer is saved.

delete-auto-save-files   Variable
> This variable is used by the function delete-auto-save-file-if-
> necessary. If it is non-nil, Emacs deletes auto-save files when a true
> save is done (in the visited file). This saves disk space and unclutters
> your directory.

rename-auto-save-file *Function*

> This function adjusts the current buffer's auto-save file name if the
> visited file name has changed. It also renames an existing auto-save
> file. If the visited file name has not changed, this function does nothing.

buffer-saved-size *Variable*

> The value of this buffer-local variable is the length of the current buffer
> as of the last time it was read in, saved, or auto-saved. This is used
> to detect a substantial decrease in size, and turn off auto-saving in
> response.
>
> If it is -1, that means auto-saving is temporarily shut off in this buffer
> due to a substantial deletion. Explicitly saving the buffer stores a
> positive value in this variable, thus reenabling auto-saving. Turning
> auto-save mode off or on also alters this variable.

auto-save-list-file-name *Variable*

> This variable (if non-`nil`) specifies a file for recording the names of all
> the auto-save files. Each time Emacs does auto-saving, it writes two
> lines into this file for each buffer that has auto-saving enabled. The
> first line gives the name of the visited file (it's empty if the buffer has
> none), and the second gives the name of the auto-save file.
>
> If Emacs exits normally, it deletes this file. If Emacs crashes, you can
> look in the file to find all the auto-save files that might contain work
> that was otherwise lost. The `recover-session` command uses these
> files.
>
> The default name for this file is in your home directory and starts with
> '`.saves-`'. It also contains the Emacs process ID and the host name.

23.3 Reverting

If you have made extensive changes to a file and then change your mind
about them, you can get rid of them by reading in the previous version of
the file with the `revert-buffer` command. See section "Reverting a Buffer"
in *The GNU Emacs Manual*.

revert-buffer &optional *check-auto-save noconfirm* *Command*

> This command replaces the buffer text with the text of the visited file
> on disk. This action undoes all changes since the file was visited or
> saved.
>
> If the argument *check-auto-save* is non-`nil`, and the latest auto-save
> file is more recent than the visited file, `revert-buffer` asks the user
> whether to use that instead. Otherwise, it always uses the text of
> the visited file itself. Interactively, *check-auto-save* is set if there is a
> numeric prefix argument.

Normally, `revert-buffer` asks for confirmation before it changes the buffer; but if the argument *noconfirm* is non-`nil`, `revert-buffer` does not ask for confirmation.

Reverting tries to preserve marker positions in the buffer by using the replacement feature of `insert-file-contents`. If the buffer contents and the file contents are identical before the revert operation, reverting preserves all the markers. If they are not identical, reverting does change the buffer; then it preserves the markers in the unchanged text (if any) at the beginning and end of the buffer. Preserving any additional markers would be problematical.

You can customize how `revert-buffer` does its work by setting these variables—typically, as buffer-local variables.

revert-buffer-function   Variable
The value of this variable is the function to use to revert this buffer. If non-`nil`, it is called as a function with no arguments to do the work of reverting. If the value is `nil`, reverting works the usual way.

Modes such as Dired mode, in which the text being edited does not consist of a file's contents but can be regenerated in some other fashion, give this variable a buffer-local value that is a function to regenerate the contents.

revert-buffer-insert-file-contents-function   Variable
The value of this variable, if non-`nil`, is the function to use to insert the updated contents when reverting this buffer. The function receives two arguments: first the file name to use; second, `t` if the user has asked to read the auto-save file.

before-revert-hook   Variable
This normal hook is run by `revert-buffer` before actually inserting the modified contents—but only if `revert-buffer-function` is `nil`.

Font Lock mode uses this hook to record that the buffer contents are no longer fontified.

after-revert-hook   Variable
This normal hook is run by `revert-buffer` after actually inserting the modified contents—but only if `revert-buffer-function` is `nil`.

Font Lock mode uses this hook to recompute the fonts for the updated buffer contents.

24 Buffers

A *buffer* is a Lisp object containing text to be edited. Buffers are used to hold the contents of files that are being visited; there may also be buffers that are not visiting files. While several buffers may exist at one time, exactly one buffer is designated the *current buffer* at any time. Most editing commands act on the contents of the current buffer. Each buffer, including the current buffer, may or may not be displayed in any windows.

24.1 Buffer Basics

Buffers in Emacs editing are objects that have distinct names and hold text that can be edited. Buffers appear to Lisp programs as a special data type. You can think of the contents of a buffer as an extendable string; insertions and deletions may occur in any part of the buffer. See Chapter 29 [Text], page 143.

A Lisp buffer object contains numerous pieces of information. Some of this information is directly accessible to the programmer through variables, while other information is accessible only through special-purpose functions. For example, the visited file name is directly accessible through a variable, while the value of point is accessible only through a primitive function.

Buffer-specific information that is directly accessible is stored in *buffer-local* variable bindings, which are variable values that are effective only in a particular buffer. This feature allows each buffer to override the values of certain variables. Most major modes override variables such as `fill-column` or `comment-column` in this way. For more information about buffer-local variables and functions related to them, see Section 10.9 [Buffer-Local Variables], page 151, vol. 1.

For functions and variables related to visiting files in buffers, see Section 22.1 [Visiting Files], page 11 and Section 22.2 [Saving Buffers], page 14. For functions and variables related to the display of buffers in windows, see Section 25.6 [Buffers and Windows], page 77.

bufferp *object*   Function
  This function returns `t` if *object* is a buffer, `nil` otherwise.

24.2 The Current Buffer

There are, in general, many buffers in an Emacs session. At any time, one of them is designated as the *current buffer*. This is the buffer in which most editing takes place, because most of the primitives for examining or changing text in a buffer operate implicitly on the current buffer (see Chapter 29 [Text], page 143). Normally the buffer that is displayed on the screen in the selected window is the current buffer, but this is not always so: a Lisp program can designate any buffer as current temporarily in order to operate on its contents, without changing what is displayed on the screen.

The way to designate a current buffer in a Lisp program is by calling `set-buffer`. The specified buffer remains current until a new one is designated.

When an editing command returns to the editor command loop, the command loop designates the buffer displayed in the selected window as current, to prevent confusion: the buffer that the cursor is in when Emacs reads a command is the buffer that the command will apply to. (See Chapter 18 [Command Loop], page 275, vol. 1.) Therefore, `set-buffer` is not the way to switch visibly to a different buffer so that the user can edit it. For this, you must use the functions described in Section 25.7 [Displaying Buffers], page 78.

However, Lisp functions that change to a different current buffer should not depend on the command loop to set it back afterwards. Editing commands written in Emacs Lisp can be called from other programs as well as from the command loop. It is convenient for the caller if the subroutine does not change which buffer is current (unless, of course, that is the subroutine's purpose). Therefore, you should normally use `set-buffer` within a `save-excursion` that will restore the current buffer when your function is done (see Section 27.3 [Excursions], page 129). Here is an example, the code for the command `append-to-buffer` (with the documentation string abridged):

```
(defun append-to-buffer (buffer start end)
  "Append to specified buffer the text of the region.
..."
  (interactive "BAppend to buffer: \nr")
  (let ((oldbuf (current-buffer)))
    (save-excursion
      (set-buffer (get-buffer-create buffer))
      (insert-buffer-substring oldbuf start end))))
```

This function binds a local variable to the current buffer, and then `save-excursion` records the values of point, the mark, and the original buffer. Next, `set-buffer` makes another buffer current. Finally, `insert-buffer-substring` copies the string from the original current buffer to the new current buffer.

If the buffer appended to happens to be displayed in some window, the next redisplay will show how its text has changed. Otherwise, you will not see the change immediately on the screen. The buffer becomes current temporarily during the execution of the command, but this does not cause it to be displayed.

If you make local bindings (with `let` or function arguments) for a variable that may also have buffer-local bindings, make sure that the same buffer is current at the beginning and at the end of the local binding's scope. Otherwise you might bind it in one buffer and unbind it in another! There are two ways to do this. In simple cases, you may see that nothing ever changes the current buffer within the scope of the binding. Otherwise, use `save-excursion` to make sure that the buffer current at the beginning is current again whenever the variable is unbound.

It is not reliable to change the current buffer back with `set-buffer`, because that won't do the job if a quit happens while the wrong buffer is current. Here is what *not* to do:

```
(let (buffer-read-only
      (obuf (current-buffer)))
  (set-buffer ...)
  ...
  (set-buffer obuf))
```

Using `save-excursion`, as shown below, handles quitting, errors, and `throw`, as well as ordinary evaluation.

```
(let (buffer-read-only)
  (save-excursion
    (set-buffer ...)
    ...))
```

current-buffer   Function
  This function returns the current buffer.

```
(current-buffer)
     ⇒ #<buffer buffers.texi>
```

set-buffer *buffer-or-name*   Function
  This function makes *buffer-or-name* the current buffer. It does not display the buffer in the currently selected window or in any other window, so the user cannot necessarily see the buffer. But Lisp programs can in any case work on it.

  This function returns the buffer identified by *buffer-or-name*. An error is signaled if *buffer-or-name* does not identify an existing buffer.

24.3 Buffer Names

Each buffer has a unique name, which is a string. Many of the functions that work on buffers accept either a buffer or a buffer name as an argument. Any argument called *buffer-or-name* is of this sort, and an error is signaled if it is neither a string nor a buffer. Any argument called *buffer* must be an actual buffer object, not a name.

Buffers that are ephemeral and generally uninteresting to the user have names starting with a space, so that the `list-buffers` and `buffer-menu` commands don't mention them. A name starting with space also initially disables recording undo information; see Section 29.9 [Undo], page 157.

buffer-name &optional *buffer*   Function
> This function returns the name of *buffer* as a string. If *buffer* is not supplied, it defaults to the current buffer.
>
> If `buffer-name` returns `nil`, it means that *buffer* has been killed. See Section 24.10 [Killing Buffers], page 66.
>
> ```
> (buffer-name)
>      ⇒ "buffers.texi"
> (setq foo (get-buffer "temp"))
>      ⇒ #<buffer temp>
> (kill-buffer foo)
>      ⇒ nil
> (buffer-name foo)
>      ⇒ nil
> foo
>      ⇒ #<killed buffer>
> ```

rename-buffer *newname* &optional *unique*   Command
> This function renames the current buffer to *newname*. An error is signaled if *newname* is not a string, or if there is already a buffer with that name. The function returns `nil`.
>
> Ordinarily, `rename-buffer` signals an error if *newname* is already in use. However, if *unique* is non-`nil`, it modifies *newname* to make a name that is not in use. Interactively, you can make *unique* non-`nil` with a numeric prefix argument.
>
> One application of this command is to rename the '`*shell*`' buffer to some other name, thus making it possible to create a second shell buffer under the name '`*shell*`'.

get-buffer *buffer-or-name*   Function
> This function returns the buffer specified by *buffer-or-name*. If *buffer-or-name* is a string and there is no buffer with that name, the value is `nil`. If *buffer-or-name* is a buffer, it is returned as given. (That is not very useful, so the argument is usually a name.) For example:
>
> ```
> (setq b (get-buffer "lewis"))
>      ⇒ #<buffer lewis>
> (get-buffer b)
>      ⇒ #<buffer lewis>
> ```

```
(get-buffer "Frazzle-nots")
     ⇒ nil
```

See also the function `get-buffer-create` in Section 24.9 [Creating Buffers], page 65.

generate-new-buffer-name *starting-name*   Function

This function returns a name that would be unique for a new buffer—but does not create the buffer. It starts with *starting-name*, and produces a name not currently in use for any buffer by appending a number inside of '<...>'.

See the related function `generate-new-buffer` in Section 24.9 [Creating Buffers], page 65.

24.4 Buffer File Name

The *buffer file name* is the name of the file that is visited in that buffer. When a buffer is not visiting a file, its buffer file name is `nil`. Most of the time, the buffer name is the same as the nondirectory part of the buffer file name, but the buffer file name and the buffer name are distinct and can be set independently. See Section 22.1 [Visiting Files], page 11.

buffer-file-name &optional *buffer*   Function

This function returns the absolute file name of the file that *buffer* is visiting. If *buffer* is not visiting any file, `buffer-file-name` returns `nil`. If *buffer* is not supplied, it defaults to the current buffer.

```
(buffer-file-name (other-buffer))
     ⇒ "/usr/user/lewis/manual/files.texi"
```

buffer-file-name   Variable

This buffer-local variable contains the name of the file being visited in the current buffer, or `nil` if it is not visiting a file. It is a permanent local, unaffected by `kill-local-variables`.

```
buffer-file-name
     ⇒ "/usr/user/lewis/manual/buffers.texi"
```

It is risky to change this variable's value without doing various other things. See the definition of `set-visited-file-name` in 'files.el'; some of the things done there, such as changing the buffer name, are not strictly necessary, but others are essential to avoid confusing Emacs.

buffer-file-truename   Variable

This buffer-local variable holds the truename of the file visited in the current buffer, or `nil` if no file is visited. It is a permanent local, un-

affected by `kill-local-variables`. See Section 22.6.3 [Truenames],
page 23.

buffer-file-number   Variable

This buffer-local variable holds the file number and directory device
number of the file visited in the current buffer, or `nil` if no file or
a nonexistent file is visited. It is a permanent local, unaffected by
`kill-local-variables`. See Section 22.6.3 [Truenames], page 23.

The value is normally a list of the form (*filenum devnum*). This pair
of numbers uniquely identifies the file among all files accessible on the
system. See the function `file-attributes`, in Section 22.6.4 [File
Attributes], page 23, for more information about them.

get-file-buffer *filename*   Function

This function returns the buffer visiting file *filename*. If there is no such
buffer, it returns `nil`. The argument *filename*, which must be a string,
is expanded (see Section 22.8.4 [File Name Expansion], page 32), then
compared against the visited file names of all live buffers.

```
(get-file-buffer "buffers.texi")
    ⇒ #<buffer buffers.texi>
```

In unusual circumstances, there can be more than one buffer visiting
the same file name. In such cases, this function returns the first such
buffer in the buffer list.

set-visited-file-name *filename*   Command

If *filename* is a non-empty string, this function changes the name of
the file visited in current buffer to *filename*. (If the buffer had no
visited file, this gives it one.) The *next time* the buffer is saved it
will go in the newly-specified file. This command marks the buffer as
modified, since it does not (as far as Emacs knows) match the contents
of *filename*, even if it matched the former visited file.

If *filename* is `nil` or the empty string, that stands for "no visited file".
In this case, `set-visited-file-name` marks the buffer as having no
visited file.

When the function `set-visited-file-name` is called interactively, it
prompts for *filename* in the minibuffer.

See also `clear-visited-file-modtime` and `verify-visited-file-modtime` in Section 24.5 [Buffer Modification], page 61.

list-buffers-directory   Variable

This buffer-local variable records a string to display in a buffer listing
in place of the visited file name, for buffers that don't have a visited
file name. Dired buffers use this variable.

24.5 Buffer Modification

Emacs keeps a flag called the *modified flag* for each buffer, to record whether you have changed the text of the buffer. This flag is set to `t` whenever you alter the contents of the buffer, and cleared to `nil` when you save it. Thus, the flag shows whether there are unsaved changes. The flag value is normally shown in the mode line (see Section 20.3.2 [Mode Line Variables], page 356, vol. 1), and controls saving (see Section 22.2 [Saving Buffers], page 14) and auto-saving (see Section 23.2 [Auto-Saving], page 50).

Some Lisp programs set the flag explicitly. For example, the function `set-visited-file-name` sets the flag to `t`, because the text does not match the newly-visited file, even if it is unchanged from the file formerly visited.

The functions that modify the contents of buffers are described in Chapter 29 [Text], page 143.

buffer-modified-p &optional *buffer*   Function
> This function returns `t` if the buffer *buffer* has been modified since it was last read in from a file or saved, or `nil` otherwise. If *buffer* is not supplied, the current buffer is tested.

set-buffer-modified-p *flag*   Function
> This function marks the current buffer as modified if *flag* is non-`nil`, or as unmodified if the flag is `nil`.
>
> Another effect of calling this function is to cause unconditional redisplay of the mode line for the current buffer. In fact, the function `force-mode-line-update` works by doing this:
>
> ```
> (set-buffer-modified-p (buffer-modified-p))
> ```

not-modified   Command
> This command marks the current buffer as unmodified, and not needing to be saved. Don't use this function in programs, since it prints a message in the echo area; use `set-buffer-modified-p` (above) instead.

buffer-modified-tick &optional *buffer*   Function
> This function returns *buffer*'s modification-count. This is a counter that increments every time the buffer is modified. If *buffer* is `nil` (or omitted), the current buffer is used.

24.6 Comparison of Modification Time

Suppose that you visit a file and make changes in its buffer, and meanwhile the file itself is changed on disk. At this point, saving the buffer would overwrite the changes in the file. Occasionally this may be what you want, but usually it would lose valuable information. Emacs therefore checks the file's modification time using the functions described below before saving the file.

verify-visited-file-modtime *buffer*   Function
This function compares what *buffer* has recorded for the modification time of its visited file against the actual modification time of the file as recorded by the operating system. The two should be the same unless some other process has written the file since Emacs visited or saved it.

The function returns t if the last actual modification time and Emacs's recorded modification time are the same, nil otherwise.

clear-visited-file-modtime   Function
This function clears out the record of the last modification time of the file being visited by the current buffer. As a result, the next attempt to save this buffer will not complain of a discrepancy in file modification times.

This function is called in set-visited-file-name and other exceptional places where the usual test to avoid overwriting a changed file should not be done.

visited-file-modtime   Function
This function returns the buffer's recorded last file modification time, as a list of the form (*high* . *low*). (This is the same format that file-attributes uses to return time values; see Section 22.6.4 [File Attributes], page 23.)

set-visited-file-modtime &optional *time*   Function
This function updates the buffer's record of the last modification time of the visited file, to the value specified by *time* if *time* is not nil, and otherwise to the last modification time of the visited file.

If *time* is not nil, it should have the form (*high* . *low*) or (*high low*), in either case containing two integers, each of which holds 16 bits of the time.

This function is useful if the buffer was not read from the file normally, or if the file itself has been changed for some known benign reason.

ask-user-about-supersession-threat *filename*   Function
This function is used to ask a user how to proceed after an attempt to modify an obsolete buffer visiting file *filename*. An *obsolete buffer* is an unmodified buffer for which the associated file on disk is newer than the last save-time of the buffer. This means some other program has probably altered the file.

Depending on the user's answer, the function may return normally, in which case the modification of the buffer proceeds, or it may signal a `file-supersession` error with data (*filename*), in which case the proposed buffer modification is not allowed.

This function is called automatically by Emacs on the proper occasions. It exists so you can customize Emacs by redefining it. See the file 'userlock.el' for the standard definition.

See also the file locking mechanism in Section 22.5 [File Locks], page 19.

24.7 Read-Only Buffers

If a buffer is *read-only*, then you cannot change its contents, although you may change your view of the contents by scrolling and narrowing.

Read-only buffers are used in two kinds of situations:

- A buffer visiting a write-protected file is normally read-only.

  Here, the purpose is to show the user that editing the buffer with the aim of saving it in the file may be futile or undesirable. The user who wants to change the buffer text despite this can do so after clearing the read-only flag with `C-x C-q`.

- Modes such as Dired and Rmail make buffers read-only when altering the contents with the usual editing commands is probably a mistake.

  The special commands of these modes bind `buffer-read-only` to `nil` (with `let`) or bind `inhibit-read-only` to `t` around the places where they change the text.

buffer-read-only   Variable
This buffer-local variable specifies whether the buffer is read-only. The buffer is read-only if this variable is non-`nil`.

inhibit-read-only   Variable
If this variable is non-`nil`, then read-only buffers and read-only characters may be modified. Read-only characters in a buffer are those that have non-`nil` `read-only` properties (either text properties or overlay properties). See Section 29.18.4 [Special Properties], page 181, for more information about text properties. See Section 35.9 [Overlays], page 284, for more information about overlays and their properties.

If `inhibit-read-only` is `t`, all `read-only` character properties have no effect. If `inhibit-read-only` is a list, then `read-only` character properties have no effect if they are members of the list (comparison is done with `eq`).

toggle-read-only   Command
This command changes whether the current buffer is read-only. It is intended for interactive use; don't use it in programs. At any given point in a program, you should know whether you want the read-only

flag on or off; so you can set `buffer-read-only` explicitly to the proper value, `t` or `nil`.

barf-if-buffer-read-only   Function
 This function signals a `buffer-read-only` error if the current buffer
 is read-only. See Section 18.3 [Interactive Call], page 281, vol. 1, for
 another way to signal an error if the current buffer is read-only.

24.8 The Buffer List

 The *buffer list* is a list of all live buffers. Creating a buffer adds it to
this list, and killing a buffer deletes it. The order of the buffers in the list
is based primarily on how recently each buffer has been displayed in the
selected window. Buffers move to the front of the list when they are selected
and to the end when they are buried. Several functions, notably `other-buffer`, use this ordering. A buffer list displayed for the user also follows
this order.

buffer-list   Function
 This function returns a list of all buffers, including those whose names
 begin with a space. The elements are actual buffers, not their names.

```
(buffer-list)
    ⇒ (#<buffer buffers.texi>
        #<buffer  *Minibuf-1*> #<buffer buffer.c>
        #<buffer *Help*> #<buffer TAGS>)

;; Note that the name of the minibuffer
;;    begins with a space!
(mapcar (function buffer-name) (buffer-list))
    ⇒ ("buffers.texi" " *Minibuf-1*"
        "buffer.c" "*Help*" "TAGS")
```

 This list is a copy of a list used inside Emacs; modifying it has no
 effect on the ordering of buffers.

other-buffer &optional *buffer-or-name visible-ok*   Function
 This function returns the first buffer in the buffer list other than *buffer-or-name*. Usually this is the buffer most recently shown in the selected
 window, aside from *buffer-or-name*. Buffers whose names start with a
 space are not considered.

 If *buffer-or-name* is not supplied (or if it is not a buffer), then `other-buffer` returns the first buffer on the buffer list that is not visible in
 any window in a visible frame.

 If the selected frame has a non-`nil` `buffer-predicate` parameter,
 then `other-buffer` uses that predicate to decide which buffers to con-

sider. It calls the predicate once for each buffer, and if the value is
nil, that buffer is ignored. See Section 26.3.3 [X Frame Parameters],
page 100.

If *visible-ok* is `nil`, `other-buffer` avoids returning a buffer visible in
any window on any visible frame, except as a last resort. If *visible-ok* is non-`nil`, then it does not matter whether a buffer is displayed
somewhere or not.

If no suitable buffer exists, the buffer '`*scratch*`' is returned (and
created, if necessary).

bury-buffer &optional *buffer-or-name*   Command
This function puts *buffer-or-name* at the end of the buffer list without
changing the order of any of the other buffers on the list. This buffer
therefore becomes the least desirable candidate for `other-buffer` to
return.

If *buffer-or-name* is `nil` or omitted, this means to bury the current
buffer. In addition, if the buffer is displayed in the selected window,
this switches to some other buffer (obtained using `other-buffer`) in
the selected window. But if the buffer is displayed in some other
window, it remains displayed there.

If you wish to replace a buffer in all the windows that display it,
use `replace-buffer-in-windows`. See Section 25.6 [Buffers and Windows], page 77.

24.9 Creating Buffers

This section describes the two primitives for creating buffers. `get-buffer-create` creates a buffer if it finds no existing buffer with the specified name; `generate-new-buffer` always creates a new buffer and gives it
a unique name.

Other functions you can use to create buffers include `with-output-to-temp-buffer` (see Section 35.8 [Temporary Displays], page 282) and `create-file-buffer` (see Section 22.1 [Visiting Files], page 11). Starting a subprocess can also create a buffer (see Chapter 33 [Processes], page 229).

get-buffer-create *name*   Function
This function returns a buffer named *name*. It returns an existing
buffer with that name, if one exists; otherwise, it creates a new buffer.
The buffer does not become the current buffer—this function does not
change which buffer is current.

An error is signaled if *name* is not a string.

```
(get-buffer-create "foo")
     ⇒ #<buffer foo>
```

The major mode for the new buffer is set to Fundamental mode. The variable `default-major-mode` is handled at a higher level. See Section 20.1.3 [Auto Major Mode], page 347, vol. 1.

generate-new-buffer *name*   Function

This function returns a newly created, empty buffer, but does not make it current. If there is no buffer named *name*, then that is the name of the new buffer. If that name is in use, this function adds suffixes of the form '<*n*>' to *name*, where *n* is an integer. It tries successive integers starting with 2 until it finds an available name.

An error is signaled if *name* is not a string.

```
(generate-new-buffer "bar")
     ⇒ #<buffer bar>
(generate-new-buffer "bar")
     ⇒ #<buffer bar<2>>
(generate-new-buffer "bar")
     ⇒ #<buffer bar<3>>
```

The major mode for the new buffer is set to Fundamental mode. The variable `default-major-mode` is handled at a higher level. See Section 20.1.3 [Auto Major Mode], page 347, vol. 1.

See the related function `generate-new-buffer-name` in Section 24.3 [Buffer Names], page 57.

24.10 Killing Buffers

Killing a buffer makes its name unknown to Emacs and makes its text space available for other use.

The buffer object for the buffer that has been killed remains in existence as long as anything refers to it, but it is specially marked so that you cannot make it current or display it. Killed buffers retain their identity, however; two distinct buffers, when killed, remain distinct according to `eq`.

If you kill a buffer that is current or displayed in a window, Emacs automatically selects or displays some other buffer instead. This means that killing a buffer can in general change the current buffer. Therefore, when you kill a buffer, you should also take the precautions associated with changing the current buffer (unless you happen to know that the buffer being killed isn't current). See Section 24.2 [Current Buffer], page 55.

If you kill a buffer that is the base buffer of one or more indirect buffers, the indirect buffers are automatically killed as well.

The `buffer-name` of a killed buffer is `nil`. You can use this feature to test whether a buffer has been killed:

```
(defun buffer-killed-p (buffer)
  "Return t if BUFFER is killed."
  (not (buffer-name buffer)))
```

kill-buffer *buffer-or-name*   Command

This function kills the buffer *buffer-or-name*, freeing all its memory for use as space for other buffers. (Emacs version 18 and older was unable to return the memory to the operating system.) It returns `nil`.

Any processes that have this buffer as the `process-buffer` are sent the `SIGHUP` signal, which normally causes them to terminate. (The basic meaning of `SIGHUP` is that a dialup line has been disconnected.) See Section 33.5 [Deleting Processes], page 235.

If the buffer is visiting a file and contains unsaved changes, `kill-buffer` asks the user to confirm before the buffer is killed. It does this even if not called interactively. To prevent the request for confirmation, clear the modified flag before calling `kill-buffer`. See Section 24.5 [Buffer Modification], page 61.

Killing a buffer that is already dead has no effect.

```
(kill-buffer "foo.unchanged")
    ⇒ nil
(kill-buffer "foo.changed")

---------- Buffer: Minibuffer ----------
Buffer foo.changed modified; kill anyway? (yes or no) yes
---------- Buffer: Minibuffer ----------

    ⇒ nil
```

kill-buffer-query-functions   Variable

After confirming unsaved changes, `kill-buffer` calls the functions in the list `kill-buffer-query-functions`, in order of appearance, with no arguments. The buffer being killed is the current buffer when they are called. The idea is that these functions ask for confirmation from the user for various nonstandard reasons. If any of them returns `nil`, `kill-buffer` spares the buffer's life.

kill-buffer-hook   Variable

This is a normal hook run by `kill-buffer` after asking all the questions it is going to ask, just before actually killing the buffer. The buffer to be killed is current when the hook functions run. See Section 20.4 [Hooks], page 360, vol. 1.

buffer-offer-save   Variable

This variable, if non-`nil` in a particular buffer, tells `save-buffers-kill-emacs` and `save-some-buffers` to offer to save that buffer, just as they offer to save file-visiting buffers. The variable `buffer-offer-save` automatically becomes buffer-local when set for any reason. See Section 10.9 [Buffer-Local Variables], page 151, vol. 1.

24.11 Indirect Buffers

An *indirect buffer* shares the text of some other buffer, which is called the *base buffer* of the indirect buffer. In some ways it is the analogue, for buffers, of a symbolic link among files. The base buffer may not itself be an indirect buffer.

The text of the indirect buffer is always identical to the text of its base buffer; changes made by editing either one are visible immediately in the other. This includes the text properties as well as the characters themselves.

But in all other respects, the indirect buffer and its base buffer are completely separate. They have different names, different values of point, different narrowing, different markers and overlays (though inserting or deleting text in either buffer relocates the markers and overlays for both), different major modes, and different local variables.

An indirect buffer cannot visit a file, but its base buffer can. If you try to save the indirect buffer, that actually works by saving the base buffer.

Killing an indirect buffer has no effect on its base buffer. Killing the base buffer effectively kills the indirect buffer in that it cannot ever again be the current buffer.

make-indirect-buffer *base-buffer name*   Command
This creates an indirect buffer named *name* whose base buffer is *base-buffer*. The argument *base-buffer* may be a buffer or a string.

If *base-buffer* is an indirect buffer, its base buffer is used as the base for the new buffer.

buffer-base-buffer *buffer*   Function
This function returns the base buffer of *buffer*. If *buffer* is not indirect, the value is `nil`. Otherwise, the value is another buffer, which is never an indirect buffer.

25 Windows

This chapter describes most of the functions and variables related to Emacs windows. See Chapter 35 [Display], page 275, for information on how text is displayed in windows.

25.1 Basic Concepts of Emacs Windows

A *window* in Emacs is the physical area of the screen in which a buffer is displayed. The term is also used to refer to a Lisp object that represents that screen area in Emacs Lisp. It should be clear from the context which is meant.

Emacs groups windows into frames. A frame represents an area of screen available for Emacs to use. Each frame always contains at least one window, but you can subdivide it vertically or horizontally into multiple nonoverlapping Emacs windows.

In each frame, at any time, one and only one window is designated as *selected within the frame*. The frame's cursor appears in that window. At ant time, one frame is the selected frame; and the window selected within that frame is *the selected window*. The selected window's buffer is usually the current buffer (except when `set-buffer` has been used). See Section 24.2 [Current Buffer], page 55.

For practical purposes, a window exists only while it is displayed in a frame. Once removed from the frame, the window is effectively deleted and should not be used, *even though there may still be references to it* from other Lisp objects. Restoring a saved window configuration is the only way for a window no longer on the screen to come back to life. (See Section 25.3 [Deleting Windows], page 73.)

Each window has the following attributes:

- containing frame
- window height
- window width
- window edges with respect to the screen or frame
- the buffer it displays
- position within the buffer at the upper left of the window
- amount of horizontal scrolling, in columns
- point
- the mark
- how recently the window was selected

Users create multiple windows so they can look at several buffers at once. Lisp libraries use multiple windows for a variety of reasons, but most often to display related information. In Rmail, for example, you can move through a summary buffer in one window while the other window shows messages one at a time as they are reached.

The meaning of "window" in Emacs is similar to what it means in the context of general-purpose window systems such as X, but not identical. The X Window System places X windows on the screen; Emacs uses one or more X windows as frames, and subdivides them into Emacs windows. When you use Emacs on a character-only terminal, Emacs treats the whole terminal screen as one frame.

Most window systems support arbitrarily located overlapping windows. In contrast, Emacs windows are *tiled*; they never overlap, and together they fill the whole screen or frame. Because of the way in which Emacs creates new windows and resizes them, you can't create every conceivable tiling of windows on an Emacs frame. See Section 25.2 [Splitting Windows], page 70, and Section 25.13 [Size of Window], page 89.

See Chapter 35 [Display], page 275, for information on how the contents of the window's buffer are displayed in the window.

windowp *object*   Function
   This function returns t if *object* is a window.

25.2 Splitting Windows

The functions described here are the primitives used to split a window into two windows. Two higher level functions sometimes split a window, but not always: `pop-to-buffer` and `display-buffer` (see Section 25.7 [Displaying Buffers], page 78).

The functions described here do not accept a buffer as an argument. The two "halves" of the split window initially display the same buffer previously visible in the window that was split.

split-window &optional *window size horizontal*   Command
   This function splits *window* into two windows. The original window *window* remains the selected window, but occupies only part of its former screen area. The rest is occupied by a newly created window which is returned as the value of this function.

   If *horizontal* is non-nil, then *window* splits into two side by side windows. The original window *window* keeps the leftmost *size* columns, and gives the rest of the columns to the new window. Otherwise, it splits into windows one above the other, and *window* keeps the upper *size* lines and gives the rest of the lines to the new window. The original window is therefore the left-hand or upper of the two, and the new window is the right-hand or lower.

If *window* is omitted or `nil`, then the selected window is split. If *size* is omitted or `nil`, then *window* is divided evenly into two parts. (If there is an odd line, it is allocated to the new window.) When `split-window` is called interactively, all its arguments are `nil`.

The following example starts with one window on a screen that is 50 lines high by 80 columns wide; then the window is split.

```
(setq w (selected-window))
     ⇒ #<window 8 on windows.texi>
(window-edges)             ; Edges in order:
     ⇒ (0 0 80 50)        ;   left–top–right–bottom
;; Returns window created
(setq w2 (split-window w 15))
     ⇒ #<window 28 on windows.texi>
(window-edges w2)
     ⇒ (0 15 80 50)       ; Bottom window;
                          ;   top is line 15
(window-edges w)
     ⇒ (0 0 80 15)        ; Top window
```

The screen looks like this:

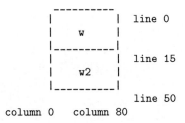

Next, the top window is split horizontally:

```
(setq w3 (split-window w 35 t))
     ⇒ #<window 32 on windows.texi>
(window-edges w3)
     ⇒ (35 0 80 15)   ; Left edge at column 35
(window-edges w)
     ⇒ (0 0 35 15)    ; Right edge at column 35
(window-edges w2)
     ⇒ (0 15 80 50)   ; Bottom window unchanged
```

Now, the screen looks like this:

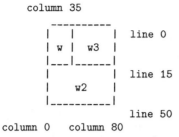

```
column 35

      ----------
     |   |      |  line 0
     | w |  w3  |
     |___|_____|
     |          |  line 15
     |    w2    |
     |_____|
                   line 50
  column 0    column 80
```

Normally, Emacs indicates the border between two side-by-side windows with a scroll bar (see Section 26.3.3 [X Frame Parameters], page 100) or '|' characters. The display table can specify alternative border characters; see Section 35.14 [Display Tables], page 294.

split-window-vertically *size*   Command
> This function splits the selected window into two windows, one above the other, leaving the selected window with *size* lines.
>
> This function is simply an interface to `split-windows`. Here is the complete function definition for it:
>
> ```
> (defun split-window-vertically (&optional arg)
>   "Split current window into two windows, one above the other."
>   (interactive "P")
>   (split-window nil (and arg (prefix-numeric-value arg))))
> ```

split-window-horizontally *size*   Command
> This function splits the selected window into two windows side-by-side, leaving the selected window with *size* columns.
>
> This function is simply an interface to `split-windows`. Here is the complete definition for `split-window-horizontally` (except for part of the documentation string):
>
> ```
> (defun split-window-horizontally (&optional arg)
>   "Split selected window into two windows, side by side..."
>   (interactive "P")
>   (split-window nil (and arg (prefix-numeric-value arg)) t))
> ```

one-window-p &optional *no-mini all-frames*   Function
> This function returns non-nil if there is only one window. The argument *no-mini*, if non-nil, means don't count the minibuffer even if it is active; otherwise, the minibuffer window is included, if active, in the total number of windows, which is compared against one.
>
> The argument *all-frames* specifies which frames to consider. Here are the possible values and their meanings:

nil   Count the windows in the selected frame, plus the mini-buffer used by that frame even if it lies in some other frame.

t   Count all windows in all existing frames.

visible   Count all windows in all visible frames.

0   Count all windows in all visible or iconified frames.

anything else
       Count precisely the windows in the selected frame, and no others.

25.3 Deleting Windows

A window remains visible on its frame unless you *delete* it by calling certain functions that delete windows. A deleted window cannot appear on the screen, but continues to exist as a Lisp object until there are no references to it. There is no way to cancel the deletion of a window aside from restoring a saved window configuration (see Section 25.16 [Window Configurations], page 94). Restoring a window configuration also deletes any windows that aren't part of that configuration.

When you delete a window, the space it took up is given to one adjacent sibling. (In Emacs version 18, the space was divided evenly among all the siblings.)

window-live-p *window*   Function
This function returns nil if *window* is deleted, and t otherwise.

Warning: Erroneous information or fatal errors may result from using a deleted window as if it were live.

delete-window &optional *window*   Command
This function removes *window* from the display. If *window* is omitted, then the selected window is deleted. An error is signaled if there is only one window when delete-window is called.

This function returns nil.

When delete-window is called interactively, *window* defaults to the selected window.

delete-other-windows &optional *window*   Command
This function makes *window* the only window on its frame, by deleting the other windows in that frame. If *window* is omitted or nil, then the selected window is used by default.

The result is nil.

delete-windows-on *buffer* &optional *frame*   Command
This function deletes all windows showing *buffer*. If there are no windows showing *buffer*, it does nothing.

`delete-windows-on` operates frame by frame. If a frame has several windows showing different buffers, then those showing *buffer* are removed, and the others expand to fill the space. If all windows in some frame are showing *buffer* (including the case where there is only one window), then the frame reverts to having a single window showing another buffer chosen with `other-buffer`. See Section 24.8 [The Buffer List], page 64.

The argument *frame* controls which frames to operate on:

- If it is `nil`, operate on the selected frame.
- If it is `t`, operate on all frames.
- If it is `visible`, operate on all visible frames.
- 0 If it is 0, operate on all visible or iconified frames.
- If it is a frame, operate on that frame.

This function always returns `nil`.

25.4 Selecting Windows

When a window is selected, the buffer in the window becomes the current buffer, and the cursor will appear in it.

selected-window   Function
This function returns the selected window. This is the window in which the cursor appears and to which many commands apply.

select-window *window*   Function
This function makes *window* the selected window. The cursor then appears in *window* (on redisplay). The buffer being displayed in *window* is immediately designated the current buffer.

The return value is *window*.

```
(setq w (next-window))
(select-window w)
     ⇒ #<window 65 on windows.texi>
```

save-selected-window *forms...*   Macro
This macro records the selected window, executes *forms* in sequence, then restores the earlier selected window. It does not save or restore anything about the sizes, arrangement or contents of windows; therefore, if the *forms* change them, the changes are permanent.

The following functions choose one of the windows on the screen, offering various criteria for the choice.

get-lru-window &optional *frame*   Function
This function returns the window least recently "used" (that is, selected). The selected window is always the most recently used window.

The selected window can be the least recently used window if it is the only window. A newly created window becomes the least recently used window until it is selected. A minibuffer window is never a candidate.

The argument *frame* controls which windows are considered.

- If it is `nil`, consider windows on the selected frame.
- If it is `t`, consider windows on all frames.
- If it is `visible`, consider windows on all visible frames.
- If it is 0, consider windows on all visible or iconified frames.
- If it is a frame, consider windows on that frame.

get-largest-window &optional *frame*   Function
This function returns the window with the largest area (height times width). If there are no side-by-side windows, then this is the window with the most lines. A minibuffer window is never a candidate.

If there are two windows of the same size, then the function returns the window that is first in the cyclic ordering of windows (see following section), starting from the selected window.

The argument *frame* controls which set of windows are considered. See `get-lru-window`, above.

25.5 Cyclic Ordering of Windows

When you use the command `C-x o` (`other-window`) to select the next window, it moves through all the windows on the screen in a specific cyclic order. For any given configuration of windows, this order never varies. It is called the *cyclic ordering of windows*.

This ordering generally goes from top to bottom, and from left to right. But it may go down first or go right first, depending on the order in which the windows were split.

If the first split was vertical (into windows one above each other), and then the subwindows were split horizontally, then the ordering is left to right in the top of the frame, and then left to right in the next lower part of the frame, and so on. If the first split was horizontal, the ordering is top to bottom in the left part, and so on. In general, within each set of siblings at any level in the window tree, the order is left to right, or top to bottom.

next-window &optional *window minibuf all-frames*   Function
This function returns the window following *window* in the cyclic ordering of windows. This is the window that C-x o would select if typed when *window* is selected. If *window* is the only window visible, then this function returns *window*. If omitted, *window* defaults to the selected window.

The value of the argument *minibuf* determines whether the minibuffer is included in the window order. Normally, when *minibuf* is nil, the minibuffer is included if it is currently active; this is the behavior of C-x o. (The minibuffer window is active while the minibuffer is in use. See Chapter 17 [Minibuffers], page 253, vol. 1.)

If *minibuf* is t, then the cyclic ordering includes the minibuffer window even if it is not active.

If *minibuf* is neither t nor nil, then the minibuffer window is not included even if it is active.

The argument *all-frames* specifies which frames to consider. Here are the possible values and their meanings:

nil   Consider all the windows in *window*'s frame, plus the minibuffer used by that frame even if it lies in some other frame.

t   Consider all windows in all existing frames.

visible   Consider all windows in all visible frames. (To get useful results, you must ensure *window* is in a visible frame.)

0   Consider all windows in all visible or iconified frames.

anything else
            Consider precisely the windows in *window*'s frame, and no others.

This example assumes there are two windows, both displaying the buffer 'windows.texi':

```
(selected-window)
     ⇒ #<window 56 on windows.texi>
(next-window (selected-window))
     ⇒ #<window 52 on windows.texi>
(next-window (next-window (selected-window)))
     ⇒ #<window 56 on windows.texi>
```

previous-window &optional *window minibuf all-frames*   Function
This function returns the window preceding *window* in the cyclic ordering of windows. The other arguments specify which windows to include in the cycle, as in next-window.

other-window *count*   Command

> This function selects the *count*th following window in the cyclic order.
> If count is negative, then it selects the −*count*th preceding window. It
> returns `nil`.
>
> In an interactive call, *count* is the numeric prefix argument.

walk-windows *proc* &optional *minibuf all-frames*   Function

> This function cycles through all windows, calling `proc` once for each
> window with the window as its sole argument.
>
> The optional arguments *minibuf* and *all-frames* specify the set of win-
> dows to include in the scan. See `next-window`, above, for details.

25.6 Buffers and Windows

This section describes low-level functions to examine windows or to display buffers in windows in a precisely controlled fashion. See the following
section for related functions that find a window to use and specify a buffer
for it. The functions described there are easier to use than these, but they
employ heuristics in choosing or creating a window; use these functions when
you need complete control.

set-window-buffer *window buffer-or-name*   Function

> This function makes *window* display *buffer-or-name* as its contents. It
> returns `nil`.
>
>   (set-window-buffer (selected-window) "foo")
>   ⇒ nil

window-buffer &optional *window*   Function

> This function returns the buffer that *window* is displaying. If *window*
> is omitted, this function returns the buffer for the selected window.
>
>   (window-buffer)
>   ⇒ #<buffer windows.texi>

get-buffer-window *buffer-or-name* &optional *all-frames*   Function

> This function returns a window currently displaying *buffer-or-name*,
> or `nil` if there is none. If there are several such windows, then the
> function returns the first one in the cyclic ordering of windows, starting
> from the selected window. See Section 25.5 [Cyclic Window Ordering],
> page 75.
>
> The argument *all-frames* controls which windows to consider.
>
> - If it is `nil`, consider windows on the selected frame.
> - If it is `t`, consider windows on all frames.
> - If it is `visible`, consider windows on all visible frames.

- If it is 0, consider windows on all visible or iconified frames.
- If it is a frame, consider windows on that frame.

25.7 Displaying Buffers in Windows

In this section we describe convenient functions that choose a window automatically and use it to display a specified buffer. These functions can also split an existing window in certain circumstances. We also describe variables that parameterize the heuristics used for choosing a window. See the preceding section for low-level functions that give you more precise control.

Do not use the functions in this section in order to make a buffer current so that a Lisp program can access or modify it; they are too drastic for that purpose, since they change the display of buffers in windows, which is gratuitous and will surprise the user. Instead, use `set-buffer` (see Section 24.2 [Current Buffer], page 55) and `save-excursion` (see Section 27.3 [Excursions], page 129), which designate buffers as current for programmed access without affecting the display of buffers in windows.

switch-to-buffer *buffer-or-name* &optional *norecord*   Command
This function makes *buffer-or-name* the current buffer, and also displays the buffer in the selected window. This means that a human can see the buffer and subsequent keyboard commands will apply to it. Contrast this with `set-buffer`, which makes *buffer-or-name* the current buffer but does not display it in the selected window. See Section 24.2 [Current Buffer], page 55.

If *buffer-or-name* does not identify an existing buffer, then a new buffer by that name is created. The major mode for the new buffer is set according to the variable `default-major-mode`. See Section 20.1.3 [Auto Major Mode], page 347, vol. 1.

Normally the specified buffer is put at the front of the buffer list. This affects the operation of `other-buffer`. However, if *norecord* is non-`nil`, this is not done. See Section 24.8 [The Buffer List], page 64.

The `switch-to-buffer` function is often used interactively, as the binding of `C-x b`. It is also used frequently in programs. It always returns `nil`.

switch-to-buffer-other-window *buffer-or-name*   Command
This function makes *buffer-or-name* the current buffer and displays it in a window not currently selected. It then selects that window. The handling of the buffer is the same as in `switch-to-buffer`.

The currently selected window is absolutely never used to do the job. If it is the only window, then it is split to make a distinct window for this purpose. If the selected window is already displaying the buffer,

then it continues to do so, but another window is nonetheless found
to display it in as well.

pop-to-buffer *buffer-or-name* &optional *other-window*   Function
This function makes *buffer-or-name* the current buffer and switches to
it in some window, preferably not the window previously selected. The
"popped-to" window becomes the selected window within its frame.

If the variable `pop-up-frames` is non-`nil`, `pop-to-buffer` looks for a
window in any visible frame already displaying the buffer; if there is
one, it returns that window and makes it be selected within its frame.
If there is none, it creates a new frame and displays the buffer in it.

If `pop-up-frames` is `nil`, then `pop-to-buffer` operates entirely within
the selected frame. (If the selected frame has just a minibuffer, `pop-
to-buffer` operates within the most recently selected frame that was
not just a minibuffer.)

If the variable `pop-up-windows` is non-`nil`, windows may be split to
create a new window that is different from the original window. For
details, see Section 25.8 [Choosing Window], page 80.

If *other-window* is non-`nil`, `pop-to-buffer` finds or creates another
window even if *buffer-or-name* is already visible in the selected window. Thus *buffer-or-name* could end up displayed in two windows. On
the other hand, if *buffer-or-name* is already displayed in the selected
window and *other-window* is `nil`, then the selected window is considered sufficient display for *buffer-or-name*, so that nothing needs to be
done.

All the variables that affect `display-buffer` affect `pop-to-buffer` as
well. See Section 25.8 [Choosing Window], page 80.

If *buffer-or-name* is a string that does not name an existing buffer, a
buffer by that name is created. The major mode for the new buffer is
set according to the variable `default-major-mode`. See Section 20.1.3
[Auto Major Mode], page 347, vol. 1.

replace-buffer-in-windows *buffer*   Command
This function replaces *buffer* with some other buffer in all windows
displaying it. The other buffer used is chosen with `other-buffer`.
In the usual applications of this function, you don't care which other
buffer is used; you just want to make sure that *buffer* is no longer
displayed.

This function returns `nil`.

25.8 Choosing a Window for Display

This section describes the basic facility that chooses a window to display a buffer in—`display-buffer`. All the higher-level functions and commands use this subroutine. Here we describe how to use `display-buffer` and how to customize it.

display-buffer *buffer-or-name* &optional   Command
        not-this-window

This command makes *buffer-or-name* appear in some window, like `pop-to-buffer`, but it does not select that window and does not make the buffer current. The identity of the selected window is unaltered by this function.

If *not-this-window* is non-`nil`, it means to display the specified buffer in a window other than the selected one, even if it is already on display in the selected window. This can cause the buffer to appear in two windows at once. Otherwise, if *buffer-or-name* is already being displayed in any window, that is good enough, so this function does nothing.

`display-buffer` returns the window chosen to display *buffer-or-name*.

Precisely how `display-buffer` finds or creates a window depends on the variables described below.

pop-up-windows   User Option

This variable controls whether `display-buffer` makes new windows. If it is non-`nil` and there is only one window, then that window is split. If it is `nil`, then `display-buffer` does not split the single window, but uses it whole.

split-height-threshold   User Option

This variable determines when `display-buffer` may split a window, if there are multiple windows. `display-buffer` always splits the largest window if it has at least this many lines. If the largest window is not this tall, it is split only if it is the sole window and `pop-up-windows` is non-`nil`.

pop-up-frames   User Option

This variable controls whether `display-buffer` makes new frames. If it is non-`nil`, `display-buffer` looks for an existing window already displaying the desired buffer, on any visible frame. If it finds one, it returns that window. Otherwise it makes a new frame. The variables `pop-up-windows` and `split-height-threshold` do not matter if `pop-up-frames` is non-`nil`.

If `pop-up-frames` is `nil`, then `display-buffer` either splits a window or reuses one.

See Chapter 26 [Frames], page 97, for more information.

pop-up-frame-function   Variable

This variable specifies how to make a new frame if `pop-up-frames` is non-`nil`.

Its value should be a function of no arguments. When `display-buffer` makes a new frame, it does so by calling that function, which should return a frame. The default value of the variable is a function that creates a frame using parameters from `pop-up-frame-alist`.

pop-up-frame-alist   Variable

This variable holds an alist specifying frame parameters used when `display-buffer` makes a new frame. See Section 26.3 [Frame Parameters], page 99, for more information about frame parameters.

special-display-buffer-names   Variable

A list of buffer names for buffers that should be displayed specially. If the buffer's name is in this list, `display-buffer` handles the buffer specially.

By default, special display means to give the buffer a dedicated frame.

If an element is a list, instead of a string, then the CAR of the list is the buffer name, and the rest of the list says how to create the frame. There are two possibilities for the rest of the list. It can be an alist, specifying frame parameters, or it can contain a function and arguments to give to it. (The function's first argument is always the buffer to be displayed; the arguments from the list come after that.)

special-display-regexps   Variable

A list of regular expressions that specify buffers that should be displayed specially. If the buffer's name matches any of the regular expressions in this list, `display-buffer` handles the buffer specially.

By default, special display means to give the buffer a dedicated frame.

If an element is a list, instead of a string, then the CAR of the list is the regular expression, and the rest of the list says how to create the frame. See above, under `special-display-buffer-names`.

special-display-function   Variable

This variable holds the function to call to display a buffer specially. It receives the buffer as an argument, and should return the window in which it is displayed.

The default value of this variable is `special-display-popup-frame`.

special-display-popup-frame *buffer*   Function

This function makes *buffer* visible in a frame of its own. If *buffer* is already displayed in a window in some frame, it makes the frame visible and raises it, to use that window. Otherwise, it creates a frame that will be dedicated to *buffer*.

This function uses an existing window displaying *buffer* whether or not it is in a frame of its own; but if you set up the above variables in your init file, before *buffer* was created, then presumably the window was previously made by this function.

special-display-frame-alist   User Option
This variable holds frame parameters for `special-display-popup-frame` to use when it creates a frame.

same-window-buffer-names   Variable
A list of buffer names for buffers that should be displayed in the selected window. If the buffer's name is in this list, `display-buffer` handles the buffer by switching to it in the selected window.

same-window-regexps   Variable
A list of regular expressions that specify buffers that should be displayed in the selected window. If the buffer's name matches any of the regular expressions in this list, `display-buffer` handles the buffer by switching to it in the selected window.

display-buffer-function   Variable
This variable is the most flexible way to customize the behavior of `display-buffer`. If it is non-`nil`, it should be a function that `display-buffer` calls to do the work. The function should accept two arguments, the same two arguments that `display-buffer` received. It should choose or create a window, display the specified buffer, and then return the window.

This hook takes precedence over all the other options and hooks described above.

A window can be marked as "dedicated" to its buffer. Then `display-buffer` does not try to use that window.

window-dedicated-p *window*   Function
This function returns `t` if *window* is marked as dedicated; otherwise `nil`.

set-window-dedicated-p *window flag*   Function
This function marks *window* as dedicated if *flag* is non-`nil`, and nondedicated otherwise.

25.9 Windows and Point

Each window has its own value of point, independent of the value of point in other windows displaying the same buffer. This makes it useful to have multiple windows showing one buffer.

- The window point is established when a window is first created; it is initialized from the buffer's point, or from the window point of another window opened on the buffer if such a window exists.

- Selecting a window sets the value of point in its buffer to the window's value of point. Conversely, deselecting a window sets the window's value of point from that of the buffer. Thus, when you switch between windows that display a given buffer, the point value for the selected window is in effect in the buffer, while the point values for the other windows are stored in those windows.

- As long as the selected window displays the current buffer, the window's point and the buffer's point always move together; they remain equal.

- See Chapter 27 [Positions], page 119, for more details on buffer positions.

As far as the user is concerned, point is where the cursor is, and when the user switches to another buffer, the cursor jumps to the position of point in that buffer.

window-point *window*   Function

This function returns the current position of point in *window*. For a nonselected window, this is the value point would have (in that window's buffer) if that window were selected.

When *window* is the selected window and its buffer is also the current buffer, the value returned is the same as point in that buffer.

Strictly speaking, it would be more correct to return the "top-level" value of point, outside of any `save-excursion` forms. But that value is hard to find.

set-window-point *window position*   Function

This function positions point in *window* at position *position* in *window*'s buffer.

25.10 The Window Start Position

Each window contains a marker used to keep track of a buffer position that specifies where in the buffer display should start. This position is called the *display-start* position of the window (or just the *start*). The character after this position is the one that appears at the upper left corner of the window. It is usually, but not inevitably, at the beginning of a text line.

window-start &optional *window*   Function

This function returns the display-start position of window *window*. If *window* is `nil`, the selected window is used. For example,

```
(window-start)
     ⇒ 7058
```

When you create a window, or display a different buffer in it, the display-start position is set to a display-start position recently used for the same buffer, or 1 if the buffer doesn't have any.

For a realistic example, see the description of `count-lines` in Section 27.2.4 [Text Lines], page 122.

window-end &optional *window*   Function

This function returns the position of the end of the display in window *window*. If *window* is `nil`, the selected window is used.

Simply changing the buffer text or moving point does not update the value that `window-end` returns. The value is updated only when Emacs redisplays and redisplay actually finishes.

If the last redisplay of *window* was preempted, and did not finish, Emacs does not know the position of the end of display in that window. In that case, this function returns a value that is not correct. In a future version, `window-end` will return `nil` in that case.

set-window-start *window position* &optional *noforce*   Function

This function sets the display-start position of *window* to *position* in *window*'s buffer. It returns *position*.

The display routines insist that the position of point be visible when a buffer is displayed. Normally, they change the display-start position (that is, scroll the window) whenever necessary to make point visible. However, if you specify the start position with this function using `nil` for *noforce*, it means you want display to start at *position* even if that would put the location of point off the screen. If this does place point off screen, the display routines move point to the left margin on the middle line in the window.

For example, if point is 1 and you set the start of the window to 2, then point would be "above" the top of the window. The display routines will automatically move point if it is still 1 when redisplay occurs. Here is an example:

```
;; Here is what 'foo' looks like before executing
;;     the set-window-start expression.
```

```
---------- Buffer: foo ----------
⋆This is the contents of buffer foo.
2
3
4
5
6
---------- Buffer: foo ----------

(set-window-start
 (selected-window)
 (1+ (window-start)))
⇒ 2
```

;; Here is what 'foo' looks like after executing
;;   the set-window-start expression.

```
---------- Buffer: foo ----------
his is the contents of buffer foo.
2
3
⋆4
5
6
---------- Buffer: foo ----------
```

If *noforce* is non-nil, and *position* would place point off screen at the next redisplay, then redisplay computes a new window-start position that works well with point, and thus *position* is not used.

pos-visible-in-window-p &optional *position window*   Function
This function returns t if *position* is within the range of text currently visible on the screen in *window*. It returns nil if *position* is scrolled vertically out of view. The argument *position* defaults to the current position of point; *window*, to the selected window. Here is an example:

```
(or (pos-visible-in-window-p
      (point) (selected-window))
    (recenter 0))
```

The pos-visible-in-window-p function considers only vertical scrolling. If *position* is out of view only because *window* has been scrolled horizontally, pos-visible-in-window-p returns t. See Section 25.12 [Horizontal Scrolling], page 88.

25.11 Vertical Scrolling

Vertical scrolling means moving the text up or down in a window. It works by changing the value of the window's display-start location. It may also change the value of `window-point` to keep it on the screen.

In the commands `scroll-up` and `scroll-down`, the directions "up" and "down" refer to the motion of the text in the buffer at which you are looking through the window. Imagine that the text is written on a long roll of paper and that the scrolling commands move the paper up and down. Thus, if you are looking at text in the middle of a buffer and repeatedly call `scroll-down`, you will eventually see the beginning of the buffer.

Some people have urged that the opposite convention be used: they imagine that the window moves over text that remains in place. Then "down" commands would take you to the end of the buffer. This view is more consistent with the actual relationship between windows and the text in the buffer, but it is less like what the user sees. The position of a window on the terminal does not move, and short scrolling commands clearly move the text up or down on the screen. We have chosen names that fit the user's point of view.

The scrolling functions (aside from `scroll-other-window`) have unpredictable results if the current buffer is different from the buffer that is displayed in the selected window. See Section 24.2 [Current Buffer], page 55.

scroll-up &optional *count*   Command
> This function scrolls the text in the selected window upward *count* lines. If *count* is negative, scrolling is actually downward.
>
> If *count* is `nil` (or omitted), then the length of scroll is `next-screen-context-lines` lines less than the usable height of the window (not counting its mode line).
>
> `scroll-up` returns `nil`.

scroll-down &optional *count*   Command
> This function scrolls the text in the selected window downward *count* lines. If *count* is negative, scrolling is actually upward.
>
> If *count* is omitted or `nil`, then the length of the scroll is `next-screen-context-lines` lines less than the usable height of the window (not counting its mode line).
>
> `scroll-down` returns `nil`.

scroll-other-window &optional *count*   Command
> This function scrolls the text in another window upward *count* lines. Negative values of *count*, or `nil`, are handled as in `scroll-up`.
>
> You can specify a buffer to scroll with the variable `other-window-scroll-buffer`. When the selected window is the minibuffer, the

next window is normally the one at the top left corner. You can specify a different window to scroll with the variable `minibuffer-scroll-window`. This variable has no effect when any other window is selected. See Section 17.8 [Minibuffer Misc], page 272, vol. 1.

When the minibuffer is active, it is the next window if the selected window is the one at the bottom right corner. In this case, `scroll-other-window` attempts to scroll the minibuffer. If the minibuffer contains just one line, it has nowhere to scroll to, so the line reappears after the echo area momentarily displays the message "Beginning of buffer".

other-window-scroll-buffer   Variable
If this variable is non-`nil`, it tells `scroll-other-window` which buffer to scroll.

scroll-step   User Option
This variable controls how scrolling is done automatically when point moves off the screen. If the value is zero, then redisplay scrolls the text to center point vertically in the window. If the value is a positive integer *n*, then redisplay brings point back on screen by scrolling *n* lines in either direction, if possible; otherwise, it centers point. The default value is zero.

next-screen-context-lines   User Option
The value of this variable is the number of lines of continuity to retain when scrolling by full screens. For example, `scroll-up` with an argument of `nil` scrolls so that this many lines at the bottom of the window appear instead at the top. The default value is 2.

recenter &optional *count*   Command
This function scrolls the selected window to put the text where point is located at a specified vertical position within the window.

If *count* is a nonnegative number, it puts the line containing point *count* lines down from the top of the window. If *count* is a negative number, then it counts upward from the bottom of the window, so that −1 stands for the last usable line in the window. If *count* is a non-`nil` list, then it stands for the line in the middle of the window.

If *count* is `nil`, `recenter` puts the line containing point in the middle of the window, then clears and redisplays the entire selected frame.

When `recenter` is called interactively, *count* is the raw prefix argument. Thus, typing C-u as the prefix sets the *count* to a non-`nil` list, while typing C-u 4 sets *count* to 4, which positions the current line four lines from the top.

With an argument of zero, `recenter` positions the current line at the top of the window. This action is so handy that some people make a separate key binding to do this. For example,

```
(defun line-to-top-of-window ()
  "Scroll current line to top of window.
Replaces three keystroke sequence C-u 0 C-l."
  (interactive)
  (recenter 0))

(global-set-key [kp-multiply] 'line-to-top-of-window)
```

25.12 Horizontal Scrolling

Because we read English first from top to bottom and second from left to right, horizontal scrolling is not like vertical scrolling. Vertical scrolling involves selection of a contiguous portion of text to display. Horizontal scrolling causes part of each line to go off screen. The amount of horizontal scrolling is therefore specified as a number of columns rather than as a position in the buffer. It has nothing to do with the display-start position returned by `window-start`.

Usually, no horizontal scrolling is in effect; then the leftmost column is at the left edge of the window. In this state, scrolling to the right is meaningless, since there is no data to the left of the screen to be revealed by it; so this is not allowed. Scrolling to the left is allowed; it scrolls the first columns of text off the edge of the window and can reveal additional columns on the right that were truncated before. Once a window has a nonzero amount of leftward horizontal scrolling, you can scroll it back to the right, but only so far as to reduce the net horizontal scroll to zero. There is no limit to how far left you can scroll, but eventually all the text will disappear off the left edge.

scroll-left *count*   Command
> This function scrolls the selected window *count* columns to the left (or to the right if *count* is negative). The return value is the total amount of leftward horizontal scrolling in effect after the change—just like the value returned by `window-hscroll` (below).

scroll-right *count*   Command
> This function scrolls the selected window *count* columns to the right (or to the left if *count* is negative). The return value is the total amount of leftward horizontal scrolling in effect after the change—just like the value returned by `window-hscroll` (below).

Once you scroll a window as far right as it can go, back to its normal position where the total leftward scrolling is zero, attempts to scroll any farther right have no effect.

window-hscroll &optional *window*   Function
This function returns the total leftward horizontal scrolling of *window*—the number of columns by which the text in *window* is scrolled left past the left margin.

The value is never negative. It is zero when no horizontal scrolling has been done in *window* (which is usually the case).

If *window* is `nil`, the selected window is used.

```
(window-hscroll)
     ⇒ 0
(scroll-left 5)
     ⇒ 5
(window-hscroll)
     ⇒ 5
```

set-window-hscroll *window columns*   Function
This function sets the number of columns from the left margin that *window* is scrolled to the value of *columns*. The argument *columns* should be zero or positive; if not, it is taken as zero.

The value returned is *columns*.

```
(set-window-hscroll (selected-window) 10)
     ⇒ 10
```

Here is how you can determine whether a given position *position* is off the screen due to horizontal scrolling:

```
(defun hscroll-on-screen (window position)
  (save-excursion
    (goto-char position)
    (and
     (>= (- (current-column) (window-hscroll window)) 0)
     (< (- (current-column) (window-hscroll window))
        (window-width window)))))
```

25.13 The Size of a Window

An Emacs window is rectangular, and its size information consists of the height (the number of lines) and the width (the number of character positions in each line). The mode line is included in the height. But the width does not count the scroll bar or the column of '|' characters that separates side-by-side windows.

The following three functions return size information about a window:

window-height &optional *window*   Function
> This function returns the number of lines in *window*, including its
> mode line. If *window* fills its entire frame, this is one less than the
> value of `frame-height` on that frame (since the last line is always
> reserved for the minibuffer).
>
> If *window* is `nil`, the function uses the selected window.
>
> ```
> (window-height)
>      ⇒ 23
> (split-window-vertically)
>      ⇒ #<window 4 on windows.texi>
> (window-height)
>      ⇒ 11
> ```

window-width &optional *window*   Function
> This function returns the number of columns in *window*. If *window*
> fills its entire frame, this is the same as the value of `frame-width` on
> that frame. The width does not include the window's scroll bar or the
> column of '|' characters that separates side-by-side windows.
>
> If *window* is `nil`, the function uses the selected window.
>
> ```
> (window-width)
>      ⇒ 80
> ```

window-edges &optional *window*   Function
> This function returns a list of the edge coordinates of *window*. If
> *window* is `nil`, the selected window is used.
>
> The order of the list is (*left top right bottom*), all elements relative
> to 0, 0 at the top left corner of the frame. The element *right* of the
> value is one more than the rightmost column used by *window*, and
> *bottom* is one more than the bottommost row used by *window* and its
> mode-line.
>
> When you have side-by-side windows, the right edge value for a win-
> dow with a neighbor on the right includes the width of the separator
> between the window and that neighbor. This separator may be a col-
> umn of '|' characters or it may be a scroll bar. Since the width of the
> window does not include this separator, the width does not equal the
> difference between the right and left edges in this case.
>
> Here is the result obtained on a typical 24-line terminal with just one
> window:
>
> ```
> (window-edges (selected-window))
>      ⇒ (0 0 80 23)
> ```

The bottom edge is at line 23 because the last line is the echo area.

If *window* is at the upper left corner of its frame, *right* and *bottom* are the same as the values returned by (window-width) and (window-height) respectively, and *top* and *bottom* are zero. For example, the edges of the following window are '0 0 5 8'. Assuming that the frame has more than 8 columns, the last column of the window (column 7) holds a border rather than text. The last row (row 4) holds the mode line, shown here with 'xxxxxxxxx'.

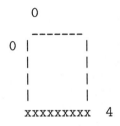

When there are side-by-side windows, any window not at the right edge of its frame has a separator in its last column or columns. The separator counts as one or two columns in the width of the window. A window never includes a separator on its left, since that belongs to the window to the left.

In the following example, let's suppose that the frame is 7 columns wide. Then the edges of the left window are '0 0 4 3' and the edges of the right window are '4 0 7 3'.

25.14 Changing the Size of a Window

The window size functions fall into two classes: high-level commands that change the size of windows and low-level functions that access window size. Emacs does not permit overlapping windows or gaps between windows, so resizing one window affects other windows.

enlarge-window *size &optional horizontal*   Command
This function makes the selected window *size* lines taller, stealing lines from neighboring windows. It takes the lines from one window at a

time until that window is used up, then takes from another. If a window from which lines are stolen shrinks below `window-min-height` lines, that window disappears.

If *horizontal* is non-`nil`, this function makes *window* wider by *size* columns, stealing columns instead of lines. If a window from which columns are stolen shrinks below `window-min-width` columns, that window disappears.

If the requested size would exceed that of the window's frame, then the function makes the window occupy the entire height (or width) of the frame.

If *size* is negative, this function shrinks the window by −*size* lines or columns. If that makes the window smaller than the minimum size (`window-min-height` and `window-min-width`), `enlarge-window` deletes the window.

`enlarge-window` returns `nil`.

enlarge-window-horizontally *columns*   Command
This function makes the selected window *columns* wider. It could be defined as follows:

```
(defun enlarge-window-horizontally (columns)
  (enlarge-window columns t))
```

shrink-window *size &optional horizontal*   Command
This function is like `enlarge-window` but negates the argument *size*, making the selected window smaller by giving lines (or columns) to the other windows. If the window shrinks below `window-min-height` or `window-min-width`, then it disappears.

If *size* is negative, the window is enlarged by −*size* lines or columns.

shrink-window-horizontally *columns*   Command
This function makes the selected window *columns* narrower. It could be defined as follows:

```
(defun shrink-window-horizontally (columns)
  (shrink-window columns t))
```

The following two variables constrain the window-size-changing functions to a minimum height and width.

window-min-height   User Option
The value of this variable determines how short a window may become before it is automatically deleted. Making a window smaller than `window-min-height` automatically deletes it, and no window may be created shorter than this. The absolute minimum height is two (allowing one line for the mode line, and one line for the buffer display).

Actions that change window sizes reset this variable to two if it is less than two. The default value is 4.

window-min-width   *User Option*
The value of this variable determines how narrow a window may become before it automatically deleted. Making a window smaller than `window-min-width` automatically deletes it, and no window may be created narrower than this. The absolute minimum width is one; any value below that is ignored. The default value is 10.

window-size-change-functions   *Variable*
This variable holds a list of functions to be called if the size of any window changes for any reason. The functions are called just once per redisplay, and just once for each frame on which size changes have occurred.

Each function receives the frame as its sole argument. There is no direct way to find out which windows changed size, or precisely how; however, if your size-change function keeps track, after each change, of the windows that interest you, you can figure out what has changed by comparing the old size data with the new.

Creating or deleting windows counts as a size change, and therefore causes these functions to be called. Changing the frame size also counts, because it changes the sizes of the existing windows.

It is not a good idea to use `save-window-excursion` in these functions, because that always counts as a size change, and it would cause these functions to be called over and over. In most cases, `save-selected-window` is what you need here.

25.15 Coordinates and Windows

This section describes how to relate screen coordinates to windows.

window-at *x y* &optional *frame*   Function
This function returns the window containing the specified cursor position in the frame *frame*. The coordinates *x* and *y* are measured in characters and count from the top left corner of the frame. If they are out of range, `window-at` returns `nil`.

If you omit *frame*, the selected frame is used.

coordinates-in-window-p *coordinates window*   Function
This function checks whether a particular frame position falls within the window *window*.

The argument *coordinates* is a cons cell of this form:

    (x . y)

The coordinates *x* and *y* are measured in characters, and count from the top left corner of the screen or frame.

The value of `coordinates-in-window-p` is non-`nil` if the coordinates are inside *window*. The value also indicates what part of the window the position is in, as follows:

(*relx* . *rely*)
> The coordinates are inside *window*. The numbers *relx* and *rely* are the equivalent window-relative coordinates for the specified position, counting from 0 at the top left corner of the window.

mode-line
> The coordinates are in the mode line of *window*.

vertical-split
> The coordinates are in the vertical line between *window* and its neighbor to the right. This value occurs only if the window doesn't have a scroll bar; positions in a scroll bar are considered outside the window.

nil
> The coordinates are not in any part of *window*.

The function `coordinates-in-window-p` does not require a frame as argument because it always uses the frame that *window* is on.

25.16 Window Configurations

A *window configuration* records the entire layout of a frame—all windows, their sizes, which buffers they contain, what part of each buffer is displayed, and the values of point and the mark. You can bring back an entire previous layout by restoring a window configuration previously saved.

If you want to record all frames instead of just one, use a frame configuration instead of a window configuration. See Section 26.12 [Frame Configurations], page 111.

current-window-configuration   Function
> This function returns a new object representing Emacs's current window configuration, namely the number of windows, their sizes and current buffers, which window is the selected window, and for each window the displayed buffer, the display-start position, and the positions of point and the mark. An exception is made for point in the current buffer, whose value is not saved.

set-window-configuration *configuration*   Function
This function restores the configuration of Emacs's windows and buffers to the state specified by *configuration*. The argument *configuration* must be a value that was previously returned by `current-window-configuration`.

This function always counts as a window size change and triggers execution of the `window-size-change-functions`. (It doesn't know how to tell whether the new configuration actually differs from the old one.)

Here is a way of using this function to get the same effect as `save-window-excursion`:

```
(let ((config (current-window-configuration)))
  (unwind-protect
      (progn (split-window-vertically nil)
             ...)
    (set-window-configuration config)))
```

save-window-excursion *forms...*   Special Form
This special form records the window configuration, executes *forms* in sequence, then restores the earlier window configuration. The window configuration includes the value of point and the portion of the buffer that is visible. It also includes the choice of selected window. However, it does not include the value of point in the current buffer; use `save-excursion` if you wish to preserve that.

Don't use this construct when `save-selected-window` is all you need.

Exit from `save-window-excursion` always triggers execution of the `window-size-change-functions`. (It doesn't know how to tell whether the restored configuration actually differs from the one in effect at the end of the *forms*.)

The return value is the value of the final form in *forms*. For example:

```
(split-window)
     ⇒ #<window 25 on control.texi>
(setq w (selected-window))
     ⇒ #<window 19 on control.texi>
(save-window-excursion
  (delete-other-windows w)
  (switch-to-buffer "foo")
  'do-something)
     ⇒ do-something
     ;; The screen is now split again.
```

window-configuration-p *object*   Function
This function returns t if *object* is a window configuration.

Primitives to look inside of window configurations would make sense, but none are implemented. It is not clear they are useful enough to be worth implementing.

26 Frames

A *frame* is a rectangle on the screen that contains one or more Emacs windows. A frame initially contains a single main window (plus perhaps a minibuffer window), which you can subdivide vertically or horizontally into smaller windows.

When Emacs runs on a text-only terminal, it starts with one *terminal frame*. If you create additional ones, Emacs displays one and only one at any given time—on the terminal screen, of course.

When Emacs communicates directly with an X server, it does not have a terminal frame; instead, it starts with a single *X window frame*. It can display multiple X window frames at the same time, each in its own X window.

framep *object*   Function
This predicate returns `t` if *object* is a frame, and `nil` otherwise.

See Chapter 35 [Display], page 275, for related information.

26.1 Creating Frames

To create a new frame, call the function `make-frame`.

make-frame *alist*   Function
This function creates a new frame. If you are using X, it makes an X window frame; otherwise, it makes a terminal frame.

The argument is an alist specifying frame parameters. Any parameters not mentioned in *alist* default according to the value of the variable `default-frame-alist`; parameters not specified even there default from the standard X defaults file and X resources.

The set of possible parameters depends in principle on what kind of window system Emacs uses to display its frames. See Section 26.3.3 [X Frame Parameters], page 100, for documentation of individual parameters you can specify.

before-make-frame-hook   Variable
A normal hook run by `make-frame` before it actually creates the frame.

after-make-frame-hook   Variable
A normal hook run by `make-frame` after it creates the frame.

26.2 Multiple Displays

A single Emacs can talk to more than one X Windows display. Initially,
Emacs uses just one display—the one chosen with the DISPLAY environment
variable or with the '--display' option (see section "Initial Options" in *The
GNU Emacs Manual*). To connect to another display, use the command
make-frame-on-display or specify the display frame parameter when you
create the frame.

Emacs treats each X server as a separate terminal, giving each one its
own selected frame and its own minibuffer windows. A few Lisp variables
have values local to the current terminal (that is, the terminal corresponding to the currently selected frame): these are default-minibuffer-frame,
defining-kbd-macro, last-kbd-macro, multiple-frames and system-
key-alist. These variables are always terminal-local and can never be
buffer-local.

A single X server can handle more than one screen. A display name
'host.server.screen' has three parts; the last part specifies the screen number
for a given server. When you use two screens belonging to one server, Emacs
knows by the similarity in their names that they share a single keyboard,
and it treats them as a single terminal.

make-frame-on-display *display* &optional   Command
   parameters
  This creates a new frame on display *display*, taking the other frame
  parameters from *parameters*. Aside from the *display* argument, it is
  like make-frame (see Section 26.1 [Creating Frames], page 97).

x-display-list   Function
  This returns a list that indicates which X displays Emacs has a connection to. The elements of the list are strings, and each one is a display
  name.

x-open-connection *display* &optional *xrm-string*   Function
  This function opens a connection to the X display *display*. It does
  not create a frame on that display, but it permits you to check that
  communication can be established with that display.

  The optional argument *resource-string*, if not nil, is a string of resource names and values, in the same format used in the '.Xresources'
  file. The values you specify override the resource values recorded in
  the X server itself; they apply to all Emacs frames created on this
  display. Here's an example of what this string might look like:

```
"*BorderWidth: 3\n*InternalBorder: 2\n"
```
  See Section 26.20 [Resources], page 117.

x-close-connection *display*   Function
  This function closes the connection to display *display*. Before you can
  do this, you must first delete all the frames that were open on that
  display (see Section 26.5 [Deleting Frames], page 106).

26.3 Frame Parameters

A frame has many parameters that control its appearance and behavior.
Just what parameters a frame has depends on what display mechanism it
uses.

Frame parameters exist for the sake of window systems. A terminal frame
has a few parameters, mostly for compatibility's sake; only the height, width
and `buffer-predicate` parameters really do something.

26.3.1 Access to Frame Parameters

These functions let you read and change the parameter values of a frame.

frame-parameters *frame*   Function
  The function `frame-parameters` returns an alist listing all the parameters of *frame* and their values.

modify-frame-parameters *frame alist*   Function
  This function alters the parameters of frame *frame* based on the elements of *alist*. Each element of *alist* has the form (*parm . value*),
  where *parm* is a symbol naming a parameter. If you don't mention a
  parameter in *alist*, its value doesn't change.

26.3.2 Initial Frame Parameters

You can specify the parameters for the initial startup frame by setting
`initial-frame-alist` in your '.emacs' file.

initial-frame-alist   Variable
  This variable's value is an alist of parameter values used when creating
  the initial X window frame. Each element has the form:

      (*parameter . value*)

  Emacs creates the initial frame before it reads your '~/.emacs' file.
  After reading that file, Emacs checks `initial-frame-alist`, and applies the parameter settings in the altered value to the already created
  initial frame.

  If these settings affect the frame geometry and appearance, you'll see
  the frame appear with the wrong ones and then change to the specified

ones. If that bothers you, you can specify the same geometry and appearance with X resources; those do take affect before the frame is created. See section "X Resources" in *The GNU Emacs Manual*.

X resource settings typically apply to all frames. If you want to specify some X resources solely for the sake of the initial frame, and you don't want them to apply to subsequent frames, here's how to achieve this. Specify parameters in `default-frame-alist` to override the X resources for subsequent frames; then, to prevent these from affecting the initial frame, specify the same parameters in `initial-frame-alist` with values that match the X resources.

If these parameters specify a separate minibuffer-only frame with `(minibuffer . nil)`, and you have not created one, Emacs creates one for you.

minibuffer-frame-alist   Variable
   This variable's value is an alist of parameter values used when creating an initial minibuffer-only frame—if such a frame is needed, according to the parameters for the main initial frame.

default-frame-alist   Variable
   This is an alist specifying default values of frame parameters for subsequent Emacs frames (not the initial ones).

See also `special-display-frame-alist`, in Section 25.8 [Choosing Window], page 80.

If you use options that specify window appearance when you invoke Emacs, they take effect by adding elements to `default-frame-alist`. One exception is '`-geometry`', which adds the specified position to `initial-frame-alist` instead. See section "Command Arguments" in *The GNU Emacs Manual*.

26.3.3 X Window Frame Parameters

Just what parameters a frame has depends on what display mechanism it uses. Here is a table of the parameters of an X window frame; of these, `name`, `height`, `width`, and `buffer-predicate` provide meaningful information in non-X frames.

name   The name of the frame. Most window managers display the frame's name in the frame's border, at the top of the frame. If you don't specify a name, and you have more than one frame, Emacs sets the frame name based on the buffer displayed in the frame's selected window.

If you specify the frame name explicitly when you create the frame, the name is also used (instead of the name of the Emacs executable) when looking up X resources for the frame.

display   The display on which to open this frame. It should be a string of the form "*host*:*dpy*.*screen*", just like the DISPLAY environment variable.

left   The screen position of the left edge, in pixels, with respect to the left edge of the screen. The value may be a positive number *pos*, or a list of the form (+ *pos*) which permits specifying a negative *pos* value.

           A negative number −*pos*, or a list of the form (- *pos*), actually specifies the position of the right edge of the window with respect to the right edge of the screen. A positive value of *pos* counts toward the left. If the parameter is a negative integer −*pos* then *pos* is positive!

top   The screen position of the top edge, in pixels, with respect to the top edge of the screen. The value may be a positive number *pos*, or a list of the form (+ *pos*) which permits specifying a negative *pos* value.

           A negative number −*pos*, or a list of the form (- *pos*), actually specifies the position of the bottom edge of the window with respect to the bottom edge of the screen. A positive value of *pos* counts toward the top. If the parameter is a negative integer −*pos* then *pos* is positive!

icon-left
           The screen position of the left edge *of the frame's icon*, in pixels, counting from the left edge of the screen. This takes effect if and when the frame is iconified.

icon-top   The screen position of the top edge *of the frame's icon*, in pixels, counting from the top edge of the screen. This takes effect if and when the frame is iconified.

user-position
           Non-nil if the screen position of the frame was explicitly requested by the user (for example, with the '-geometry' option). Nothing automatically makes this parameter non-nil; it is up to Lisp programs that call make-frame to specify this parameter as well as specifying the left and top parameters.

height   The height of the frame contents, in characters. (To get the height in pixels, call frame-pixel-height; see Section 26.3.4 [Size and Position], page 104.)

width   The width of the frame contents, in characters. (To get the
               height in pixels, call `frame-pixel-width`; see Section 26.3.4
               [Size and Position], page 104.)

window-id
               The number of the X window for the frame.

minibuffer
               Whether this frame has its own minibuffer. The value t means
               yes, `nil` means no, `only` means this frame is just a minibuffer.
               If the value is a minibuffer window (in some other frame), the
               new frame uses that minibuffer.

buffer-predicate
               The buffer-predicate function for this frame. The function
               `other-buffer` uses this predicate (from the selected frame) to
               decide which buffers it should consider, if the predicate is not
               `nil`. It calls the predicate with one arg, a buffer, once for each
               buffer; if the predicate returns a non-`nil` value, it considers that
               buffer.

font   The name of the font for displaying text in the frame. This is a
               string.

auto-raise
               Whether selecting the frame raises it (non-`nil` means yes).

auto-lower
               Whether deselecting the frame lowers it (non-`nil` means yes).

vertical-scroll-bars
               Whether the frame has scroll bars for vertical scrolling (non-`nil`
               means yes).

horizontal-scroll-bars
               Whether the frame has scroll bars for horizontal scrolling (non-
               nil means yes). (Horizontal scroll bars are not currently imple-
               mented.)

scroll-bar-width
               The width of the vertical scroll bar, in pixels.

icon-type
               The type of icon to use for this frame when it is iconified. If
               the value is a string, that specifies a file containing a bitmap to
               use. Any other non-`nil` value specifies the default bitmap icon
               (a picture of a gnu); `nil` specifies a text icon.

icon-name
               The name to use in the icon for this frame, when and if the icon
               appears. If this is `nil`, the frame's title is used.

`foreground-color`

> The color to use for the image of a character. This is a string; the X server defines the meaningful color names.

`background-color`

> The color to use for the background of characters.

`mouse-color`

> The color for the mouse pointer.

`cursor-color`

> The color for the cursor that shows point.

`border-color`

> The color for the border of the frame.

`cursor-type`

> The way to display the cursor. The legitimate values are `bar`, `box`, and `(bar . width)`. The symbol `box` specifies an ordinary black box overlaying the character after point; that is the default. The symbol `bar` specifies a vertical bar between characters as the cursor. `(bar . width)` specifies a bar *width* pixels wide.

`border-width`

> The width in pixels of the window border.

`internal-border-width`

> The distance in pixels between text and border.

`unsplittable`

> If non-`nil`, this frame's window is never split automatically.

`visibility`

> The state of visibility of the frame. There are three possibilities: `nil` for invisible, `t` for visible, and `icon` for iconified. See Section 26.10 [Visibility of Frames], page 110.

`menu-bar-lines`

> The number of lines to allocate at the top of the frame for a menu bar. The default is 1. See Section 19.12.5 [Menu Bar], page 337, vol. 1. (In Emacs versions that use the X toolkit, there is only one menu bar line; all that matters about the number you specify is whether it is greater than zero.)

`parent-id`

> The X window number of the window that should be the parent of this one. Specifying this lets you create an Emacs window inside some other application's window. (It is not certain this will be implemented; try it and see if it works.)

26.3.4 Frame Size And Position

You can read or change the size and position of a frame using the frame parameters `left`, `top`, `height`, and `width`. Whatever geometry parameters you don't specify are chosen by the window manager in its usual fashion.

Here are some special features for working with sizes and positions:

set-frame-position *frame left top*   Function

> This function sets the position of the top left corner of *frame* to *left* and *top*. These arguments are measured in pixels, and count from the top left corner of the screen. Negative parameter values count up or rightward from the top left corner of the screen.

frame-height &optional *frame*   Function
frame-width &optional *frame*   Function

> These functions return the height and width of *frame*, measured in characters. If you don't supply *frame*, they use the selected frame.

frame-pixel-height &optional *frame*   Function
frame-pixel-width &optional *frame*   Function

> These functions return the height and width of *frame*, measured in pixels. If you don't supply *frame*, they use the selected frame.

frame-char-height &optional *frame*   Function
frame-char-width &optional *frame*   Function

> These functions return the height and width of a character in *frame*, measured in pixels. The values depend on the choice of font. If you don't supply *frame*, these functions use the selected frame.

set-frame-size *frame cols rows*   Function

> This function sets the size of *frame*, measured in characters; *cols* and *rows* specify the new width and height.
>
> To set the size based on values measured in pixels, use `frame-char-height` and `frame-char-width` to convert them to units of characters.

The old-fashioned functions `set-screen-height` and `set-screen-width`, which were used to specify the height and width of the screen in Emacs versions that did not support multiple frames, are still usable. They apply to the selected frame. See Section 35.2 [Screen Size], page 275.

x-parse-geometry *geom*   Function

> The function `x-parse-geometry` converts a standard X windows geometry string to an alist that you can use as part of the argument to `make-frame`.
>
> The alist describes which parameters were specified in *geom*, and gives the values specified for them. Each element looks like (*parameter* .

value). The possible *parameter* values are `left`, `top`, `width`, and `height`.

For the size parameters, the value must be an integer. The position parameter names `left` and `top` are not totally accurate, because some values indicate the position of the right or bottom edges instead. These are the *value* possibilities for the position parameters:

an integer   A positive integer relates the left edge or top edge of the window to the left or top edge of the screen. A negative integer relates the right or bottom edge of the window to the right or bottom edge of the screen.

(+ *position*)
            This specifies the position of the left or top edge of the window relative to the left or top edge of the screen. The integer *position* may be positive or negative; a negative value specifies a position outside the screen.

(- *position*)
            This specifies the position of the right or bottom edge of the window relative to the right or bottom edge of the screen. The integer *position* may be positive or negative; a negative value specifies a position outside the screen.

Here is an example:

```
(x-parse-geometry "35x70+0-0")
    ⇒ ((width . 35) (height . 70)
       (left . 0) (top - 0))
```

26.4 Frame Titles

Every frame has a title; most window managers display the frame title at the top of the frame. You can specify an explicit title with the `name` frame property. But normally you don't specify this explicitly, and Emacs computes the title automatically.

Emacs computes the frame title based on a template stored in the variable `frame-title-format`.

frame-title-format   Variable
    This variable specifies how to compute a title for a frame when you have not explicitly specified one.

    The variable's value is actually a mode line construct, just like `mode-line-format`. See Section 20.3.1 [Mode Line Data], page 354, vol. 1.

icon-title-format   Variable
> This variable specifies how to compute the title for an iconified frame,
> when you have not explicitly specified the frame title. This title ap-
> pears in the icon itself.

multiple-frames   Variable
> This variable is set automatically by Emacs. Its value is t when
> there are two or more frames (not counting minibuffer-only frames
> or invisible frames). The default value of `frame-title-format` uses
> `multiple-frames` so as to put the buffer name in the frame title only
> when there is more than one frame.
>
> The variable is always local to the current terminal and cannot be
> buffer-local. See Section 26.2 [Multiple Displays], page 98.

26.5 Deleting Frames

Frames remain potentially visible until you explicitly *delete* them. A
deleted frame cannot appear on the screen, but continues to exist as a Lisp
object until there are no references to it. There is no way to cancel the
deletion of a frame aside from restoring a saved frame configuration (see
Section 26.12 [Frame Configurations], page 111); this is similar to the way
windows behave.

delete-frame &optional *frame*   Command
> This function deletes the frame *frame*. By default, *frame* is the selected
> frame.

frame-live-p *frame*   Function
> The function `frame-live-p` returns non-`nil` if the frame *frame* has
> not been deleted.

Some window managers provide a command to delete a window. These
work by sending a special message to the program that operates the window.
When Emacs gets one of these commands, it generates a `delete-frame`
event, whose normal definition is a command that calls the function `delete-`
`frame`. See Section 18.5.10 [Misc Events], page 293, vol. 1.

26.6 Finding All Frames

frame-list   Function
> The function `frame-list` returns a list of all the frames that have not
> been deleted. It is analogous to `buffer-list` for buffers. The list that
> you get is newly created, so modifying the list doesn't have any effect
> on the internals of Emacs.

visible-frame-list   Function

This function returns a list of just the currently visible frames. See Section 26.10 [Visibility of Frames], page 110. (Terminal frames always count as "visible", even though only the selected one is actually displayed.)

next-frame &optional *frame minibuf*   Function

The function `next-frame` lets you cycle conveniently through all the frames from an arbitrary starting point. It returns the "next" frame after *frame* in the cycle. If *frame* is omitted or `nil`, it defaults to the selected frame.

The second argument, *minibuf*, says which frames to consider:

`nil`   Exclude minibuffer-only frames.

`visible`   Consider all visible frames.

0   Consider all visible or iconified frames.

a window   Consider only the frames using that particular window as their minibuffer.

anything else
                Consider all frames.

previous-frame &optional *frame minibuf*   Function

Like `next-frame`, but cycles through all frames in the opposite direction.

See also `next-window` and `previous-window`, in Section 25.5 [Cyclic Window Ordering], page 75.

26.7 Frames and Windows

Each window is part of one and only one frame; you can get the frame with `window-frame`.

window-frame *window*   Function

This function returns the frame that *window* is on.

All the non-minibuffer windows in a frame are arranged in a cyclic order. The order runs from the frame's top window, which is at the upper left corner, down and to the right, until it reaches the window at the lower right corner (always the minibuffer window, if the frame has one), and then it moves back to the top.

frame-top-window *frame*   Function

This returns the topmost, leftmost window of frame *frame*.

At any time, exactly one window on any frame is *selected within the frame*. The significance of this designation is that selecting the frame also selects this window. You can get the frame's current selected window with `frame-selected-window`.

frame-selected-window *frame*   Function
> This function returns the window on *frame* that is selected within *frame*.

Conversely, selecting a window for Emacs with `select-window` also makes that window selected within its frame. See Section 25.4 [Selecting Windows], page 74.

Another function that (usually) returns one of the windows in a frame is `minibuffer-window`. See Section 17.8 [Minibuffer Misc], page 272, vol. 1.

26.8 Minibuffers and Frames

Normally, each frame has its own minibuffer window at the bottom, which is used whenever that frame is selected. If the frame has a minibuffer, you can get it with `minibuffer-window` (see Section 17.8 [Minibuffer Misc], page 272, vol. 1).

However, you can also create a frame with no minibuffer. Such a frame must use the minibuffer window of some other frame. When you create the frame, you can specify explicitly the minibuffer window to use (in some other frame). If you don't, then the minibuffer is found in the frame which is the value of the variable `default-minibuffer-frame`. Its value should be a frame that does have a minibuffer.

If you use a minibuffer-only frame, you might want that frame to raise when you enter the minibuffer. If so, set the variable `minibuffer-auto-raise` to t. See Section 26.11 [Raising and Lowering], page 111.

default-minibuffer-frame   Variable
> This variable specifies the frame to use for the minibuffer window, by default. It is always local to the current terminal and cannot be buffer-local. See Section 26.2 [Multiple Displays], page 98.

26.9 Input Focus

At any time, one frame in Emacs is the *selected frame*. The selected window always resides on the selected frame.

selected-frame   Function
> This function returns the selected frame.

The X server normally directs keyboard input to the X window that the mouse is in. Some window managers use mouse clicks or keyboard events to *shift the focus* to various X windows, overriding the normal behavior of the server.

Lisp programs can switch frames "temporarily" by calling the function `select-frame`. This does not override the window manager; rather, it escapes from the window manager's control until that control is somehow reasserted.

When using a text-only terminal, there is no window manager; therefore, `switch-frame` is the only way to switch frames, and the effect lasts until overridden by a subsequent call to `switch-frame`. Only the selected terminal frame is actually displayed on the terminal. Each terminal screen except for the initial one has a number, and the number of the selected frame appears in the mode line after the word 'Emacs' (see Section 20.3.2 [Mode Line Variables], page 356, vol. 1).

select-frame *frame*   Function
    This function selects frame *frame*, temporarily disregarding the focus
    of the X server if any. The selection of *frame* lasts until the next time
    the user does something to select a different frame, or until the next
    time this function is called.

Emacs cooperates with the X server and the window managers by arranging to select frames according to what the server and window manager ask for. It does so by generating a special kind of input event, called a *focus* event. The command loop handles a focus event by calling `handle-select-frame`. See Section 18.5.9 [Focus Events], page 293, vol. 1.

handle-switch-frame *frame*   Command
    This function handles a focus event by selecting frame *frame*.

    Focus events normally do their job by invoking this command. Don't
    call it for any other reason.

redirect-frame-focus *frame focus-frame*   Function
    This function redirects focus from *frame* to *focus-frame*. This means
    that *focus-frame* will receive subsequent keystrokes intended for *frame*.
    After such an event, the value of `last-event-frame` will be *focus-frame*. Also, switch-frame events specifying *frame* will instead select
    focus-frame.

    If *focus-frame* is `nil`, that cancels any existing redirection for *frame*,
    which therefore once again receives its own events.

    One use of focus redirection is for frames that don't have minibuffers.
    These frames use minibuffers on other frames. Activating a minibuffer
    on another frame redirects focus to that frame. This puts the focus

on the minibuffer's frame, where it belongs, even though the mouse remains in the frame that activated the minibuffer.

Selecting a frame can also change focus redirections. Selecting frame `bar`, when `foo` had been selected, changes any redirections pointing to `foo` so that they point to `bar` instead. This allows focus redirection to work properly when the user switches from one frame to another using `select-window`.

This means that a frame whose focus is redirected to itself is treated differently from a frame whose focus is not redirected. `select-frame` affects the former but not the latter.

The redirection lasts until `redirect-frame-focus` is called to change it.

26.10 Visibility of Frames

An X window frame may be *visible*, *invisible*, or *iconified*. If it is visible, you can see its contents. If it is iconified, the frame's contents do not appear on the screen, but an icon does. If the frame is invisible, it doesn't show on the screen, not even as an icon.

Visibility is meaningless for terminal frames, since only the selected one is actually displayed in any case.

make-frame-visible &optional *frame*   Command
This function makes frame *frame* visible. If you omit *frame*, it makes the selected frame visible.

make-frame-invisible &optional *frame*   Command
This function makes frame *frame* invisible. If you omit *frame*, it makes the selected frame invisible.

iconify-frame &optional *frame*   Command
This function iconifies frame *frame*. If you omit *frame*, it iconifies the selected frame.

frame-visible-p *frame*   Function
This returns the visibility status of frame *frame*. The value is `t` if *frame* is visible, `nil` if it is invisible, and `icon` if it is iconified.

The visibility status of a frame is also available as a frame parameter. You can read or change it as such. See Section 26.3.3 [X Frame Parameters], page 100.

The user can iconify and deiconify frames with the window manager. This happens below the level at which Emacs can exert any control, but Emacs does provide events that you can use to keep track of such changes. See Section 18.5.10 [Misc Events], page 293, vol. 1.

26.11 Raising and Lowering Frames

The X Window System uses a desktop metaphor. Part of this metaphor is the idea that windows are stacked in a notional third dimension perpendicular to the screen surface, and thus ordered from "highest" to "lowest". Where two windows overlap, the one higher up covers the one underneath. Even a window at the bottom of the stack can be seen if no other window overlaps it.

A window's place in this ordering is not fixed; in fact, users tend to change the order frequently. *Raising* a window means moving it "up", to the top of the stack. *Lowering* a window means moving it to the bottom of the stack. This motion is in the notional third dimension only, and does not change the position of the window on the screen.

You can raise and lower Emacs's X windows with these functions:

raise-frame *frame*   Command
> This function raises frame *frame*.

lower-frame *frame*   Command
> This function lowers frame *frame*.

minibuffer-auto-raise   User Option
> If this is non-`nil`, activation of the minibuffer raises the frame that the minibuffer window is in.

You can also enable auto-raise (raising automatically when a frame is selected) or auto-lower (lowering automatically when it is deselected) for any frame using frame parameters. See Section 26.3.3 [X Frame Parameters], page 100.

26.12 Frame Configurations

A *frame configuration* records the current arrangement of frames, all their properties, and the window configuration of each one.

current-frame-configuration   Function
> This function returns a frame configuration list that describes the current arrangement of frames and their contents.

set-frame-configuration *configuration*   Function
> This function restores the state of frames described in *configuration*.

26.13 Mouse Tracking

Sometimes it is useful to *track* the mouse, which means to display something to indicate where the mouse is and move the indicator as the mouse moves. For efficient mouse tracking, you need a way to wait until the mouse actually moves.

The convenient way to track the mouse is to ask for events to represent mouse motion. Then you can wait for motion by waiting for an event. In addition, you can easily handle any other sorts of events that may occur. That is useful, because normally you don't want to track the mouse forever— only until some other event, such as the release of a button.

track-mouse *body...*   Special Form
> Execute *body*, meanwhile generating input events for mouse motion. The code in *body* can read these events with `read-event` or `read-key-sequence`. See Section 18.5.8 [Motion Events], page 292, vol. 1, for the format of mouse motion events.
>
> The value of `track-mouse` is that of the last form in *body*.

The usual purpose of tracking mouse motion is to indicate on the screen the consequences of pushing or releasing a button at the current position.

In many cases, you can avoid the need to track the mouse by using the `mouse-face` text property (see Section 29.18.4 [Special Properties], page 181). That works at a much lower level and runs more smoothly than Lisp-level mouse tracking.

26.14 Mouse Position

The functions `mouse-position` and `set-mouse-position` give access to the current position of the mouse.

mouse-position   Function
> This function returns a description of the position of the mouse. The value looks like (*frame x . y*), where *x* and *y* are integers giving the position in characters relative to the top left corner of the inside of *frame*.

set-mouse-position *frame x y*   Function
> This function *warps the mouse* to position *x, y* in frame *frame*. The arguments *x* and *y* are integers, giving the position in characters relative to the top left corner of the inside of *frame*.

mouse-pixel-position   Function
> This function is like `mouse-position` except that it returns coordinates in units of pixels rather than units of characters.

set-mouse-pixel-position *frame x y*   Function
    This function warps the mouse like `set-mouse-position` except that
    x and *y* are in units of pixels rather than units of characters. These
    coordinates are not required to be within the frame.

26.15 Pop-Up Menus

    When using X windows, a Lisp program can pop up a menu which the
user can choose from with the mouse.

x-popup-menu *position menu*   Function
    This function displays a pop-up menu and returns an indication of
    what selection the user makes.

    The argument *position* specifies where on the screen to put the menu.
    It can be either a mouse button event (which says to put the menu
    where the user actuated the button) or a list of this form:

        ((*xoffset yoffset*) *window*)

    where *xoffset* and *yoffset* are coordinates, measured in pixels, counting
    from the top left corner of *window*'s frame.

    If *position* is `t`, it means to use the current mouse position. If *position*
    is `nil`, it means to precompute the key binding equivalents for the
    keymaps specified in *menu*, without actually displaying or popping up
    the menu.

    The argument *menu* says what to display in the menu. It can be
    a keymap or a list of keymaps (see Section 19.12 [Menu Keymaps],
    page 334, vol. 1). Alternatively, it can have the following form:

        (*title pane1 pane2*...)

    where each pane is a list of form

        (*title* (*line . item*)...)

    Each *line* should be a string, and each *item* should be the value to
    return if that *line* is chosen.

    Usage note: Don't use `x-popup-menu` to display a menu if a prefix key
with a menu keymap would do the job. If you use a menu keymap to implement a menu, `C-h c` and `C-h a` can see the individual items in that menu
and provide help for them. If instead you implement the menu by defining
a command that calls `x-popup-menu`, the help facilities cannot know what
happens inside that command, so they cannot give any help for the menu's
items. This is the reason why all the menu bar items are normally implemented with menu keymaps (see Section 19.12 [Menu Keymaps], page 334,
vol. 1).

26.16 Dialog Boxes

A dialog box is a variant of a pop-up menu. It looks a little different (if Emacs uses an X toolkit), it always appears in the center of a frame, and it has just one level and one pane. The main use of dialog boxes is for asking questions that the user can answer with "yes", "no", and a few other alternatives. The functions y-or-n-p and yes-or-no-p use dialog boxes instead of the keyboard, when called from commands invoked by mouse clicks.

x-popup-dialog *position contents*   Function

This function displays a pop-up dialog box and returns an indication of what selection the user makes. The argument *contents* specifies the alternatives to offer; it has this format:

> (*title* (*string* . *value*)...)

which looks like the list that specifies a single pane for x-popup-menu.

The return value is *value* from the chosen alternative.

An element of the list may be just a string instead of a cons cell (*string* . *value*). That makes a box that cannot be selected.

If nil appears in the list, it separates the left-hand items from the right-hand items; items that precede the nil appear on the left, and items that follow the nil appear on the right. If you don't include a nil in the list, then approximately half the items appear on each side.

Dialog boxes always appear in the center of a frame; the argument *position* specifies which frame. The possible values are as in x-popup-menu, but the precise coordinates don't matter; only the frame matters.

If your Emacs executable does not use an X toolkit, then it cannot display a real dialog box; so instead it displays the same items in a pop-up menu in the center of the frame.

26.17 Pointer Shapes

These variables specify which shape to use for the mouse pointer in various situations:

x-pointer-shape

This variable specifies the pointer shape to use ordinarily in the Emacs frame.

x-sensitive-text-pointer-shape

This variable specifies the pointer shape to use when the mouse is over mouse-sensitive text.

These variables affect newly created frames. They do not normally affect existing frames; however, if you set the mouse color of a frame, that also updates its pointer shapes based on the current values of these variables. See Section 26.3.3 [X Frame Parameters], page 100.

The values you can use, to specify either of these pointer shapes, are defined in the file 'lisp/x-win.el'. Use M-x apropos RET x-pointer RET to see a list of them.

26.18 X Selections

The X server records a set of *selections* which permit transfer of data between application programs. The various selections are distinguished by *selection types*, represented in Emacs by symbols. X clients including Emacs can read or set the selection for any given type.

x-set-selection *type data*   Function
> This function sets a "selection" in the X server. It takes two arguments: a selection type *type*, and the value to assign to it, *data*. If *data* is nil, it means to clear out the selection. Otherwise, *data* may be a string, a symbol, an integer (or a cons of two integers or list of two integers), an overlay, or a cons of two markers pointing to the same buffer. An overlay or a pair of markers stands for text in the overlay or between the markers.
>
> The data may also be a vector of valid non-vector selection values.
>
> Each possible *type* has its own selection value, which changes independently. The usual values of *type* are PRIMARY and SECONDARY; these are symbols with upper-case names, in accord with X Window System conventions. The default is PRIMARY.

x-get-selection &optional *type data-type*   Function
> This function accesses selections set up by Emacs or by other X clients. It takes two optional arguments, *type* and *data-type*. The default for *type*, the selection type, is PRIMARY.
>
> The *data-type* argument specifies the form of data conversion to use, to convert the raw data obtained from another X client into Lisp data. Meaningful values include TEXT, STRING, TARGETS, LENGTH, DELETE, FILE_NAME, CHARACTER_POSITION, LINE_NUMBER, COLUMN_NUMBER, OWNER_OS, HOST_NAME, USER, CLASS, NAME, ATOM, and INTEGER. (These are symbols with upper-case names in accord with X conventions.) The default for *data-type* is STRING.

The X server also has a set of numbered *cut buffers* which can store text or other data being moved between applications. Cut buffers are considered obsolete, but Emacs supports them for the sake of X clients that still use them.

x-get-cut-buffer *n*   Function
    This function returns the contents of cut buffer number *n*.

x-set-cut-buffer *string*   Function
    This function stores *string* into the first cut buffer (cut buffer 0), moving the other values down through the series of cut buffers, much like the way successive kills in Emacs move down the kill ring.

26.19 Color Names

x-color-defined-p *color*   Function
    This function reports whether a color name is meaningful. It returns t if so; otherwise, nil.

    Note that this does not tell you whether the display you are using really supports that color. You can ask for any defined color on any kind of display, and you will get some result—that is how the X server works. Here's an approximate way to test whether your display supports the color *color*:

```
(defun x-color-supported-p (color)
  (and (x-color-defined-p color)
       (or (x-display-color-p)
           (member color '("black" "white"))
           (and (> (x-display-planes) 1)
                (equal color "gray")))))
```

x-color-values *color*   Function
    This function returns a value that describes what *color* should ideally look like. If *color* is defined, the value is a list of three integers, which give the amount of red, the amount of green, and the amount of blue. Each integer ranges in principle from 0 to 65535, but in practice no value seems to be above 65280. If *color* is not defined, the value is nil.

```
(x-color-values "black")
     ⇒ (0 0 0)
(x-color-values "white")
     ⇒ (65280 65280 65280)
(x-color-values "red")
     ⇒ (65280 0 0)
(x-color-values "pink")
     ⇒ (65280 49152 51968)
```

```
(x-color-values "hungry")
     ⇒ nil
```

26.20 X Resources

x-get-resource *attribute class* &optional *component*   Function
        subclass
The function `x-get-resource` retrieves a resource value from the X Windows defaults database.

Resources are indexed by a combination of a *key* and a *class*. This function searches using a key of the form '*instance.attribute*' (where *instance* is the name under which Emacs was invoked), and using '`Emacs.`*class*' as the class.

The optional arguments *component* and *subclass* add to the key and the class, respectively. You must specify both of them or neither. If you specify them, the key is '*instance.component.attribute*', and the class is '`Emacs.`*class.subclass*'.

See section "X Resources" in *The GNU Emacs Manual*.

26.21 Data about the X Server

This section describes functions and a variable that you can use to get information about the capabilities and origin of an X display that Emacs is using. Each of these functions lets you specify the display you are interested in: the *display* argument can be either a display name, or a frame (meaning use the display that frame is on). If you omit the *display* argument, or specify `nil`, that means to use the selected frame's display.

x-display-screens &optional *display*   Function
This function returns the number of screens associated with the display.

x-server-version &optional *display*   Function
This function returns the list of version numbers of the X server running the display.

x-server-vendor &optional *display*   Function
This function returns the vendor that provided the X server software.

x-display-pixel-height &optional *display*   Function
This function returns the height of the screen in pixels.

x-display-mm-height &optional *display*   Function
This function returns the height of the screen in millimeters.

x-display-pixel-width &optional *display*   Function
This function returns the width of the screen in pixels.

x-display-mm-width &optional *display*   Function
This function returns the width of the screen in millimeters.

x-display-backing-store &optional *display*   Function
This function returns the backing store capability of the screen. Values
can be the symbols `always`, `when-mapped`, or `not-useful`.

x-display-save-under &optional *display*   Function
This function returns non-`nil` if the display supports the SaveUnder
feature.

x-display-planes &optional *display*   Function
This function returns the number of planes the display supports.

x-display-visual-class &optional *display*   Function
This function returns the visual class for the screen. The value is one
of the symbols `static-gray`, `gray-scale`, `static-color`, `pseudo-
color`, `true-color`, and `direct-color`.

x-display-grayscale-p &optional *display*   Function
This function returns `t` if the screen can display shades of gray.

x-display-color-p &optional *display*   Function
This function returns `t` if the screen is a color screen.

x-display-color-cells &optional *display*   Function
This function returns the number of color cells the screen supports.

27 Positions

A *position* is the index of a character in the text of a buffer. More precisely, a position identifies the place between two characters (or before the first character, or after the last character), so we can speak of the character before or after a given position. However, we often speak of the character "at" a position, meaning the character after that position.

Positions are usually represented as integers starting from 1, but can also be represented as *markers*—special objects that relocate automatically when text is inserted or deleted so they stay with the surrounding characters. See Chapter 28 [Markers], page 133.

27.1 Point

Point is a special buffer position used by many editing commands, including the self-inserting typed characters and text insertion functions. Other commands move point through the text to allow editing and insertion at different places.

Like other positions, point designates a place between two characters (or before the first character, or after the last character), rather than a particular character. Usually terminals display the cursor over the character that immediately follows point; point is actually before the character on which the cursor sits.

The value of point is a number between 1 and the buffer size plus 1. If narrowing is in effect (see Section 27.4 [Narrowing], page 130), then point is constrained to fall within the accessible portion of the buffer (possibly at one end of it).

Each buffer has its own value of point, which is independent of the value of point in other buffers. Each window also has a value of point, which is independent of the value of point in other windows on the same buffer. This is why point can have different values in various windows that display the same buffer. When a buffer appears in only one window, the buffer's point and the window's point normally have the same value, so the distinction is rarely important. See Section 25.9 [Window Point], page 83, for more details.

point   Function
   This function returns the value of point in the current buffer, as an integer.

     (point)
       ⇒ 175

point-min   Function
This function returns the minimum accessible value of point in the current buffer. This is normally 1, but if narrowing is in effect, it is the position of the start of the region that you narrowed to. (See Section 27.4 [Narrowing], page 130.)

point-max   Function
This function returns the maximum accessible value of point in the current buffer. This is (1+ (buffer-size)), unless narrowing is in effect, in which case it is the position of the end of the region that you narrowed to. (See Section 27.4 [Narrowing], page 130).

buffer-end *flag*   Function
This function returns (point-min) if *flag* is less than 1, (point-max) otherwise. The argument *flag* must be a number.

buffer-size   Function
This function returns the total number of characters in the current buffer. In the absence of any narrowing (see Section 27.4 [Narrowing], page 130), point-max returns a value one larger than this.

```
(buffer-size)
    ⇒ 35
(point-max)
    ⇒ 36
```

27.2 Motion

Motion functions change the value of point, either relative to the current value of point, relative to the beginning or end of the buffer, or relative to the edges of the selected window. See Section 27.1 [Point], page 119.

27.2.1 Motion by Characters

These functions move point based on a count of characters. goto-char is the fundamental primitive; the other functions use that.

goto-char *position*   Command
This function sets point in the current buffer to the value *position*. If *position* is less than 1, it moves point to the beginning of the buffer. If *position* is greater than the length of the buffer, it moves point to the end.

If narrowing is in effect, *position* still counts from the beginning of the buffer, but point cannot go outside the accessible portion. If *position* is out of range, `goto-char` moves point to the beginning or the end of the accessible portion.

When this function is called interactively, *position* is the numeric prefix argument, if provided; otherwise it is read from the minibuffer.

`goto-char` returns *position*.

forward-char &optional *count*   Command
:   This function moves point *count* characters forward, towards the end of the buffer (or backward, towards the beginning of the buffer, if *count* is negative). If the function attempts to move point past the beginning or end of the buffer (or the limits of the accessible portion, when narrowing is in effect), an error is signaled with error code `beginning-of-buffer` or `end-of-buffer`.

:   In an interactive call, *count* is the numeric prefix argument.

backward-char &optional *count*   Command
:   This function moves point *count* characters backward, towards the beginning of the buffer (or forward, towards the end of the buffer, if *count* is negative). If the function attempts to move point past the beginning or end of the buffer (or the limits of the accessible portion, when narrowing is in effect), an error is signaled with error code `beginning-of-buffer` or `end-of-buffer`.

:   In an interactive call, *count* is the numeric prefix argument.

27.2.2 Motion by Words

These functions for parsing words use the syntax table to decide whether a given character is part of a word. See Chapter 31 [Syntax Tables], page 211.

forward-word *count*   Command
:   This function moves point forward *count* words (or backward if *count* is negative). Normally it returns `t`. If this motion encounters the beginning or end of the buffer, or the limits of the accessible portion when narrowing is in effect, point stops there and the value is `nil`.

:   In an interactive call, *count* is set to the numeric prefix argument.

backward-word *count*   Command
:   This function is just like `forward-word`, except that it moves backward until encountering the front of a word, rather than forward.

:   In an interactive call, *count* is set to the numeric prefix argument.

:   This function is rarely used in programs, as it is more efficient to call `forward-word` with a negative argument.

words-include-escapes   *Variable*
> This variable affects the behavior of `forward-word` and everything
> that uses it. If it is non-`nil`, then characters in the "escape" and
> "character quote" syntax classes count as part of words. Otherwise,
> they do not.

27.2.3 Motion to an End of the Buffer

To move point to the beginning of the buffer, write:

```
(goto-char (point-min))
```

Likewise, to move to the end of the buffer, use:

```
(goto-char (point-max))
```

Here are two commands that users use to do these things. They are
documented here to warn you not to use them in Lisp programs, because
they set the mark and display messages in the echo area.

beginning-of-buffer &optional *n*   *Command*
> This function moves point to the beginning of the buffer (or the limits
> of the accessible portion, when narrowing is in effect), setting the mark
> at the previous position. If *n* is non-`nil`, then it puts point *n* tenths
> of the way from the beginning of the buffer.
>
> In an interactive call, *n* is the numeric prefix argument, if provided;
> otherwise *n* defaults to `nil`.
>
> Don't use this function in Lisp programs!

end-of-buffer &optional *n*   *Command*
> This function moves point to the end of the buffer (or the limits of the
> accessible portion, when narrowing is in effect), setting the mark at
> the previous position. If *n* is non-`nil`, then it puts point *n* tenths of
> the way from the end of the buffer.
>
> In an interactive call, *n* is the numeric prefix argument, if provided;
> otherwise *n* defaults to `nil`.
>
> Don't use this function in Lisp programs!

27.2.4 Motion by Text Lines

Text lines are portions of the buffer delimited by newline characters,
which are regarded as part of the previous line. The first text line begins
at the beginning of the buffer, and the last text line ends at the end of the
buffer whether or not the last character is a newline. The division of the
buffer into text lines is not affected by the width of the window, by line
continuation in display, or by how tabs and control characters are displayed.

goto-line *line*   Command

This function moves point to the front of the *line*th line, counting from
line 1 at beginning of the buffer. If *line* is less than 1, it moves point
to the beginning of the buffer. If *line* is greater than the number of
lines in the buffer, it moves point to the end of the buffer—that is,
the *end of the last line* of the buffer. This is the only case in which
`goto-line` does not necessarily move to the beginning of a line.

If narrowing is in effect, then *line* still counts from the beginning of the
buffer, but point cannot go outside the accessible portion. So `goto-line` moves point to the beginning or end of the accessible portion, if
the line number specifies an inaccessible position.

The return value of `goto-line` is the difference between *line* and the
line number of the line to which point actually was able to move (in
the full buffer, before taking account of narrowing). Thus, the value
is positive if the scan encounters the real end of the buffer. The value
is zero if scan encounters the end of the accessible portion but not the
real end of the buffer.

In an interactive call, *line* is the numeric prefix argument if one has
been provided. Otherwise *line* is read in the minibuffer.

beginning-of-line &optional *count*   Command

This function moves point to the beginning of the current line. With
an argument *count* not `nil` or 1, it moves forward *count*−1 lines and
then to the beginning of the line.

If this function reaches the end of the buffer (or of the accessible portion, if narrowing is in effect), it positions point there. No error is
signaled.

end-of-line &optional *count*   Command

This function moves point to the end of the current line. With an
argument *count* not `nil` or 1, it moves forward *count*−1 lines and
then to the end of the line.

If this function reaches the end of the buffer (or of the accessible portion, if narrowing is in effect), it positions point there. No error is
signaled.

forward-line &optional *count*   Command

This function moves point forward *count* lines, to the beginning of the
line. If *count* is negative, it moves point −*count* lines backward, to the
beginning of a line. If *count* is zero, it moves point to the beginning
of the current line.

If `forward-line` encounters the beginning or end of the buffer (or of
the accessible portion) before finding that many lines, it sets point
there. No error is signaled.

`forward-line` returns the difference between *count* and the number of lines actually moved. If you attempt to move down five lines from the beginning of a buffer that has only three lines, point stops at the end of the last line, and the value will be 2.

In an interactive call, *count* is the numeric prefix argument.

count-lines *start end*   Function

This function returns the number of lines between the positions *start* and *end* in the current buffer. If *start* and *end* are equal, then it returns 0. Otherwise it returns at least 1, even if *start* and *end* are on the same line. This is because the text between them, considered in isolation, must contain at least one line unless it is empty.

Here is an example of using `count-lines`:

```
(defun current-line ()
  "Return the vertical position of point..."
  (+ (count-lines (window-start) (point))
     (if (= (current-column) 0) 1 0)
     -1))
```

Also see the functions `bolp` and `eolp` in Section 29.1 [Near Point], page 143. These functions do not move point, but test whether it is already at the beginning or end of a line.

27.2.5 Motion by Screen Lines

The line functions in the previous section count text lines, delimited only by newline characters. By contrast, these functions count screen lines, which are defined by the way the text appears on the screen. A text line is a single screen line if it is short enough to fit the width of the selected window, but otherwise it may occupy several screen lines.

In some cases, text lines are truncated on the screen rather than continued onto additional screen lines. In these cases, `vertical-motion` moves point much like `forward-line`. See Section 35.3 [Truncation], page 276.

Because the width of a given string depends on the flags that control the appearance of certain characters, `vertical-motion` behaves differently, for a given piece of text, depending on the buffer it is in, and even on the selected window (because the width, the truncation flag, and display table may vary between windows). See Section 35.13 [Usual Display], page 293.

These functions scan text to determine where screen lines break, and thus take time proportional to the distance scanned. If you intend to use them heavily, Emacs provides caches which may improve the performance of your code. See Section 27.2.4 [Text Lines], page 122.

vertical-motion *count* &optional *window*   Function

This function moves point to the start of the screen line *count* screen lines down from the screen line containing point. If *count* is negative, it moves up instead.

`vertical-motion` returns the number of lines moved. The value may be less in absolute value than *count* if the beginning or end of the buffer was reached.

The window *window* is used for obtaining parameters such as the width, the horizontal scrolling, and the display table. But `vertical-motion` always operates on the current buffer, even if *window* currently displays some other buffer.

move-to-window-line *count*   Command

This function moves point with respect to the text currently displayed in the selected window. It moves point to the beginning of the screen line *count* screen lines from the top of the window. If *count* is negative, that specifies a position −*count* lines from the bottom (or the last line of the buffer, if the buffer ends above the specified screen position).

If *count* is `nil`, then point moves to the beginning of the line in the middle of the window. If the absolute value of *count* is greater than the size of the window, then point moves to the place that would appear on that screen line if the window were tall enough. This will probably cause the next redisplay to scroll to bring that location onto the screen.

In an interactive call, *count* is the numeric prefix argument.

The value returned is the window line number point has moved to, with the top line in the window numbered 0.

compute-motion *from frompos to topos width offsets*   Function
   window

This function scans the current buffer, calculating screen positions. It scans the buffer forward from position *from*, assuming that is at screen coordinates *frompos*, to position *to* or coordinates *topos*, whichever comes first. It returns the ending buffer position and screen coordinates.

The coordinate arguments *frompos* and *topos* are cons cells of the form (*hpos* . *vpos*).

The argument *width* is the number of columns available to display text; this affects handling of continuation lines. Use the value returned by `window-width` for the window of your choice; normally, use (`window-width` *window*).

The argument *offsets* is either `nil` or a cons cell of the form (*hscroll* . *tab-offset*). Here *hscroll* is the number of columns not being displayed at the left margin; most callers get this from `window-hscroll`. Meanwhile, *tab-offset* is the offset between column numbers on the screen and column numbers in the buffer. This can be nonzero in a continuation line, when the previous screen lines' widths do not add up to a multiple of `tab-width`. It is always zero in a non-continuation line.

The window *window* serves only to specify which display table to use. `compute-motion` always operates on the current buffer, regardless of what buffer is displayed in *window*.

The return value is a list of five elements:

(*pos vpos hpos prevhpos contin*)

Here *pos* is the buffer position where the scan stopped, *vpos* is the vertical screen position, and *hpos* is the horizontal screen position.

The result *prevhpos* is the horizontal position one character back from *pos*. The result *contin* is t if the last line was continued after (or within) the previous character.

For example, to find the buffer position of column *col* of line *line* of a certain window, pass the window's display start location as *from* and the window's upper-left coordinates as *frompos*. Pass the buffer's (`point-max`) as *to*, to limit the scan to the end of the accessible portion of the buffer, and pass *line* and *col* as *topos*. Here's a function that does this:

```
(defun coordinates-of-position (col line)
  (car (compute-motion (window-start)
                       '(0 . 0)
                       (point-max)
                       (cons col line)
                       (window-width)
                       (cons (window-hscroll) 0)
                       (selected-window))))
```

When you use `compute-motion` for the minibuffer, you need to use `minibuffer-prompt-width` to get the horizontal position of the beginning of the first screen line. See Section 17.8 [Minibuffer Misc], page 272, vol. 1.

27.2.6 Moving over Balanced Expressions

Here are several functions concerned with balanced-parenthesis expressions (also called *sexps* in connection with moving across them in Emacs). The syntax table controls how these functions interpret various characters; see Chapter 31 [Syntax Tables], page 211. See Section 31.5 [Parsing Expressions], page 218, for lower-level primitives for scanning sexps or parts of sexps. For user-level commands, see section "Lists and Sexps" in *GNU Emacs Manual*.

forward-list *arg*   Command
  This function moves forward across *arg* balanced groups of parentheses. (Other syntactic entities such as words or paired string quotes are
  ignored.)

backward-list *arg*   Command
  This function moves backward across *arg* balanced groups of parentheses. (Other syntactic entities such as words or paired string quotes
  are ignored.)

up-list *arg*   Command
  This function moves forward out of *arg* levels of parentheses. A negative argument means move backward but still to a less deep spot.

down-list *arg*   Command
  This function moves forward into *arg* levels of parentheses. A negative
  argument means move backward but still go deeper in parentheses
  (−*arg* levels).

forward-sexp *arg*   Command
  This function moves forward across *arg* balanced expressions. Balanced expressions include both those delimited by parentheses and
  other kinds, such as words and string constants. For example,

```
---------- Buffer: foo ----------
(concat* "foo " (car x) y z)
---------- Buffer: foo ----------

(forward-sexp 3)
     ⇒ nil


---------- Buffer: foo ----------
(concat "foo " (car x) y* z)
---------- Buffer: foo ----------
```

backward-sexp *arg*   Command
  This function moves backward across *arg* balanced expressions.

beginning-of-defun *arg*   Command
  This function moves back to the *arg*th beginning of a defun. If *arg* is
  negative, this actually moves forward, but it still moves to the beginning of a defun, not to the end of one.

end-of-defun *arg*   Command
  This function moves forward to the *arg*th end of a defun. If *arg* is
  negative, this actually moves backward, but it still moves to the end
  of a defun, not to the beginning of one.

defun-prompt-regexp   User Option

    If non-`nil`, this variable holds a regular expression that specifies what
text can appear before the open-parenthesis that starts a defun. That
is to say, a defun begins on a line that starts with a match for this regular expression, followed by a character with open-parenthesis syntax.

27.2.7 Skipping Characters

    The following two functions move point over a specified set of characters.
For example, they are often used to skip whitespace. For related functions,
see Section 31.4 [Motion and Syntax], page 218.

skip-chars-forward *character-set* &optional *limit*   Function

    This function moves point in the current buffer forward, skipping over a
given set of characters. It examines the character following point, then
advances point if the character matches *character-set*. This continues
until it reaches a character that does not match. The function returns
`nil`.

    The argument *character-set* is like the inside of a '[...]' in a regular
expression except that ']' is never special and '\' quotes '^', '-' or
'\'. Thus, `"a-zA-Z"` skips over all letters, stopping before the first
nonletter, and `"^a-zA-Z"` skips nonletters stopping before the first
letter. See Section 30.2 [Regular Expressions], page 193.

    If *limit* is supplied (it must be a number or a marker), it specifies the
maximum position in the buffer that point can be skipped to. Point
will stop at or before *limit*.

    In the following example, point is initially located directly before the
'T'. After the form is evaluated, point is located at the end of that
line (between the 't' of 'hat' and the newline). The function skips all
letters and spaces, but not newlines.

```
---------- Buffer: foo ----------
I read "*The cat in the hat
comes back" twice.
---------- Buffer: foo ----------

(skip-chars-forward "a-zA-Z ")
     ⇒ nil

---------- Buffer: foo ----------
I read "The cat in the hat*
comes back" twice.
---------- Buffer: foo ----------
```

skip-chars-backward *character-set* &optional *limit*   Function
  This function moves point backward, skipping characters that match
  character-set, until *limit*. It just like `skip-chars-forward` except for
  the direction of motion.

27.3 Excursions

It is often useful to move point "temporarily" within a localized portion
of the program, or to switch buffers temporarily. This is called an *excursion*,
and it is done with the `save-excursion` special form. This construct saves
the current buffer and its values of point and the mark so they can be restored
after the completion of the excursion.

The forms for saving and restoring the configuration of windows are described elsewhere (see Section 25.16 [Window Configurations], page 94, and
see Section 26.12 [Frame Configurations], page 111).

save-excursion *forms...*   Special Form
  The `save-excursion` special form saves the identity of the current
  buffer and the values of point and the mark in it, evaluates *forms*, and
  finally restores the buffer and its saved values of point and the mark.
  All three saved values are restored even in case of an abnormal exit
  via `throw` or error (see Section 9.5 [Nonlocal Exits], page 125, vol. 1).

  The `save-excursion` special form is the standard way to switch
  buffers or move point within one part of a program and avoid affecting
  the rest of the program. It is used more than 500 times in the Lisp
  sources of Emacs.

  `save-excursion` does not save the values of point and the mark for
  other buffers, so changes in other buffers remain in effect after `save-`
  `excursion` exits.

  Likewise, `save-excursion` does not restore window-buffer correspondences altered by functions such as `switch-to-buffer`. One way to
  restore these correspondences, and the selected window, is to use `save-`
  `window-excursion` inside `save-excursion` (see Section 25.16 [Win-
  dow Configurations], page 94).

  The value returned by `save-excursion` is the result of the last of
  forms, or `nil` if no *forms* are given.

```
(save-excursion
  forms)
≡
(let ((old-buf (current-buffer))
      (old-pnt (point-marker))
      (old-mark (copy-marker (mark-marker))))
   (unwind-protect
       (progn forms)
     (set-buffer old-buf)
     (goto-char old-pnt)
     (set-marker (mark-marker) old-mark)))
```

27.4 Narrowing

Narrowing means limiting the text addressable by Emacs editing commands to a limited range of characters in a buffer. The text that remains addressable is called the *accessible portion* of the buffer.

Narrowing is specified with two buffer positions which become the beginning and end of the accessible portion. For most editing commands and most Emacs primitives, these positions replace the values of the beginning and end of the buffer. While narrowing is in effect, no text outside the accessible portion is displayed, and point cannot move outside the accessible portion.

Values such as positions or line numbers, which usually count from the beginning of the buffer, do so despite narrowing, but the functions which use them refuse to operate on text that is inaccessible.

The commands for saving buffers are unaffected by narrowing; they save the entire buffer regardless of any narrowing.

narrow-to-region *start end*   Command
This function sets the accessible portion of the current buffer to start at *start* and end at *end*. Both arguments should be character positions.

In an interactive call, *start* and *end* are set to the bounds of the current region (point and the mark, with the smallest first).

narrow-to-page *move-count*   Command
This function sets the accessible portion of the current buffer to include just the current page. An optional first argument *move-count* non-`nil` means to move forward or backward by *move-count* pages and then narrow. The variable **page-delimiter** specifies where pages start and end (see Section 30.8 [Standard Regexps], page 209).

In an interactive call, *move-count* is set to the numeric prefix argument.

widen   Command
   This function cancels any narrowing in the current buffer, so that the
   entire contents are accessible. This is called *widening*. It is equivalent
   to the following expression:

```
(narrow-to-region 1 (1+ (buffer-size)))
```

save-restriction *body...*   Special Form
   This special form saves the current bounds of the accessible portion,
   evaluates the *body* forms, and finally restores the saved bounds, thus
   restoring the same state of narrowing (or absence thereof) formerly
   in effect. The state of narrowing is restored even in the event of an
   abnormal exit via `throw` or error (see Section 9.5 [Nonlocal Exits],
   page 125, vol. 1). Therefore, this construct is a clean way to narrow a
   buffer temporarily.

   The value returned by `save-restriction` is that returned by the last
   form in *body*, or `nil` if no body forms were given.

   Caution: it is easy to make a mistake when using the `save-`
   `restriction` construct. Read the entire description here before you
   try it.

   If *body* changes the current buffer, `save-restriction` still restores
   the restrictions on the original buffer (the buffer whose restructions it
   saved from), but it does not restore the identity of the current buffer.

   `save-restriction` does *not* restore point and the mark; use `save-`
   `excursion` for that. If you use both `save-restriction` and `save-`
   `excursion` together, `save-excursion` should come first (on the outside). Otherwise, the old point value would be restored with temporary
   narrowing still in effect. If the old point value were outside the limits
   of the temporary narrowing, this would fail to restore it accurately.

   The `save-restriction` special form records the values of the beginning and end of the accessible portion as distances from the beginning
   and end of the buffer. In other words, it records the amount of inaccessible text before and after the accessible portion.

   This method yields correct results if *body* does further narrowing.
   However, `save-restriction` can become confused if the body widens
   and then make changes outside the range of the saved narrowing.
   When this is what you want to do, `save-restriction` is not the right
   tool for the job. Here is what you must use instead:

```
(let ((beg (point-min-marker))
      (end (point-max-marker)))
  (unwind-protect
      (progn body)
    (save-excursion
      (set-buffer (marker-buffer beg))
      (narrow-to-region beg end))))
```

Here is a simple example of correct use of `save-restriction`:

```
---------- Buffer: foo ----------
This is the contents of foo
This is the contents of foo
This is the contents of foo*
---------- Buffer: foo ----------

(save-excursion
  (save-restriction
    (goto-char 1)
    (forward-line 2)
    (narrow-to-region 1 (point))
    (goto-char (point-min))
    (replace-string "foo" "bar")))

---------- Buffer: foo ----------
This is the contents of bar
This is the contents of bar
This is the contents of foo*
---------- Buffer: foo ----------
```

28 Markers

A *marker* is a Lisp object used to specify a position in a buffer relative to the surrounding text. A marker changes its offset from the beginning of the buffer automatically whenever text is inserted or deleted, so that it stays with the two characters on either side of it.

28.1 Overview of Markers

A marker specifies a buffer and a position in that buffer. The marker can be used to represent a position in the functions that require one, just as an integer could be used. See Chapter 27 [Positions], page 119, for a complete description of positions.

A marker has two attributes: the marker position, and the marker buffer. The marker position is an integer that is equivalent (at a given time) to the marker as a position in that buffer. But the marker's position value can change often during the life of the marker. Insertion and deletion of text in the buffer relocate the marker. The idea is that a marker positioned between two characters remains between those two characters despite insertion and deletion elsewhere in the buffer. Relocation changes the integer equivalent of the marker.

Deleting text around a marker's position leaves the marker between the characters immediately before and after the deleted text. Inserting text at the position of a marker normally leaves the marker in front of the new text—unless it is inserted with `insert-before-markers` (see Section 29.4 [Insertion], page 146).

Insertion and deletion in a buffer must check all the markers and relocate them if necessary. This slows processing in a buffer with a large number of markers. For this reason, it is a good idea to make a marker point nowhere if you are sure you don't need it any more. Unreferenced markers are garbage collected eventually, but until then will continue to use time if they do point somewhere.

Because it is common to perform arithmetic operations on a marker position, most of the arithmetic operations (including + and -) accept markers as arguments. In such cases, the marker stands for its current position.

Here are examples of creating markers, setting markers, and moving point to markers:

```
;; Make a new marker that initially does not point anywhere:
(setq m1 (make-marker))
     ⇒ #<marker in no buffer>
```

```
;; Set m1 to point between the 99th and 100th characters
;;    in the current buffer:
(set-marker m1 100)
        ⇒ #<marker at 100 in markers.texi>
```

```
;; Now insert one character at the beginning of the buffer:
(goto-char (point-min))
        ⇒ 1
(insert "Q")
        ⇒ nil
```

```
;; m1 is updated appropriately.
m1
        ⇒ #<marker at 101 in markers.texi>
```

```
;; Two markers that point to the same position
;;    are not eq, but they are equal.
(setq m2 (copy-marker m1))
        ⇒ #<marker at 101 in markers.texi>
(eq m1 m2)
        ⇒ nil
(equal m1 m2)
        ⇒ t
```

```
;; When you are finished using a marker, make it point nowhere.
(set-marker m1 nil)
        ⇒ #<marker in no buffer>
```

28.2 Predicates on Markers

You can test an object to see whether it is a marker, or whether it is either an integer or a marker. The latter test is useful in connection with the arithmetic functions that work with both markers and integers.

markerp *object*   Function
> This function returns t if *object* is a marker, nil otherwise. Note that integers are not markers, even though many functions will accept either a marker or an integer.

integer-or-marker-p *object*   Function
> This function returns t if *object* is an integer or a marker, nil otherwise.

number-or-marker-p *object*   Function
> This function returns t if *object* is a number (either kind) or a marker, nil otherwise.

28.3 Functions That Create Markers

When you create a new marker, you can make it point nowhere, or point to the present position of point, or to the beginning or end of the accessible portion of the buffer, or to the same place as another given marker.

make-marker   *Function*
This functions returns a newly created marker that does not point anywhere.

```
(make-marker)
     ⇒ #<marker in no buffer>
```

point-marker   *Function*
This function returns a new marker that points to the present position of point in the current buffer. See Section 27.1 [Point], page 119. For an example, see `copy-marker`, below.

point-min-marker   *Function*
This function returns a new marker that points to the beginning of the accessible portion of the buffer. This will be the beginning of the buffer unless narrowing is in effect. See Section 27.4 [Narrowing], page 130.

point-max-marker   *Function*
This function returns a new marker that points to the end of the accessible portion of the buffer. This will be the end of the buffer unless narrowing is in effect. See Section 27.4 [Narrowing], page 130.

Here are examples of this function and `point-min-marker`, shown in a buffer containing a version of the source file for the text of this chapter.

```
(point-min-marker)
     ⇒ #<marker at 1 in markers.texi>
(point-max-marker)
     ⇒ #<marker at 15573 in markers.texi>

(narrow-to-region 100 200)
     ⇒ nil
(point-min-marker)
     ⇒ #<marker at 100 in markers.texi>
(point-max-marker)
     ⇒ #<marker at 200 in markers.texi>
```

copy-marker *marker-or-integer*   *Function*
If passed a marker as its argument, `copy-marker` returns a new marker that points to the same place and the same buffer as does *marker-or-integer*. If passed an integer as its argument, `copy-marker` returns a

new marker that points to position *marker-or-integer* in the current buffer.

If passed an integer argument less than 1, `copy-marker` returns a new marker that points to the beginning of the current buffer. If passed an integer argument greater than the length of the buffer, `copy-marker` returns a new marker that points to the end of the buffer.

An error is signaled if *marker* is neither a marker nor an integer.

```
(setq p (point-marker))
     ⇒ #<marker at 2139 in markers.texi>

(setq q (copy-marker p))
     ⇒ #<marker at 2139 in markers.texi>

(eq p q)
     ⇒ nil

(equal p q)
     ⇒ t

(copy-marker 0)
     ⇒ #<marker at 1 in markers.texi>

(copy-marker 20000)
     ⇒ #<marker at 7572 in markers.texi>
```

28.4 Information from Markers

This section describes the functions for accessing the components of a marker object.

marker-position *marker*   Function
This function returns the position that *marker* points to, or `nil` if it points nowhere.

marker-buffer *marker*   Function
This function returns the buffer that *marker* points into, or `nil` if it points nowhere.

```
(setq m (make-marker))
     ⇒ #<marker in no buffer>
(marker-position m)
     ⇒ nil
(marker-buffer m)
     ⇒ nil

(set-marker m 3770 (current-buffer))
     ⇒ #<marker at 3770 in markers.texi>
```

```
(marker-buffer m)
    ⇒ #<buffer markers.texi>
(marker-position m)
    ⇒ 3770
```

Two distinct markers are considered `equal` (even though not `eq`) to each other if they have the same position and buffer, or if they both point nowhere.

28.5 Changing Marker Positions

This section describes how to change the position of an existing marker. When you do this, be sure you know whether the marker is used outside of your program, and, if so, what effects will result from moving it—otherwise, confusing things may happen in other parts of Emacs.

set-marker *marker position* &optional *buffer*   Function
    This function moves *marker* to *position* in *buffer*. If *buffer* is not provided, it defaults to the current buffer.

    If *position* is less than 1, `set-marker` moves *marker* to the beginning of the buffer. If *position* is greater than the size of the buffer, `set-marker` moves marker to the end of the buffer. If *position* is `nil` or a marker that points nowhere, then *marker* is set to point nowhere.

    The value returned is *marker*.

```
(setq m (point-marker))
    ⇒ #<marker at 4714 in markers.texi>
(set-marker m 55)
    ⇒ #<marker at 55 in markers.texi>
(setq b (get-buffer "foo"))
    ⇒ #<buffer foo>
(set-marker m 0 b)
    ⇒ #<marker at 1 in foo>
```

move-marker *marker position* &optional *buffer*   Function
    This is another name for `set-marker`.

28.6 The Mark

One special marker in each buffer is designated *the mark*. It records a position for the user for the sake of commands such as `C-w` and `C-x TAB`. Lisp programs should set the mark only to values that have a potential use to the user, and never for their own internal purposes. For example, the `replace-regexp` command sets the mark to the value of point before doing any replacements, because this enables the user to move back there conveniently after the replace is finished.

   Many commands are designed so that when called interactively they operate on the text between point and the mark. If you are writing such a command, don't examine the mark directly; instead, use `interactive` with the 'r' specification. This provides the values of point and the mark as arguments to the command in an interactive call, but permits other Lisp programs to specify arguments explicitly. See Section 18.2.2 [Interactive Codes], page 278, vol. 1.

   Each buffer has its own value of the mark that is independent of the value of the mark in other buffers. When a buffer is created, the mark exists but does not point anywhere. We consider this state as "the absence of a mark in that buffer."

   Once the mark "exists" in a buffer, it normally never ceases to exist. However, it may become *inactive*, if Transient Mark mode is enabled. The variable `mark-active`, which is always local in all buffers, indicates whether the mark is active: non-`nil` means yes. A command can request deactivation of the mark upon return to the editor command loop by setting `deactivate-mark` to a non-`nil` value (but this causes deactivation only if Transient Mark mode is enabled).

   The main motivation for using Transient Mark mode is that this mode also enables highlighting of the region when the mark is active. See Chapter 35 [Display], page 275.

   In addition to the mark, each buffer has a *mark ring* which is a list of markers containing previous values of the mark. When editing commands change the mark, they should normally save the old value of the mark on the mark ring. The variable `mark-ring-max` specifies the maximum number of entries in the mark ring; once the list becomes this long, adding a new element deletes the last element.

mark &optional *force*   Function
   This function returns the current buffer's mark position as an integer.

   If the mark is inactive, `mark` normally signals an error. However, if *force* is non-`nil`, then `mark` returns the mark position anyway—or `nil`, if the mark is not yet set for this buffer.

mark-marker   Function
   This function returns the current buffer's mark. This is the very marker that records the mark location inside Emacs, not a copy. Therefore, changing this marker's position will directly affect the position of the mark. Don't do it unless that is the effect you want.

```
(setq m (mark-marker))
     ⇒ #<marker at 3420 in markers.texi>
```

```
(set-marker m 100)
    ⇒ #<marker at 100 in markers.texi>
(mark-marker)
    ⇒ #<marker at 100 in markers.texi>
```

Like any marker, this marker can be set to point at any buffer you like. We don't recommend that you make it point at any buffer other than the one of which it is the mark. If you do, it will yield perfectly consistent, but rather odd, results.

set-mark *position*   Function
This function sets the mark to *position*, and activates the mark. The old value of the mark is *not* pushed onto the mark ring.

Please note: Use this function only if you want the user to see that the mark has moved, and you want the previous mark position to be lost. Normally, when a new mark is set, the old one should go on the mark-ring. For this reason, most applications should use push-mark and pop-mark, not set-mark.

Novice Emacs Lisp programmers often try to use the mark for the wrong purposes. The mark saves a location for the user's convenience. An editing command should not alter the mark unless altering the mark is part of the user-level functionality of the command. (And, in that case, this effect should be documented.) To remember a location for internal use in the Lisp program, store it in a Lisp variable. For example:

```
(let ((beg (point)))
  (forward-line 1)
  (delete-region beg (point))).
```

push-mark &optional *position nomsg activate*   Function
This function sets the current buffer's mark to *position*, and pushes a copy of the previous mark onto mark-ring. If *position* is nil, then the value of point is used. push-mark returns nil.

The function push-mark normally *does not* activate the mark. To do that, specify t for the argument *activate*.

A 'Mark set' message is displayed unless *nomsg* is non-nil.

pop-mark   Function
This function pops off the top element of mark-ring and makes that mark become the buffer's actual mark. This does not move point in the buffer, and it does nothing if mark-ring is empty. It deactivates the mark.

The return value is not meaningful.

transient-mark-mode   User Option
> This variable if non-`nil` enables Transient Mark mode, in which every buffer-modifying primitive sets `deactivate-mark`. The consequence of this is that commands that modify the buffer normally make the mark inactive.

deactivate-mark   Variable
> If an editor command sets this variable non-`nil`, then the editor command loop deactivates the mark after the command returns, but only if Transient Mark mode is enabled.

deactivate-mark   Function
> This function deactivates the mark, but only if Transient Mark mode is enabled.

mark-active   Variable
> The mark is active when this variable is non-`nil`. This variable is always local in each buffer.

activate-mark-hook   Variable
deactivate-mark-hook   Variable
> These normal hooks are run, respectively, when the mark becomes active and when it becomes inactive. The hook `activate-mark-hook` is also run at the end of a command if the mark is active and the region may have changed.

mark-ring   Variable
> The value of this buffer-local variable is the list of saved former marks of the current buffer, most recent first.
>
> ```
> mark-ring
> ⇒ (#<marker at 11050 in markers.texi>
>     #<marker at 10832 in markers.texi>
>     ...)
> ```

mark-ring-max   User Option
> The value of this variable is the maximum size of `mark-ring`. If more marks than this are pushed onto the `mark-ring`, `push-mark` discards an old mark when it adds a new one.

28.7 The Region

The text between point and the mark is known as *the region*. Various functions operate on text delimited by point and the mark, but only those functions specifically related to the region itself are described here.

region-beginning   Function
This function returns the position of the beginning of the region (as an integer). This is the position of either point or the mark, whichever is smaller.

If the mark does not point anywhere, an error is signaled.

region-end   Function
This function returns the position of the end of the region (as an integer). This is the position of either point or the mark, whichever is larger.

If the mark does not point anywhere, an error is signaled.

Few programs need to use the `region-beginning` and `region-end` functions. A command designed to operate on a region should normally use `interactive` with the 'r' specification to find the beginning and end of the region. This lets other Lisp programs specify the bounds explicitly as arguments. (See Section 18.2.2 [Interactive Codes], page 278, vol. 1.)

29 Text

This chapter describes the functions that deal with the text in a buffer. Most examine, insert, or delete text in the current buffer, often in the vicinity of point. Many are interactive. All the functions that change the text provide for undoing the changes (see Section 29.9 [Undo], page 157).

Many text-related functions operate on a region of text defined by two buffer positions passed in arguments named *start* and *end*. These arguments should be either markers (see Chapter 28 [Markers], page 133) or numeric character positions (see Chapter 27 [Positions], page 119). The order of these arguments does not matter; it is all right for *start* to be the end of the region and *end* the beginning. For example, (delete-region 1 10) and (delete-region 10 1) are equivalent. An args-out-of-range error is signaled if either *start* or *end* is outside the accessible portion of the buffer. In an interactive call, point and the mark are used for these arguments.

Throughout this chapter, "text" refers to the characters in the buffer, together with their properties (when relevant).

29.1 Examining Text Near Point

Many functions are provided to look at the characters around point. Several simple functions are described here. See also looking-at in Section 30.3 [Regexp Search], page 199.

char-after *position*   Function

This function returns the character in the current buffer at (i.e., immediately after) position *position*. If *position* is out of range for this purpose, either before the beginning of the buffer, or at or beyond the end, then the value is nil.

In the following example, assume that the first character in the buffer is '@':

```
(char-to-string (char-after 1))
     ⇒ "@"
```

following-char   Function

This function returns the character following point in the current buffer. This is similar to (char-after (point)). However, if point is at the end of the buffer, then following-char returns 0.

Remember that point is always between characters, and the terminal cursor normally appears over the character following point. Therefore, the character returned by following-char is the character the cursor is over.

In this example, point is between the 'a' and the 'c'.

```
---------- Buffer: foo ----------
Gentlemen may cry ''Pea⋆ce! Peace!,''
but there is no peace.
---------- Buffer: foo ----------

(char-to-string (preceding-char))
     ⇒ "a"
(char-to-string (following-char))
     ⇒ "c"
```

preceding-char   Function
> This function returns the character preceding point in the current
> buffer. See above, under `following-char`, for an example. If point is
> at the beginning of the buffer, `preceding-char` returns 0.

bobp   Function
> This function returns `t` if point is at the beginning of the buffer. If nar-
> rowing is in effect, this means the beginning of the accessible portion
> of the text. See also `point-min` in Section 27.1 [Point], page 119.

eobp   Function
> This function returns `t` if point is at the end of the buffer. If narrowing
> is in effect, this means the end of accessible portion of the text. See
> also `point-max` in See Section 27.1 [Point], page 119.

bolp   Function
> This function returns `t` if point is at the beginning of a line. See
> Section 27.2.4 [Text Lines], page 122. The beginning of the buffer (or
> its accessible portion) always counts as the beginning of a line.

eolp   Function
> This function returns `t` if point is at the end of a line. The end of the
> buffer (or of its accessible portion) is always considered the end of a
> line.

29.2 Examining Buffer Contents

This section describes two functions that allow a Lisp program to convert
any portion of the text in the buffer into a string.

buffer-substring *start end*   Function
> This function returns a string containing a copy of the text of the
> region defined by positions *start* and *end* in the current buffer. If the
> arguments are not positions in the accessible portion of the buffer,
> `buffer-substring` signals an `args-out-of-range` error.

It is not necessary for *start* to be less than *end*; the arguments can be given in either order. But most often the smaller argument is written first.

If the text being copied has any text properties, these are copied into the string along with the characters they belong to. See Section 29.18 [Text Properties], page 176. However, overlays (see Section 35.9 [Overlays], page 284) in the buffer and their properties are ignored, not copied.

```
---------- Buffer: foo ----------
This is the contents of buffer foo

---------- Buffer: foo ----------

(buffer-substring 1 10)
⇒ "This is t"
(buffer-substring (point-max) 10)
⇒ "he contents of buffer foo
"
```

buffer-substring-without-properties *start end*   Function

This is like `buffer-substring`, except that it does not copy text properties, just the characters themselves. See Section 29.18 [Text Properties], page 176. Here's an example of using this function to get a word to look up in an alist:

```
(setq flammable
      (assoc (buffer-substring start end)
             '(("wood" . t) ("paper" . t)
               ("steel" . nil) ("asbestos" . nil))))
```

If this were written using `buffer-substring` instead, it would not work reliably; any text properties that happened to be in the word copied from the buffer would make the comparisons fail.

buffer-string   Function

This function returns the contents of the accessible portion of the current buffer as a string. This is the portion between (`point-min`) and (`point-max`) (see Section 27.4 [Narrowing], page 130).

```
---------- Buffer: foo ----------
This is the contents of buffer foo

---------- Buffer: foo ----------

(buffer-string)
     ⇒ "This is the contents of buffer foo
"
```

29.3 Comparing Text

This function lets you compare portions of the text in a buffer, without copying them into strings first.

compare-buffer-substrings *buffer1 start1 end1*   Function
        buffer2 start2 end2

This function lets you compare two substrings of the same buffer or two different buffers. The first three arguments specify one substring, giving a buffer and two positions within the buffer. The last three arguments specify the other substring in the same way. You can use nil for *buffer1*, *buffer2*, or both to stand for the current buffer.

The value is negative if the first substring is less, positive if the first is greater, and zero if they are equal. The absolute value of the result is one plus the index of the first differing characters within the substrings.

This function ignores case when comparing characters if `case-fold-search` is non-`nil`. It always ignores text properties.

Suppose the current buffer contains the text 'foobarbar haha!rara!'; then in this example the two substrings are 'rbar ' and 'rara!'. The value is 2 because the first substring is greater at the second character.

```
(compare-buffer-substring nil 6 11 nil 16 21)
     ⇒ 2
```

29.4 Inserting Text

Insertion means adding new text to a buffer. The inserted text goes at point—between the character before point and the character after point.

Insertion relocates markers that point at positions after the insertion point, so that they stay with the surrounding text (see Chapter 28 [Markers], page 133). When a marker points at the place of insertion, insertion normally doesn't relocate the marker, so that it points to the beginning of the inserted text; however, certain special functions such as `insert-before-markers` relocate such markers to point after the inserted text.

Some insertion functions leave point before the inserted text, while other functions leave it after. We call the former insertion *after point* and the latter insertion *before point*.

Insertion functions signal an error if the current buffer is read-only.

These functions copy text characters from strings and buffers along with their properties. The inserted characters have exactly the same properties as the characters they were copied from. By contrast, characters specified as separate arguments, not part of a string or buffer, inherit their text properties from the neighboring text.

insert &rest *args*   *Function*

This function inserts the strings and/or characters *args* into the current buffer, at point, moving point forward. In other words, it inserts the text before point. An error is signaled unless all *args* are either strings or characters. The value is `nil`.

insert-before-markers &rest *args*   *Function*

This function inserts the strings and/or characters *args* into the current buffer, at point, moving point forward. An error is signaled unless all *args* are either strings or characters. The value is `nil`.

This function is unlike the other insertion functions in that it relocates markers initially pointing at the insertion point, to point after the inserted text.

insert-char *character count* &optional *inherit*   *Function*

This function inserts *count* instances of *character* into the current buffer before point. The argument *count* must be a number, and *character* must be a character. The value is `nil`.

If *inherit* is non-`nil`, then the inserted characters inherit sticky text properties from the two characters before and after the insertion point. See Section 29.18.6 [Sticky Properties], page 184.

insert-buffer-substring *from-buffer-or-name*   *Function*
        &optional *start end*

This function inserts a portion of buffer *from-buffer-or-name* (which must already exist) into the current buffer before point. The text inserted is the region from *start* and *end*. (These arguments default to the beginning and end of the accessible portion of that buffer.) This function returns `nil`.

In this example, the form is executed with buffer 'bar' as the current buffer. We assume that buffer 'bar' is initially empty.

```
---------- Buffer: foo ----------
We hold these truths to be self-evident, that all
---------- Buffer: foo ----------

(insert-buffer-substring "foo" 1 20)
     ⇒ nil

---------- Buffer: bar ----------
We hold these truth*
---------- Buffer: bar ----------
```

See Section 29.18.6 [Sticky Properties], page 184, for other insertion functions that inherit text properties from the nearby text in addition to inserting it. Whitespace inserted by indentation functions also inherits text properties.

29.5 User-Level Insertion Commands

This section describes higher-level commands for inserting text, commands intended primarily for the user but useful also in Lisp programs.

insert-buffer *from-buffer-or-name*   Command
> This command inserts the entire contents of *from-buffer-or-name* (which must exist) into the current buffer after point. It leaves the mark after the inserted text. The value is `nil`.

self-insert-command *count*   Command
> This command inserts the last character typed; it does so *count* times, before point, and returns `nil`. Most printing characters are bound to this command. In routine use, `self-insert-command` is the most frequently called function in Emacs, but programs rarely use it except to install it on a keymap.
>
> In an interactive call, *count* is the numeric prefix argument.
>
> This command calls `auto-fill-function` whenever that is non-`nil` and the character inserted is a space or a newline (see Section 29.13 [Auto Filling], page 164).
>
> This command performs abbrev expansion if Abbrev mode is enabled and the inserted character does not have word-constituent syntax. (See Chapter 32 [Abbrevs], page 223, and Section 31.2.1 [Syntax Class Table], page 212.)
>
> This is also responsible for calling `blink-paren-function` when the inserted character has close parenthesis syntax (see Section 35.11 [Blinking], page 291).

newline &optional *number-of-newlines*   Command
> This command inserts newlines into the current buffer before point. If *number-of-newlines* is supplied, that many newline characters are inserted.
>
> This function calls `auto-fill-function` if the current column number is greater than the value of `fill-column` and *number-of-newlines* is `nil`. Typically what `auto-fill-function` does is insert a newline; thus, the overall result in this case is to insert two newlines at different places: one at point, and another earlier in the line. `newline` does not auto-fill if *number-of-newlines* is non-`nil`.
>
> This command indents to the left margin if that is not zero. See Section 29.12 [Margins], page 163.

The value returned is `nil`. In an interactive call, *count* is the numeric prefix argument.

split-line   Command

This command splits the current line, moving the portion of the line after point down vertically so that it is on the next line directly below where it was before. Whitespace is inserted as needed at the beginning of the lower line, using the `indent-to` function. `split-line` returns the position of point.

Programs hardly ever use this function.

overwrite-mode   Variable

This variable controls whether overwrite mode is in effect: a non-`nil` value enables the mode. It is automatically made buffer-local when set in any fashion.

29.6 Deleting Text

Deletion means removing part of the text in a buffer, without saving it in the kill ring (see Section 29.8 [The Kill Ring], page 152). Deleted text can't be yanked, but can be reinserted using the undo mechanism (see Section 29.9 [Undo], page 157). Some deletion functions do save text in the kill ring in some special cases.

All of the deletion functions operate on the current buffer, and all return a value of `nil`.

erase-buffer   Function

This function deletes the entire text of the current buffer, leaving it empty. If the buffer is read-only, it signals a `buffer-read-only` error. Otherwise, it deletes the text without asking for any confirmation. It returns `nil`.

Normally, deleting a large amount of text from a buffer inhibits further auto-saving of that buffer "because it has shrunk". However, `erase-buffer` does not do this, the idea being that the future text is not really related to the former text, and its size should not be compared with that of the former text.

delete-region *start end*   Command

This command deletes the text in the current buffer in the region defined by *start* and *end*. The value is `nil`.

delete-char *count* &optional *killp*   Command

This command deletes *count* characters directly after point, or before point if *count* is negative. If *killp* is non-`nil`, then it saves the deleted characters in the kill ring.

In an interactive call, *count* is the numeric prefix argument, and *killp* is the unprocessed prefix argument. Therefore, if a prefix argument is supplied, the text is saved in the kill ring. If no prefix argument is supplied, then one character is deleted, but not saved in the kill ring.

The value returned is always `nil`.

delete-backward-char *count &optional killp*   Command
> This command deletes *count* characters directly before point, or after point if *count* is negative. If *killp* is non-`nil`, then it saves the deleted characters in the kill ring.
>
> In an interactive call, *count* is the numeric prefix argument, and *killp* is the unprocessed prefix argument. Therefore, if a prefix argument is supplied, the text is saved in the kill ring. If no prefix argument is supplied, then one character is deleted, but not saved in the kill ring.
>
> The value returned is always `nil`.

backward-delete-char-untabify *count &optional*   Command
>   *killp*
> This command deletes *count* characters backward, changing tabs into spaces. When the next character to be deleted is a tab, it is first replaced with the proper number of spaces to preserve alignment and then one of those spaces is deleted instead of the tab. If *killp* is non-`nil`, then the command saves the deleted characters in the kill ring.
>
> Conversion of tabs to spaces happens only if *count* is positive. If it is negative, exactly −*count* characters after point are deleted.
>
> In an interactive call, *count* is the numeric prefix argument, and *killp* is the unprocessed prefix argument. Therefore, if a prefix argument is supplied, the text is saved in the kill ring. If no prefix argument is supplied, then one character is deleted, but not saved in the kill ring.
>
> The value returned is always `nil`.

29.7 User-Level Deletion Commands

This section describes higher-level commands for deleting text, commands intended primarily for the user but useful also in Lisp programs.

delete-horizontal-space   Command
> This function deletes all spaces and tabs around point. It returns `nil`.
>
> In the following examples, we call `delete-horizontal-space` four times, once on each line, with point between the second and third characters on the line each time.

```
---------- Buffer: foo ----------
I ⋆thought
I ⋆      thought
We⋆ thought
Yo⋆u thought
---------- Buffer: foo ----------
```

```
(delete-horizontal-space)     ; Four times.
     ⇒ nil
```

```
---------- Buffer: foo ----------
Ithought
Ithought
Wethought
You thought
---------- Buffer: foo ----------
```

delete-indentation &optional *join-following-p*   Command

This function joins the line point is on to the previous line, deleting
any whitespace at the join and in some cases replacing it with one
space. If *join-following-p* is non-nil, `delete-indentation` joins this
line to the following line instead. The value is `nil`.

If there is a fill prefix, and the second of the lines being joined starts
with the prefix, then `delete-indentation` deletes the fill prefix before
joining the lines. See Section 29.12 [Margins], page 163.

In the example below, point is located on the line starting 'events',
and it makes no difference if there are trailing spaces in the preceding
line.

```
---------- Buffer: foo ----------
When in the course of human
⋆     events, it becomes necessary
---------- Buffer: foo ----------
```

```
(delete-indentation)
     ⇒ nil
```

```
---------- Buffer: foo ----------
When in the course of human⋆ events, it becomes necessary
---------- Buffer: foo ----------
```

After the lines are joined, the function `fixup-whitespace` is responsible for deciding whether to leave a space at the junction.

fixup-whitespace   Function

This function replaces all the white space surrounding point with either
one space or no space, according to the context. It returns `nil`.

At the beginning or end of a line, the appropriate amount of space is none. Before a character with close parenthesis syntax, or after a character with open parenthesis or expression-prefix syntax, no space is also appropriate. Otherwise, one space is appropriate. See Section 31.2.1 [Syntax Class Table], page 212.

In the example below, `fixup-whitespace` is called the first time with point before the word 'spaces' in the first line. For the second invocation, point is directly after the '('.

```
---------- Buffer: foo ----------
This has too many     *spaces
This has too many spaces at the start of (*   this list)
---------- Buffer: foo ----------

(fixup-whitespace)
     ⇒ nil
(fixup-whitespace)
     ⇒ nil

---------- Buffer: foo ----------
This has too many spaces
This has too many spaces at the start of (this list)
---------- Buffer: foo ----------
```

just-one-space   Command

This command replaces any spaces and tabs around point with a single space. It returns `nil`.

delete-blank-lines   Command

This function deletes blank lines surrounding point. If point is on a blank line with one or more blank lines before or after it, then all but one of them are deleted. If point is on an isolated blank line, then it is deleted. If point is on a nonblank line, the command deletes all blank lines following it.

A blank line is defined as a line containing only tabs and spaces.

`delete-blank-lines` returns `nil`.

29.8 The Kill Ring

Kill functions delete text like the deletion functions, but save it so that the user can reinsert it by *yanking*. Most of these functions have 'kill-' in their name. By contrast, the functions whose names start with 'delete-' normally do not save text for yanking (though they can still be undone); these are "deletion" functions.

Most of the kill commands are primarily for interactive use, and are not described here. What we do describe are the functions provided for use in writing such commands. You can use these functions to write commands for killing text. When you need to delete text for internal purposes within a Lisp function, you should normally use deletion functions, so as not to disturb the kill ring contents. See Section 29.6 [Deletion], page 149.

Killed text is saved for later yanking in the *kill ring*. This is a list that holds a number of recent kills, not just the last text kill. We call this a "ring" because yanking treats it as having elements in a cyclic order. The list is kept in the variable `kill-ring`, and can be operated on with the usual functions for lists; there are also specialized functions, described in this section, that treat it as a ring.

Some people think this use of the word "kill" is unfortunate, since it refers to operations that specifically *do not* destroy the entities "killed". This is in sharp contrast to ordinary life, in which death is permanent and "killed" entities do not come back to life. Therefore, other metaphors have been proposed. For example, the term "cut ring" makes sense to people who, in pre-computer days, used scissors and paste to cut up and rearrange manuscripts. However, it would be difficult to change the terminology now.

29.8.1 Kill Ring Concepts

The kill ring records killed text as strings in a list, most recent first. A short kill ring, for example, might look like this:

```
("some text" "a different piece of text" "even older text")
```

When the list reaches `kill-ring-max` entries in length, adding a new entry automatically deletes the last entry.

When kill commands are interwoven with other commands, each kill command makes a new entry in the kill ring. Multiple kill commands in succession build up a single entry in the kill ring, which would be yanked as a unit; the second and subsequent consecutive kill commands add text to the entry made by the first one.

For yanking, one entry in the kill ring is designated the "front" of the ring. Some yank commands "rotate" the ring by designating a different element as the "front." But this virtual rotation doesn't change the list itself—the most recent entry always comes first in the list.

29.8.2 Functions for Killing

`kill-region` is the usual subroutine for killing text. Any command that calls this function is a "kill command" (and should probably have 'kill' in its name). `kill-region` puts the newly killed text in a new element at the beginning of the kill ring or adds it to the most recent element. It uses the `last-command` variable to determine whether the previous command was a kill command, and if so appends the killed text to the most recent entry.

kill-region *start end*   Command

This function kills the text in the region defined by *start* and *end*. The text is deleted but saved in the kill ring, along with its text properties. The value is always `nil`.

In an interactive call, *start* and *end* are point and the mark.

If the buffer is read-only, `kill-region` modifies the kill ring just the same, then signals an error without modifying the buffer. This is convenient because it lets the user use all the kill commands to copy text into the kill ring from a read-only buffer.

copy-region-as-kill *start end*   Command

This command saves the region defined by *start* and *end* on the kill ring (including text properties), but does not delete the text from the buffer. It returns `nil`. It also indicates the extent of the text copied by moving the cursor momentarily, or by displaying a message in the echo area.

The command does not set `this-command` to `kill-region`, so a subsequent kill command does not append to the same kill ring entry.

Don't call `copy-region-as-kill` in Lisp programs unless you aim to support Emacs 18. For Emacs 19, it is better to use `kill-new` or `kill-append` instead. See Section 29.8.4 [Low-Level Kill Ring], page 155.

29.8.3 Functions for Yanking

Yanking means reinserting an entry of previously killed text from the kill ring. The text properties are copied too.

yank &optional *arg*   Command

This command inserts before point the text in the first entry in the kill ring. It positions the mark at the beginning of that text, and point at the end.

If *arg* is a list (which occurs interactively when the user types `C-u` with no digits), then `yank` inserts the text as described above, but puts point before the yanked text and puts the mark after it.

If *arg* is a number, then `yank` inserts the *arg*th most recently killed text—the *arg*th element of the kill ring list.

`yank` does not alter the contents of the kill ring or rotate it. It returns `nil`.

yank-pop *arg*   Command

This command replaces the just-yanked entry from the kill ring with a different entry from the kill ring.

This is allowed only immediately after a `yank` or another `yank-pop`. At such a time, the region contains text that was just inserted by yanking. `yank-pop` deletes that text and inserts in its place a different piece of killed text. It does not add the deleted text to the kill ring, since it is already in the kill ring somewhere.

If *arg* is `nil`, then the replacement text is the previous element of the kill ring. If *arg* is numeric, the replacement is the *arg*th previous kill. If *arg* is negative, a more recent kill is the replacement.

The sequence of kills in the kill ring wraps around, so that after the oldest one comes the newest one, and before the newest one goes the oldest.

The value is always `nil`.

29.8.4 Low-Level Kill Ring

These functions and variables provide access to the kill ring at a lower level, but still convenient for use in Lisp programs. They take care of interaction with X Window selections. They do not exist in Emacs version 18.

current-kill *n* &optional *do-not-move*   Function
The function `current-kill` rotates the yanking pointer which designates the "front" of the kill ring by *n* places (from newer kills to older ones), and returns the text at that place in the ring.

If the optional second argument *do-not-move* is non-`nil`, then `current-kill` doesn't alter the yanking pointer; it just returns the *n*th kill, counting from the current yanking pointer.

If *n* is zero, indicating a request for the latest kill, `current-kill` calls the value of `interprogram-paste-function` (documented below) before consulting the kill ring.

kill-new *string*   Function
This function puts the text *string* into the kill ring as a new entry at the front of the ring. It discards the oldest entry if appropriate. It also invokes the value of `interprogram-cut-function` (see below).

kill-append *string before-p*   Function
This function appends the text *string* to the first entry in the kill ring. Normally *string* goes at the end of the entry, but if *before-p* is non-`nil`, it goes at the beginning. This function also invokes the value of `interprogram-cut-function` (see below).

interprogram-paste-function   Variable
> This variable provides a way of transferring killed text from other
> programs, when you are using a window system. Its value should be
> nil or a function of no arguments.
>
> If the value is a function, current-kill calls it to get the "most recent
> kill". If the function returns a non-nil value, then that value is used
> as the "most recent kill". If it returns nil, then the first element of
> kill-ring is used.
>
> The normal use of this hook is to get the X server's primary selection
> as the most recent kill, even if the selection belongs to another X client.
> See Section 26.18 [X Selections], page 115.

interprogram-cut-function   Variable
> This variable provides a way of communicating killed text to other
> programs, when you are using a window system. Its value should be
> nil or a function of one argument.
>
> If the value is a function, kill-new and kill-append call it with the
> new first element of the kill ring as an argument.
>
> The normal use of this hook is to set the X server's primary selection
> to the newly killed text.

29.8.5 Internals of the Kill Ring

The variable kill-ring holds the kill ring contents, in the form of a list
of strings. The most recent kill is always at the front of the list.

The kill-ring-yank-pointer variable points to a link in the kill ring
list, whose CAR is the text to yank next. We say it identifies the "front"
of the ring. Moving kill-ring-yank-pointer to a different link is called
rotating the kill ring. We call the kill ring a "ring" because the functions
that move the yank pointer wrap around from the end of the list to the
beginning, or vice-versa. Rotation of the kill ring is virtual; it does not
change the value of kill-ring.

Both kill-ring and kill-ring-yank-pointer are Lisp variables whose
values are normally lists. The word "pointer" in the name of the kill-
ring-yank-pointer indicates that the variable's purpose is to identify one
element of the list for use by the next yank command.

The value of kill-ring-yank-pointer is always eq to one of the links
in the kill ring list. The element it identifies is the CAR of that link. Kill
commands, which change the kill ring, also set this variable to the value of
kill-ring. The effect is to rotate the ring so that the newly killed text is
at the front.

Here is a diagram that shows the variable `kill-ring-yank-pointer` pointing to the second entry in the kill ring (`"some text" "a different piece of text" "yet older text"`).

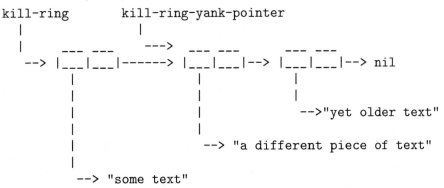

This state of affairs might occur after `C-y` (yank) immediately followed by `M-y` (yank-pop).

kill-ring   *Variable*
> This variable holds the list of killed text sequences, most recently killed first.

kill-ring-yank-pointer   *Variable*
> This variable's value indicates which element of the kill ring is at the "front" of the ring for yanking. More precisely, the value is a tail of the value of `kill-ring`, and its CAR is the kill string that `C-y` should yank.

kill-ring-max   *User Option*
> The value of this variable is the maximum length to which the kill ring can grow, before elements are thrown away at the end. The default value for `kill-ring-max` is 30.

29.9 Undo

Most buffers have an *undo list*, which records all changes made to the buffer's text so that they can be undone. (The buffers that don't have one are usually special-purpose buffers for which Emacs assumes that undoing is not useful.) All the primitives that modify the text in the buffer automatically add elements to the front of the undo list, which is in the variable `buffer-undo-list`.

buffer-undo-list   *Variable*
> This variable's value is the undo list of the current buffer. A value of `t` disables the recording of undo information.

Here are the kinds of elements an undo list can have:

integer   This kind of element records a previous value of point. Ordinary
             cursor motion does not get any sort of undo record, but deletion
             commands use these entries to record where point was before
             the command.

(*beg* . *end*)

             This kind of element indicates how to delete text that was in-
             serted. Upon insertion, the text occupied the range *beg–end* in
             the buffer.

(*text* . *position*)

             This kind of element indicates how to reinsert text that was
             deleted. The deleted text itself is the string *text*. The place to
             reinsert it is (abs *position*).

(t *high* . *low*)

             This kind of element indicates that an unmodified buffer became
             modified. The elements *high* and *low* are two integers, each
             recording 16 bits of the visited file's modification time as of when
             it was previously visited or saved. primitive-undo uses those
             values to determine whether to mark the buffer as unmodified
             once again; it does so only if the file's modification time matches
             those numbers.

(nil *property value beg* . *end*)

             This kind of element records a change in a text property. Here's
             how you might undo the change:

                 (put-text-property *beg end property value*)

position   This element indicates where point was at an earlier time. Un-
             doing this element sets point to *position*. Deletion normally
             creates an element of this kind as well as a reinsertion element.

nil   This element is a boundary. The elements between two bound-
             aries are called a *change group*; normally, each change group
             corresponds to one keyboard command, and undo commands
             normally undo an entire group as a unit.

undo-boundary   Function
   This function places a boundary element in the undo list. The undo
   command stops at such a boundary, and successive undo commands
   undo to earlier and earlier boundaries. This function returns nil.

   The editor command loop automatically creates an undo boundary
   before each key sequence is executed. Thus, each undo normally undoes the effects of one command. Self-inserting input characters are
   an exception. The command loop makes a boundary for the first such

character; the next 19 consecutive self-inserting input characters do
not make boundaries, and then the 20th does, and so on as long as
self-inserting characters continue.

All buffer modifications add a boundary whenever the previous undoable change was made in some other buffer. This way, a command that modifies several buffers makes a boundary in each buffer it
changes.

Calling this function explicitly is useful for splitting the effects of a
command into more than one unit. For example, `query-replace` calls
`undo-boundary` after each replacement, so that the user can undo
individual replacements one by one.

primitive-undo *count list*   Function
This is the basic function for undoing elements of an undo list. It
undoes the first *count* elements of *list*, returning the rest of *list*. You
could write this function in Lisp, but it is convenient to have it in C.

`primitive-undo` adds elements to the buffer's undo list when it
changes the buffer. Undo commands avoid confusion by saving the
undo list value at the beginning of a sequence of undo operations.
Then the undo operations use and update the saved value. The new
elements added by undoing are not part of this saved value, so they
don't interfere with continuing to undo.

29.10 Maintaining Undo Lists

This section describes how to enable and disable undo information for a
given buffer. It also explains how the undo list is truncated automatically
so it doesn't get too big.

Recording of undo information in a newly created buffer is normally enabled to start with; but if the buffer name starts with a space, the undo
recording is initially disabled. You can explicitly enable or disable undo
recording with the following two functions, or by setting `buffer-undo-list`
yourself.

buffer-enable-undo &optional *buffer-or-name*   Command
This command enables recording undo information for buffer *buffer-
or-name*, so that subsequent changes can be undone. If no argument is
supplied, then the current buffer is used. This function does nothing
if undo recording is already enabled in the buffer. It returns `nil`.

In an interactive call, *buffer-or-name* is the current buffer. You cannot
specify any other buffer.

buffer-disable-undo &optional *buffer*   Function
buffer-flush-undo &optional *buffer*   Function
> This function discards the undo list of *buffer*, and disables further
> recording of undo information. As a result, it is no longer possible to
> undo either previous changes or any subsequent changes. If the undo
> list of *buffer* is already disabled, this function has no effect.
>
> This function returns `nil`. It cannot be called interactively.
>
> The name `buffer-flush-undo` is not considered obsolete, but the pre-
> ferred name `buffer-disable-undo` is new as of Emacs versions 19.

As editing continues, undo lists get longer and longer. To prevent them
from using up all available memory space, garbage collection trims them
back to size limits you can set. (For this purpose, the "size" of an undo
list measures the cons cells that make up the list, plus the strings of deleted
text.) Two variables control the range of acceptable sizes: `undo-limit` and
`undo-strong-limit`.

undo-limit   Variable
> This is the soft limit for the acceptable size of an undo list. The change
> group at which this size is exceeded is the last one kept.

undo-strong-limit   Variable
> This is the upper limit for the acceptable size of an undo list. The
> change group at which this size is exceeded is discarded itself (along
> with all older change groups). There is one exception: the very latest
> change group is never discarded no matter how big it is.

29.11 Filling

Filling means adjusting the lengths of lines (by moving the line breaks)
so that they are nearly (but no greater than) a specified maximum width.
Additionally, lines can be *justified*, which means inserting spaces to make
the left and/or right margins line up precisely. The width is controlled by
the variable `fill-column`. For ease of reading, lines should be no longer
than 70 or so columns.

You can use Auto Fill mode (see Section 29.13 [Auto Filling], page 164)
to fill text automatically as you insert it, but changes to existing text may
leave it improperly filled. Then you must fill the text explicitly.

Most of the commands in this section return values that are not meaningful. All the functions that do filling take note of the current left margin,
current right margin, and current justification style (see Section 29.12 [Mar-
gins], page 163). If the current justification style is `none`, the filling functions
don't actually do anything.

Several of the filling functions have an argument *justify*. If it is non-`nil`, that requests some kind of justification. It can be `left`, `right`, `full`, or `center`, to request a specific style of justification. If it is `t`, that means to use the current justification style for this part of the text (see `current-justification`, below).

When you call the filling functions interactively, using a prefix argument implies the value `full` for *justify*.

fill-paragraph *justify*   Command
> This command fills the paragraph at or after point. If *justify* is non-`nil`, each line is justified as well. It uses the ordinary paragraph motion commands to find paragraph boundaries. See section "Paragraphs" in *The Emacs Manual*.

fill-region *start end* &optional *justify*   Command
> This command fills each of the paragraphs in the region from *start* to *end*. It justifies as well if *justify* is non-`nil`.
>
> The variable `paragraph-separate` controls how to distinguish paragraphs. See Section 30.8 [Standard Regexps], page 209.

fill-individual-paragraphs *start end* &optional   Command
> *justify mail-flag*
> This command fills each paragraph in the region according to its individual fill prefix. Thus, if the lines of a paragraph were indented with spaces, the filled paragraph will remain indented in the same fashion.
>
> The first two arguments, *start* and *end*, are the beginning and end of the region to be filled. The third and fourth arguments, *justify* and *mail-flag*, are optional. If *justify* is non-`nil`, the paragraphs are justified as well as filled. If *mail-flag* is non-`nil`, it means the function is operating on a mail message and therefore should not fill the header lines.
>
> Ordinarily, `fill-individual-paragraphs` regards each change in indentation as starting a new paragraph. If `fill-individual-varying-indent` is non-`nil`, then only separator lines separate paragraphs. That mode can handle indented paragraphs with additional indentation on the first line.

fill-individual-varying-indent   User Option
> This variable alters the action of `fill-individual-paragraphs` as described above.

fill-region-as-paragraph *start end* &optional *justify*   Command
> This command considers a region of text as a paragraph and fills it. If the region was made up of many paragraphs, the blank lines between

paragraphs are removed. This function justifies as well as filling when *justify* is non-`nil`.

In an interactive call, any prefix argument requests justification.

In Adaptive Fill mode, which is enabled by default, `fill-region-as-paragraph` on an indented paragraph when there is no fill prefix uses the indentation of the second line of the paragraph as the fill prefix.

justify-current-line *how eop nosqueeze*   Command
This command inserts spaces between the words of the current line so that the line ends exactly at `fill-column`. It returns `nil`.

The argument *how*, if non-`nil` specifies explicitly the style of justification. It can be `left`, `right`, `full`, `center`, or `none`. If it is `t`, that means to do follow specified justification style (see `current-justification`, below). `nil` means to do full justification.

If *eop* is non-`nil`, that means do left-justification when `current-justification` specifies full justification. This is used for the last line of a paragraph; even if the paragraph as a whole is fully justified, the last line should not be.

If *nosqueeze* is non-`nil`, that means do not change interior whitespace.

default-justification   User Option
This variable's value specifies the style of justification to use for text that doesn't specify a style with a text property. The possible values are `left`, `right`, `full`, `center`, or `none`. The default value is `left`.

current-justification   Function
This function returns the proper justification style to use for filling the text around point.

fill-paragraph-function   Variable
This variable provides a way for major modes to override the filling of paragraphs. If the value is non-`nil`, `fill-paragraph` calls this function to do the work. If the function returns a non-`nil` value, `fill-paragraph` assumes the job is done, and immediately returns that value.

The usual use of this feature is to fill comments in programming language modes. If the function needs to fill a paragraph in the usual way, it can do so as follows:

```
(let ((fill-paragraph-function nil))
  (fill-paragraph arg))
```

use-hard-newlines   Variable
If this variable is non-`nil`, the filling functions do not delete newlines that have the `hard` text property. These "hard newlines" act as paragraph separators.

29.12 Margins for Filling

fill-prefix   User Option

This variable specifies a string of text that appears at the beginning
of normal text lines and should be disregarded when filling them. Any
line that fails to start with the fill prefix is considered the start of a
paragraph; so is any line that starts with the fill prefix followed by
additional whitespace. Lines that start with the fill prefix but no additional whitespace are ordinary text lines that can be filled together.
The resulting filled lines also start with the fill prefix.

The fill prefix follows the left margin whitespace, if any.

fill-column   User Option

This buffer-local variable specifies the maximum width of filled lines.
Its value should be an integer, which is a number of columns. All
the filling, justification and centering commands are affected by this
variable, including Auto Fill mode (see Section 29.13 [Auto Filling],
page 164).

As a practical matter, if you are writing text for other people to read,
you should set `fill-column` to no more than 70. Otherwise the line
will be too long for people to read comfortably, and this can make the
text seem clumsy.

default-fill-column   Variable

The value of this variable is the default value for `fill-column` in
buffers that do not override it. This is the same as (`default-value`
`'fill-column`).

The default value for `default-fill-column` is 70.

set-left-margin *from to margin*   Command

This sets the `left-margin` property on the text from *from* to *to* to the
value *margin*. If Auto Fill mode is enabled, this command also refills
the region to fit the new margin.

set-right-margin *from to margin*   Command

This sets the `right-margin` property on the text from *from* to *to* to
the value *margin*. If Auto Fill mode is enabled, this command also
refills the region to fit the new margin.

current-left-margin   Function

This function returns the proper left margin value to use for filling the
text around point. The value is the sum of the `left-margin` property
of the character at the start of the current line (or zero if none), and
the value of the variable `left-margin`.

current-fill-column   *Function*
> This function returns the proper fill column value to use for filling the
> text around point. The value is the value of the `fill-column` variable,
> minus the value of the `right-margin` property of the character after
> point.

move-to-left-margin &optional *n force*   *Command*
> This function moves point to the left margin of the current line. The
> column moved to is determined by calling the function `current-left-
> margin`. If the argument *n* is non-`nil`, `move-to-left-margin` moves
> forward *n*−1 lines first.
>
> If *force* is non-`nil`, that says to fix the line's indentation if that doesn't
> match the left margin value.

delete-to-left-margin *from to*   *Function*
> This function removes left margin indentation from the text between
> *from* and *to*. The amount of indentation to delete is determined by
> calling `current-left-margin`. In no case does this function delete
> non-whitespace.

indent-to-left-margin   *Function*
> This is the default `indent-line-function`, used in Fundamental
> mode, Text mode, etc. Its effect is to adjust the indentation at the
> beginning of the current line to the value specified by the variable
> `left-margin`. This may involve either inserting or deleting whites-
> pace.

left-margin   *Variable*
> This variable specifies the base left margin column. In Fundamen-
> tal mode, LFD indents to this column. This variable automatically
> becomes buffer-local when set in any fashion.

29.13 Auto Filling

Auto Fill mode is a minor mode that fills lines automatically as text
is inserted. This section describes the hook used by Auto Fill mode. For a
description of functions that you can call explicitly to fill and justify existing
text, see Section 29.11 [Filling], page 160.

Auto Fill mode also enables the functions that change the margins and
justification style to refill portions of the text. See Section 29.12 [Margins],
page 163.

auto-fill-function   *Variable*
> The value of this variable should be a function (of no arguments) to
> be called after self-inserting a space or a newline. It may be `nil`, in
> which case nothing special is done in that case.

The value of `auto-fill-function` is `do-auto-fill` when Auto-Fill mode is enabled. That is a function whose sole purpose is to implement the usual strategy for breaking a line.

> In older Emacs versions, this variable was named `auto-fill-hook`, but since it is not called with the standard convention for hooks, it was renamed to `auto-fill-function` in version 19.

29.14 Sorting Text

The sorting functions described in this section all rearrange text in a buffer. This is in contrast to the function `sort`, which rearranges the order of the elements of a list (see Section 5.6.3 [Rearrangement], page 82, vol. 1). The values returned by these functions are not meaningful.

sort-subr *reverse nextrecfun endrecfun* &optional **Function**
  startkeyfun endkeyfun
This function is the general text-sorting routine that divides a buffer into records and sorts them. Most of the commands in this section use this function.

To understand how `sort-subr` works, consider the whole accessible portion of the buffer as being divided into disjoint pieces called *sort records*. The records may or may not be contiguous; they may not overlap. A portion of each sort record (perhaps all of it) is designated as the sort key. Sorting rearranges the records in order by their sort keys.

Usually, the records are rearranged in order of ascending sort key. If the first argument to the `sort-subr` function, *reverse*, is non-`nil`, the sort records are rearranged in order of descending sort key.

The next four arguments to `sort-subr` are functions that are called to move point across a sort record. They are called many times from within `sort-subr`.

1. *nextrecfun* is called with point at the end of a record. This function moves point to the start of the next record. The first record is assumed to start at the position of point when `sort-subr` is called. Therefore, you should usually move point to the beginning of the buffer before calling `sort-subr`.

   This function can indicate there are no more sort records by leaving point at the end of the buffer.

2. *endrecfun* is called with point within a record. It moves point to the end of the record.

3. *startkeyfun* is called to move point from the start of a record to the start of the sort key. This argument is optional; if it is omitted,

the whole record is the sort key. If supplied, the function should either return a non-nil value to be used as the sort key, or return nil to indicate that the sort key is in the buffer starting at point. In the latter case, *endkeyfun* is called to find the end of the sort key.

4. *endkeyfun* is called to move point from the start of the sort key to the end of the sort key. This argument is optional. If *startkey-fun* returns nil and this argument is omitted (or nil), then the sort key extends to the end of the record. There is no need for *endkeyfun* if *startkeyfun* returns a non-nil value.

As an example of `sort-subr`, here is the complete function definition for `sort-lines`:

```
;; Note that the first two lines of doc string
;; are effectively one line when viewed by a user.
(defun sort-lines (reverse beg end)
   "Sort lines in region alphabetically.
Called from a program, there are three arguments:
REVERSE (non-nil means reverse order),
and BEG and END (the region to sort)."
   (interactive "P\nr")
   (save-restriction
      (narrow-to-region beg end)
      (goto-char (point-min))
      (sort-subr reverse
                 'forward-line
                 'end-of-line)))
```

Here `forward-line` moves point to the start of the next record, and `end-of-line` moves point to the end of record. We do not pass the arguments *startkeyfun* and *endkeyfun*, because the entire record is used as the sort key.

The `sort-paragraphs` function is very much the same, except that its `sort-subr` call looks like this:

```
(sort-subr reverse
           (function
            (lambda ()
              (skip-chars-forward "\n \t\f")))
           'forward-paragraph)
```

sort-regexp-fields *reverse record-regexp key-regexp*   Command
       start end

This command sorts the region between *start* and *end* alphabetically as specified by *record-regexp* and *key-regexp*. If *reverse* is a negative integer, then sorting is in reverse order.

Alphabetical sorting means that two sort keys are compared by comparing the first characters of each, the second characters of each, and so on. If a mismatch is found, it means that the sort keys are unequal; the sort key whose character is less at the point of first mismatch is the lesser sort key. The individual characters are compared according to their numerical values. Since Emacs uses the ASCII character set, the ordering in that set determines alphabetical order.

The value of the *record-regexp* argument specifies how to divide the buffer into sort records. At the end of each record, a search is done for this regular expression, and the text that matches it is the next record. For example, the regular expression '`^.+$`', which matches lines with at least one character besides a newline, would make each such line into a sort record. See Section 30.2 [Regular Expressions], page 193, for a description of the syntax and meaning of regular expressions.

The value of the *key-regexp* argument specifies what part of each record is the sort key. The *key-regexp* could match the whole record, or only a part. In the latter case, the rest of the record has no effect on the sorted order of records, but it is carried along when the record moves to its new position.

The *key-regexp* argument can refer to the text matched by a subexpression of *record-regexp*, or it can be a regular expression on its own.

If *key-regexp* is:

'`\digit`'   then the text matched by the *digit*th '`\(...\)`' parenthesis grouping in *record-regexp* is the sort key.

'`\&`'   then the whole record is the sort key.

a regular expression

      then `sort-regexp-fields` searches for a match for the regular expression within the record. If such a match is found, it is the sort key. If there is no match for *key-regexp* within a record then that record is ignored, which means its position in the buffer is not changed. (The other records may move around it.)

For example, if you plan to sort all the lines in the region by the first word on each line starting with the letter '`f`', you should set *record-regexp* to '`^.*$`' and set *key-regexp* to '`\<f\w*\>`'. The resulting expression looks like this:

```
(sort-regexp-fields nil "^.*$" "\\<f\\w*\\>"
                    (region-beginning)
                    (region-end))
```

If you call `sort-regexp-fields` interactively, it prompts for *record-regexp* and *key-regexp* in the minibuffer.

sort-lines *reverse start end*   Command
> This command alphabetically sorts lines in the region between *start* and *end*. If *reverse* is non-`nil`, the sort is in reverse order.

sort-paragraphs *reverse start end*   Command
> This command alphabetically sorts paragraphs in the region between *start* and *end*. If *reverse* is non-`nil`, the sort is in reverse order.

sort-pages *reverse start end*   Command
> This command alphabetically sorts pages in the region between *start* and *end*. If *reverse* is non-`nil`, the sort is in reverse order.

sort-fields *field start end*   Command
> This command sorts lines in the region between *start* and *end*, comparing them alphabetically by the *field*th field of each line. Fields are separated by whitespace and numbered starting from 1. If *field* is negative, sorting is by the −*field*th field from the end of the line. This command is useful for sorting tables.

sort-numeric-fields *field start end*   Command
> This command sorts lines in the region between *start* and *end*, comparing them numerically by the *field*th field of each line. The specified field must contain a number in each line of the region. Fields are separated by whitespace and numbered starting from 1. If *field* is negative, sorting is by the −*field*th field from the end of the line. This command is useful for sorting tables.

sort-columns *reverse &optional beg end*   Command
> This command sorts the lines in the region between *beg* and *end*, comparing them alphabetically by a certain range of columns. The column positions of *beg* and *end* bound the range of columns to sort on.
>
> If *reverse* is non-`nil`, the sort is in reverse order.
>
> One unusual thing about this command is that the entire line containing position *beg*, and the entire line containing position *end*, are included in the region sorted.
>
> Note that `sort-columns` uses the `sort` utility program, and so cannot work properly on text containing tab characters. Use M-x `untabify` to convert tabs to spaces before sorting.

29.15 Counting Columns

The column functions convert between a character position (counting characters from the beginning of the buffer) and a column position (counting screen characters from the beginning of a line).

A character counts according to the number of columns it occupies on the screen. This means control characters count as occupying 2 or 4 columns, depending upon the value of `ctl-arrow`, and tabs count as occupying a number of columns that depends on the value of `tab-width` and on the column where the tab begins. See Section 35.13 [Usual Display], page 293.

Column number computations ignore the width of the window and the amount of horizontal scrolling. Consequently, a column value can be arbitrarily high. The first (or leftmost) column is numbered 0.

current-column   Function
    This function returns the horizontal position of point, measured in columns, counting from 0 at the left margin. The column position is the sum of the widths of all the displayed representations of the characters between the start of the current line and point.

    For an example of using `current-column`, see the description of `count-lines` in Section 27.2.4 [Text Lines], page 122.

move-to-column *column* &optional *force*   Function
    This function moves point to *column* in the current line. The calculation of *column* takes into account the widths of the displayed representations of the characters between the start of the line and point.

    If column *column* is beyond the end of the line, point moves to the end of the line. If *column* is negative, point moves to the beginning of the line.

    If it is impossible to move to column *column* because that is in the middle of a multicolumn character such as a tab, point moves to the end of that character. However, if *force* is non-`nil`, and *column* is in the middle of a tab, then `move-to-column` converts the tab into spaces so that it can move precisely to column *column*. Other multicolumn characters can cause anomalies despite *force*, since there is no way to split them.

    The argument *force* also has an effect if the line isn't long enough to reach column *column*; in that case, it says to add whitespace at the end of the line to reach that column.

    If *column* is not an integer, an error is signaled.

    The return value is the column number actually moved to.

29.16 Indentation

The indentation functions are used to examine, move to, and change whitespace that is at the beginning of a line. Some of the functions can also change whitespace elsewhere on a line. Columns and indentation count from zero at the left margin.

29.16.1 Indentation Primitives

This section describes the primitive functions used to count and insert indentation. The functions in the following sections use these primitives.

current-indentation   Function
  This function returns the indentation of the current line, which is the horizontal position of the first nonblank character. If the contents are entirely blank, then this is the horizontal position of the end of the line.

indent-to *column* &optional *minimum*   Command
  This function indents from point with tabs and spaces until *column* is reached. If *minimum* is specified and non-nil, then at least that many spaces are inserted even if this requires going beyond *column*. Otherwise the function does nothing if point is already beyond *column*. The value is the column at which the inserted indentation ends.

  The inserted whitespace characters inherit text properties from the surrounding text (usually, from the preceding text only). See Section 29.18.6 [Sticky Properties], page 184.

indent-tabs-mode   User Option
  If this variable is non-nil, indentation functions can insert tabs as well as spaces. Otherwise, they insert only spaces. Setting this variable automatically makes it local to the current buffer.

29.16.2 Indentation Controlled by Major Mode

An important function of each major mode is to customize the TAB key to indent properly for the language being edited. This section describes the mechanism of the TAB key and how to control it. The functions in this section return unpredictable values.

indent-line-function   Variable
  This variable's value is the function to be used by TAB (and various commands) to indent the current line. The command indent-according-to-mode does no more than call this function.

In Lisp mode, the value is the symbol `lisp-indent-line`; in C mode, `c-indent-line`; in Fortran mode, `fortran-indent-line`. In Fundamental mode, Text mode, and many other modes with no standard for indentation, the value is `indent-to-left-margin` (which is the default value).

indent-according-to-mode   Command
This command calls the function in `indent-line-function` to indent the current line in a way appropriate for the current major mode.

indent-for-tab-command   Command
This command calls the function in `indent-line-function` to indent the current line; except that if that function is `indent-to-left-margin`, it calls `insert-tab` instead. (That is a trivial command that inserts a tab character.)

newline-and-indent   Command
This function inserts a newline, then indents the new line (the one following the newline just inserted) according to the major mode.

It does indentation by calling the current `indent-line-function`. In programming language modes, this is the same thing TAB does, but in some text modes, where TAB inserts a tab, `newline-and-indent` indents to the column specified by `left-margin`.

reindent-then-newline-and-indent   Command
This command reindents the current line, inserts a newline at point, and then reindents the new line (the one following the newline just inserted).

This command does indentation on both lines according to the current major mode, by calling the current value of `indent-line-function`. In programming language modes, this is the same thing TAB does, but in some text modes, where TAB inserts a tab, `reindent-then-newline-and-indent` indents to the column specified by `left-margin`.

29.16.3 Indenting an Entire Region

This section describes commands that indent all the lines in the region. They return unpredictable values.

indent-region *start end to-column*   Command
This command indents each nonblank line starting between *start* (inclusive) and *end* (exclusive). If *to-column* is `nil`, `indent-region` indents each nonblank line by calling the current mode's indentation function, the value of `indent-line-function`.

If *to-column* is non-`nil`, it should be an integer specifying the number of columns of indentation; then this function gives each line exactly that much indentation, by either adding or deleting whitespace.

If there is a fill prefix, `indent-region` indents each line by making it start with the fill prefix.

indent-region-function   Variable

The value of this variable is a function that can be used by `indent-region` as a short cut. You should design the function so that it will produce the same results as indenting the lines of the region one by one, but presumably faster.

If the value is `nil`, there is no short cut, and `indent-region` actually works line by line.

A short-cut function is useful in modes such as C mode and Lisp mode, where the `indent-line-function` must scan from the beginning of the function definition: applying it to each line would be quadratic in time. The short cut can update the scan information as it moves through the lines indenting them; this takes linear time. In a mode where indenting a line individually is fast, there is no need for a short cut.

`indent-region` with a non-`nil` argument *to-column* has a different meaning and does not use this variable.

indent-rigidly *start end count*   Command

This command indents all lines starting between *start* (inclusive) and *end* (exclusive) sideways by *count* columns. This "preserves the shape" of the affected region, moving it as a rigid unit. Consequently, this command is useful not only for indenting regions of unindented text, but also for indenting regions of formatted code.

For example, if *count* is 3, this command adds 3 columns of indentation to each of the lines beginning in the region specified.

In Mail mode, `C-c C-y` (`mail-yank-original`) uses `indent-rigidly` to indent the text copied from the message being replied to.

indent-code-rigidly *start end columns* &optional   Function
          nochange-regexp

This is like `indent-rigidly`, except that it doesn't alter lines that start within strings or comments.

In addition, it doesn't alter a line if *nochange-regexp* matches at the beginning of the line (if *nochange-regexp* is non-`nil`).

29.16.4 Indentation Relative to Previous Lines

This section describes two commands that indent the current line based on the contents of previous lines.

indent-relative &optional *unindented-ok*   Command

This command inserts whitespace at point, extending to the same column as the next *indent point* of the previous nonblank line. An indent point is a non-whitespace character following whitespace. The next indent point is the first one at a column greater than the current column of point. For example, if point is underneath and to the left of the first non-blank character of a line of text, it moves to that column by inserting whitespace.

If the previous nonblank line has no next indent point (i.e., none at a great enough column position), `indent-relative` either does nothing (if *unindented-ok* is non-`nil`) or calls `tab-to-tab-stop`. Thus, if point is underneath and to the right of the last column of a short line of text, this command ordinarily moves point to the next tab stop by inserting whitespace.

The return value of `indent-relative` is unpredictable.

In the following example, point is at the beginning of the second line:

```
            This line is indented twelve spaces.
     *The quick brown fox jumped.
```

Evaluation of the expression `(indent-relative nil)` produces the following:

```
            This line is indented twelve spaces.
            *The quick brown fox jumped.
```

In this example, point is between the 'm' and 'p' of 'jumped':

```
            This line is indented twelve spaces.
     The quick brown fox jum*ped.
```

Evaluation of the expression `(indent-relative nil)` produces the following:

```
            This line is indented twelve spaces.
     The quick brown fox jum  *ped.
```

indent-relative-maybe   Command

This command indents the current line like the previous nonblank line. It calls `indent-relative` with `t` as the *unindented-ok* argument. The return value is unpredictable.

If the previous nonblank line has no indent points beyond the current column, this command does nothing.

29.16.5 Adjustable "Tab Stops"

This section explains the mechanism for user-specified "tab stops" and the mechanisms that use and set them. The name "tab stops" is used because the feature is similar to that of the tab stops on a typewriter. The feature works by inserting an appropriate number of spaces and tab characters to reach the next tab stop column; it does not affect the display of tab characters in the buffer (see Section 35.13 [Usual Display], page 293). Note that the TAB character as input uses this tab stop feature only in a few major modes, such as Text mode.

tab-to-tab-stop   Command
> This command inserts spaces or tabs up to the next tab stop column defined by `tab-stop-list`. It searches the list for an element greater than the current column number, and uses that element as the column to indent to. It does nothing if no such element is found.

tab-stop-list   User Option
> This variable is the list of tab stop columns used by `tab-to-tab-stops`. The elements should be integers in increasing order. The tab stop columns need not be evenly spaced.
>
> Use `M-x edit-tab-stops` to edit the location of tab stops interactively.

29.16.6 Indentation-Based Motion Commands

These commands, primarily for interactive use, act based on the indentation in the text.

back-to-indentation   Command
> This command moves point to the first non-whitespace character in the current line (which is the line in which point is located). It returns `nil`.

backward-to-indentation *arg*   Command
> This command moves point backward *arg* lines and then to the first nonblank character on that line. It returns `nil`.

forward-to-indentation *arg*   Command
> This command moves point forward *arg* lines and then to the first nonblank character on that line. It returns `nil`.

29.17 Case Changes

The case change commands described here work on text in the current buffer. See Section 4.7 [Character Case], page 67, vol. 1, for case conversion commands that work on strings and characters. See Section 4.8 [Case Table], page 68, vol. 1, for how to customize which characters are upper or lower case and how to convert them.

capitalize-region *start end*   Command

This function capitalizes all words in the region defined by *start* and *end*. To capitalize means to convert each word's first character to upper case and convert the rest of each word to lower case. The function returns `nil`.

If one end of the region is in the middle of a word, the part of the word within the region is treated as an entire word.

When `capitalize-region` is called interactively, *start* and *end* are point and the mark, with the smallest first.

```
---------- Buffer: foo ----------
This is the contents of the 5th foo.
---------- Buffer: foo ----------

(capitalize-region 1 44)
⇒ nil


---------- Buffer: foo ----------
This Is The Contents Of The 5th Foo.
---------- Buffer: foo ----------
```

downcase-region *start end*   Command

This function converts all of the letters in the region defined by *start* and *end* to lower case. The function returns `nil`.

When `downcase-region` is called interactively, *start* and *end* are point and the mark, with the smallest first.

upcase-region *start end*   Command

This function converts all of the letters in the region defined by *start* and *end* to upper case. The function returns `nil`.

When `upcase-region` is called interactively, *start* and *end* are point and the mark, with the smallest first.

capitalize-word *count*   Command

This function capitalizes *count* words after point, moving point over as it does. To capitalize means to convert each word's first character to upper case and convert the rest of each word to lower case. If *count* is negative, the function capitalizes the −*count* previous words but does not move point. The value is `nil`.

If point is in the middle of a word, the part of the word before point is ignored when moving forward. The rest is treated as an entire word.

When `capitalize-word` is called interactively, *count* is set to the numeric prefix argument.

downcase-word *count*   Command

This function converts the *count* words after point to all lower case, moving point over as it does. If *count* is negative, it converts the −*count* previous words but does not move point. The value is `nil`.

When `downcase-word` is called interactively, *count* is set to the numeric prefix argument.

upcase-word *count*   Command

This function converts the *count* words after point to all upper case, moving point over as it does. If *count* is negative, it converts the −*count* previous words but does not move point. The value is `nil`.

When `upcase-word` is called interactively, *count* is set to the numeric prefix argument.

29.18 Text Properties

Each character position in a buffer or a string can have a *text property list*, much like the property list of a symbol (see Section 7.4 [Property Lists], page 104, vol. 1). The properties belong to a particular character at a particular place, such as, the letter 'T' at the beginning of this sentence or the first 'o' in 'foo'—if the same character occurs in two different places, the two occurrences generally have different properties.

Each property has a name and a value. Both of these can be any Lisp object, but the name is normally a symbol. The usual way to access the property list is to specify a name and ask what value corresponds to it.

If a character has a `category` property, we call it the *category* of the character. It should be a symbol. The properties of the symbol serve as defaults for the properties of the character.

Copying text between strings and buffers preserves the properties along with the characters; this includes such diverse functions as `substring`, `insert`, and `buffer-substring`.

29.18.1 Examining Text Properties

The simplest way to examine text properties is to ask for the value of a particular property of a particular character. For that, use `get-text-property`. Use `text-properties-at` to get the entire property list of a character. See Section 29.18.3 [Property Search], page 179, for functions to examine the properties of a number of characters at once.

These functions handle both strings and buffers. Keep in mind that positions in a string start from 0, whereas positions in a buffer start from 1.

get-text-property *pos prop* &optional *object*   Function
> This function returns the value of the *prop* property of the character after position *pos* in *object* (a buffer or string). The argument *object* is optional and defaults to the current buffer.
>
> If there is no *prop* property strictly speaking, but the character has a category that is a symbol, then `get-text-property` returns the *prop* property of that symbol.

get-char-property *pos prop* &optional *object*   Function
> This function is like `get-text-property`, except that it checks overlays first and then text properties. See Section 35.9 [Overlays], page 284.
>
> The argument *object* may be a string, a buffer, or a window. If it is a window, then the buffer displayed in that window is used for text properties and overlays, but only the overlays active for that window are considered. If *object* is a buffer, then all overlays in that buffer are considered, as well as text properties. If *object* is a string, only text properties are considered, since strings never have overlays.

text-properties-at *position* &optional *object*   Function
> This function returns the entire property list of the character at *position* in the string or buffer *object*. If *object* is `nil`, it defaults to the current buffer.

default-text-properties   Variable
> This variable holds a property list giving default values for text properties. Whenever a character does not specify a value for a property, neither directly nor through a category symbol, the value stored in this list is used instead. Here is an example:
>
> ```
> (setq default-text-properties '(foo 69))
> ;; Make sure character 1 has no properties of its own.
> (set-text-properties 1 2 nil)
> ;; What we get, when we ask, is the default value.
> (get-text-property 1 'foo)
>      ⇒ 69
> ```

29.18.2 Changing Text Properties

The primitives for changing properties apply to a specified range of text. The function `set-text-properties` (see end of section) sets the entire property list of the text in that range; more often, it is useful to add, change, or delete just certain properties specified by name.

Since text properties are considered part of the buffer's contents, and can affect how the buffer looks on the screen, any change in the text properties is considered a buffer modification. Buffer text property changes are undoable (see Section 29.9 [Undo], page 157).

put-text-property *start end prop value* &optional   Function
> *object*

This function sets the *prop* property to *value* for the text between *start* and *end* in the string or buffer *object*. If *object* is `nil`, it defaults to the current buffer.

add-text-properties *start end props* &optional *object*   Function

This function modifies the text properties for the text between *start* and *end* in the string or buffer *object*. If *object* is `nil`, it defaults to the current buffer.

The argument *props* specifies which properties to change. It should have the form of a property list (see Section 7.4 [Property Lists], page 104, vol. 1): a list whose elements include the property names followed alternately by the corresponding values.

The return value is `t` if the function actually changed some property's value; `nil` otherwise (if *props* is `nil` or its values agree with those in the text).

For example, here is how to set the `comment` and `face` properties of a range of text:

```
(add-text-properties start end
                     '(comment t face highlight))
```

remove-text-properties *start end props* &optional   Function
> *object*

This function deletes specified text properties from the text between *start* and *end* in the string or buffer *object*. If *object* is `nil`, it defaults to the current buffer.

The argument *props* specifies which properties to delete. It should have the form of a property list (see Section 7.4 [Property Lists], page 104, vol. 1): a list whose elements are property names alternating with corresponding values. But only the names matter—the values that accompany them are ignored. For example, here's how to remove the `face` property.

```
(remove-text-properties start end '(face nil))
```

The return value is `t` if the function actually changed some property's value; `nil` otherwise (if *props* is `nil` or if no character in the specified text had any of those properties).

set-text-properties *start end props* &optional *object*   Function
This function completely replaces the text property list for the text
between *start* and *end* in the string or buffer *object*. If *object* is `nil`,
it defaults to the current buffer.

The argument *props* is the new property list. It should be a list whose
elements are property names alternating with corresponding values.

After `set-text-properties` returns, all the characters in the specified
range have identical properties.

If *props* is `nil`, the effect is to get rid of all properties from the specified
range of text. Here's an example:

    (set-text-properties *start end* nil)

See also the function `buffer-substring-without-properties` (see Section 29.2 [Buffer Contents], page 144) which copies text from the buffer but
does not copy its properties.

29.18.3 Property Search Functions

In typical use of text properties, most of the time several or many consecutive characters have the same value for a property. Rather than writing
your programs to examine characters one by one, it is much faster to process
chunks of text that have the same property value.

Here are functions you can use to do this. They use `eq` for comparing
property values. In all cases, *object* defaults to the current buffer.

For high performance, it's very important to use the *limit* argument
to these functions, especially the ones that search for a single property—
otherwise, they may spend a long time scanning to the end of the buffer, if
the property you are interested in does not change.

Remember that a position is always between two characters; the position returned by these functions is between two characters with different
properties.

next-property-change *pos* &optional *object limit*   Function
The function scans the text forward from position *pos* in the string or
buffer *object* till it finds a change in some text property, then returns
the position of the change. In other words, it returns the position of
the first character beyond *pos* whose properties are not identical to
those of the character just after *pos*.

If *limit* is non-`nil`, then the scan ends at position *limit*. If there is no
property change before that point, `next-property-change` returns
limit.

The value is `nil` if the properties remain unchanged all the way to the
end of *object* and *limit* is `nil`. If the value is non-`nil`, it is a position

greater than or equal to *pos*. The value equals *pos* only when *limit* equals *pos*.

Here is an example of how to scan the buffer by chunks of text within which all properties are constant:

```
(while (not (eobp))
  (let ((plist (text-properties-at (point)))
        (next-change
         (or (next-property-change (point) (current-buffer))
             (point-max))))
    Process text from point to next-change...
    (goto-char next-change)))
```

next-single-property-change *pos prop* &optional   Function
         object limit
The function scans the text forward from position *pos* in the string or buffer *object* till it finds a change in the *prop* property, then returns the position of the change. In other words, it returns the position of the first character beyond *pos* whose *prop* property differs from that of the character just after *pos*.

If *limit* is non-nil, then the scan ends at position *limit*. If there is no property change before that point, `next-single-property-change` returns *limit*.

The value is `nil` if the property remains unchanged all the way to the end of *object* and *limit* is `nil`. If the value is non-nil, it is a position greater than or equal to *pos*; it equals *pos* only if *limit* equals *pos*.

previous-property-change *pos* &optional *object limit*   Function
This is like `next-property-change`, but scans back from *pos* instead of forward. If the value is non-nil, it is a position less than or equal to *pos*; it equals *pos* only if *limit* equals *pos*.

previous-single-property-change *pos prop*   Function
         &optional *object limit*
This is like `next-single-property-change`, but scans back from *pos* instead of forward. If the value is non-nil, it is a position less than or equal to *pos*; it equals *pos* only if *limit* equals *pos*.

text-property-any *start end prop value* &optional   Function
         object
This function returns non-nil if at least one character between *start* and *end* has a property *prop* whose value is *value*. More precisely, it returns the position of the first such character. Otherwise, it returns `nil`.

The optional fifth argument, *object*, specifies the string or buffer to scan. Positions are relative to *object*. The default for *object* is the current buffer.

text-property-not-all *start end prop value* &optional   Function
       object
    This function returns non-`nil` if at least one character between *start*
and *end* has a property *prop* whose value differs from *value*. More
precisely, it returns the position of the first such character. Otherwise,
it returns `nil`.

    The optional fifth argument, *object*, specifies the string or buffer to
scan. Positions are relative to *object*. The default for *object* is the
current buffer.

29.18.4 Properties with Special Meanings

    Here is a table of text property names that have special built-in meanings.
The following section lists a few more special property names that are used
to control filling. All other names have no standard meaning, and you can
use them as you like.

category   If a character has a `category` property, we call it the *category*
            of the character. It should be a symbol. The properties of the
            symbol serve as defaults for the properties of the character.

face   You can use the property `face` to control the font and color of
            text. Its value is a face name or a list of face names. See Sec-
            tion 35.10 [Faces], page 288, for more information. This feature
            may be temporary; in the future, we may replace it with other
            ways of specifying how to display text.

mouse-face
            The property `mouse-face` is used instead of `face` when the
            mouse is on or near the character. For this purpose, "near"
            means that all text between the character and where the mouse
            is have the same `mouse-face` property value.

local-map
            You can specify a different keymap for a portion of the text by
            means of a `local-map` property. The property's value for the
            character after point, if non-`nil`, replaces the buffer's local map.
            See Section 19.6 [Active Keymaps], page 320, vol. 1.

read-only
            If a character has the property `read-only`, then modifying that
            character is not allowed. Any command that would do so gets
            an error.

            Insertion next to a read-only character is an error if inserting
            ordinary text there would inherit the `read-only` property due
            to stickiness. Thus, you can control permission to insert next to

read-only text by controlling the stickiness. See Section 29.18.6 [Sticky Properties], page 184.

Since changing properties counts as modifying the buffer, it is not possible to remove a `read-only` property unless you know the special trick: bind `inhibit-read-only` to a non-`nil` value and then remove the property. See Section 24.7 [Read Only Buffers], page 63.

`invisible`

A non-`nil` `invisible` property can make a character invisible on the screen. See Section 35.5 [Invisible Text], page 279, for details.

`intangible`

If a group of consecutive characters have equal and non-`nil` `intangible` properties, then you cannot place point between them. If you try to move point forward into the group, point actually moves to the end of the group. If you try to move point backward into the group, point actually moves to the start of the group.

When the variable `inhibit-point-motion-hooks` is non-`nil`, the `intangible` property is ignored.

`modification-hooks`

If a character has the property `modification-hooks`, then its value should be a list of functions; modifying that character calls all of those functions. Each function receives two arguments: the beginning and end of the part of the buffer being modified. Note that if a particular modification hook function appears on several characters being modified by a single primitive, you can't predict how many times the function will be called.

`insert-in-front-hooks`
`insert-behind-hooks`

The operation of inserting text in a buffer, before actually modifying the buffer, calls the functions listed in the `insert-in-front-hooks` property of the following character and in the `insert-behind-hooks` property of the preceding character. These functions receive two arguments, the beginning and end of the inserted text.

See also Section 29.22 [Change Hooks], page 189, for other hooks that are called when you change text in a buffer.

```
point-entered
point-left
```
> The special properties `point-entered` and `point-left` record hook functions that report motion of point. Each time point moves, Emacs compares these two property values:
>
> - the `point-left` property of the character after the old location, and
> - the `point-entered` property of the character after the new location.
>
> If these two values differ, each of them is called (if not `nil`) with two arguments: the old value of point, and the new one.
>
> The same comparison is made for the characters before the old and new locations. The result may be to execute two `point-left` functions (which may be the same function) and/or two `point-entered` functions (which may be the same function). In any case, all the `point-left` functions are called first, followed by all the `point-entered` functions.
>
> A primitive function may examine characters at various positions without moving point to those positions. Only an actual change in the value of point runs these hook functions.

inhibit-point-motion-hooks   Variable
> When this variable is non-`nil`, `point-left` and `point-entered` hooks are not run, and the `intangible` property has no effect.

29.18.5 Formatted Text Properties

These text properties affect the behavior of the fill commands. They are used for representing formatted text. See Section 29.11 [Filling], page 160, and Section 29.12 [Margins], page 163.

`hard`   If a newline character has this property, it is a "hard" newline. The fill commands do not alter hard newlines and do not move words across them. However, this property takes effect only if the variable `use-hard-newlines` is non-`nil`.

```
right-margin
```
> This property specifies an extra right margin for filling this part of the text.

```
left-margin
```
> This property specifies an extra left margin for filling this part of the text.

`justification`
> This property specifies the style of justification for filling this part of the text.

29.18.6 Stickiness of Text Properties

Self-inserting characters normally take on the same properties as the preceding character. This is called *inheritance* of properties.

In a Lisp program, you can do insertion with inheritance or without, depending on your choice of insertion primitive. The ordinary text insertion functions such as `insert` do not inherit any properties. They insert text with precisely the properties of the string being inserted, and no others. This is correct for programs that copy text from one context to another—for example, into or out of the kill ring. To insert with inheritance, use the special primitives described in this section. Self-inserting characters inherit properties because they work using these primitives.

When you do insertion with inheritance, *which* properties are inherited depends on two specific properties: `front-sticky` and `rear-nonsticky`.

Insertion after a character inherits those of its properties that are *rear-sticky*. Insertion before a character inherits those of its properties that are *front-sticky*. By default, a text property is rear-sticky but not front-sticky. Thus, the default is to inherit all the properties of the preceding character, and nothing from the following character. You can request different behavior by specifying the stickiness of certain properties.

If a character's `front-sticky` property is t, then all its properties are front-sticky. If the `front-sticky` property is a list, then the sticky properties of the character are those whose names are in the list. For example, if a character has a `front-sticky` property whose value is (`face read-only`), then insertion before the character can inherit its `face` property and its `read-only` property, but no others.

The `rear-nonsticky` works the opposite way. Every property is rear-sticky by default, so the `rear-nonsticky` property says which properties are *not* rear-sticky. If a character's `rear-nonsticky` property is t, then none of its properties are rear-sticky. If the `rear-nonsticky` property is a list, properties are rear-sticky *unless* their names are in the list.

When you insert text with inheritance, it inherits all the rear-sticky properties of the preceding character, and all the front-sticky properties of the following character. The previous character's properties take precedence when both sides offer different sticky values for the same property.

Here are the functions that insert text with inheritance of properties:

insert-and-inherit &rest *strings*   Function
   Insert the strings *strings*, just like the function `insert`, but inherit
   any sticky properties from the adjoining text.

insert-before-markers-and-inherit &rest *strings*   Function
   Insert the strings *strings*, just like the function `insert-before-`
   `markers`, but inherit any sticky properties from the adjoining text.

29.18.7 Saving Text Properties in Files

You can save text properties in files, and restore text properties when
inserting the files, using these two hooks:

write-region-annotate-functions   Variable
   This variable's value is a list of functions for `write-region` to run
   to encode text properties in some fashion as annotations to the text
   being written in the file. See Section 22.4 [Writing to Files], page 18.

   Each function in the list is called with two arguments: the start and
   end of the region to be written. These functions should not alter the
   contents of the buffer. Instead, they should return lists indicating
   annotations to write in the file in addition to the text in the buffer.

   Each function should return a list of elements of the form (*position* .
   string), where *position* is an integer specifying the relative position in
   the text to be written, and *string* is the annotation to add there.

   Each list returned by one of these functions must be already sorted
   in increasing order by *position*. If there is more than one function,
   `write-region` merges the lists destructively into one sorted list.

   When `write-region` actually writes the text from the buffer to the file,
   it intermixes the specified annotations at the corresponding positions.
   All this takes place without modifying the buffer.

after-insert-file-functions   Variable
   This variable holds a list of functions for `insert-file-contents` to
   call after inserting a file's contents. These functions should scan the
   inserted text for annotations, and convert them to the text properties
   they stand for.

   Each function receives one argument, the length of the inserted text;
   point indicates the start of that text. The function should scan that
   text for annotations, delete them, and create the text properties that
   the annotations specify. The function should return the updated
   length of the inserted text, as it stands after those changes. The value
   returned by one function becomes the argument to the next function.

   These functions should always return with point at the beginning of
   the inserted text.

The intended use of `after-insert-file-functions` is for converting some sort of textual annotations into actual text properties. But other uses may be possible.

We invite users to write Lisp programs to store and retrieve text properties in files, using these hooks, and thus to experiment with various data formats and find good ones. Eventually we hope users will produce good, general extensions we can install in Emacs.

We suggest not trying to handle arbitrary Lisp objects as property names or property values—because a program that general is probably difficult to write, and slow. Instead, choose a set of possible data types that are reasonably flexible, and not too hard to encode.

See Section 22.12 [Format Conversion], page 40, for a related feature.

29.18.8 Why Text Properties are not Intervals

Some editors that support adding attributes to text in the buffer do so by letting the user specify "intervals" within the text, and adding the properties to the intervals. Those editors permit the user or the programmer to determine where individual intervals start and end. We deliberately provided a different sort of interface in Emacs Lisp to avoid certain paradoxical behavior associated with text modification.

If the actual subdivision into intervals is meaningful, that means you can distinguish between a buffer that is just one interval with a certain property, and a buffer containing the same text subdivided into two intervals, both of which have that property.

Suppose you take the buffer with just one interval and kill part of the text. The text remaining in the buffer is one interval, and the copy in the kill ring (and the undo list) becomes a separate interval. Then if you yank back the killed text, you get two intervals with the same properties. Thus, editing does not preserve the distinction between one interval and two.

Suppose we "fix" this problem by coalescing the two intervals when the text is inserted. That works fine if the buffer originally was a single interval. But suppose instead that we have two adjacent intervals with the same properties, and we kill the text of one interval and yank it back. The same interval-coalescence feature that rescues the other case causes trouble in this one: after yanking, we have just one interval. One again, editing does not preserve the distinction between one interval and two.

Insertion of text at the border between intervals also raises questions that have no satisfactory answer.

However, it is easy to arrange for editing to behave consistently for questions of the form, "What are the properties of this character?" So we have decided these are the only questions that make sense; we have not implemented asking questions about where intervals start or end.

In practice, you can usually use the property search functions in place of explicit interval boundaries. You can think of them as finding the boundaries of intervals, assuming that intervals are always coalesced whenever possible. See Section 29.18.3 [Property Search], page 179.

Emacs also provides explicit intervals as a presentation feature; see Section 35.9 [Overlays], page 284.

29.19 Substituting for a Character Code

The following functions replace characters within a specified region based on their character codes.

subst-char-in-region *start end old-char new-char*   Function
       &optional *noundo*
This function replaces all occurrences of the character *old-char* with the character *new-char* in the region of the current buffer defined by *start* and *end*.

If *noundo* is non-`nil`, then `subst-char-in-region` does not record the change for undo and does not mark the buffer as modified. This feature is used for controlling selective display (see Section 35.6 [Selective Display], page 280).

`subst-char-in-region` does not move point and returns `nil`.

```
---------- Buffer: foo ----------
This is the contents of the buffer before.
---------- Buffer: foo ----------

(subst-char-in-region 1 20 ?i ?X)
     ⇒ nil


---------- Buffer: foo ----------
ThXs Xs the contents of the buffer before.
---------- Buffer: foo ----------
```

translate-region *start end table*   Function
This function applies a translation table to the characters in the buffer between positions *start* and *end*.

The translation table *table* is a string; (`aref` *table ochar*) gives the translated character corresponding to *ochar*. If the length of *table* is less than 256, any characters with codes larger than the length of *table* are not altered by the translation.

The return value of `translate-region` is the number of characters that were actually changed by the translation. This does not count characters that were mapped into themselves in the translation table.

29.20 Registers

A register is a sort of variable used in Emacs editing that can hold a marker, a string, a rectangle, a window configuration (of one frame), or a frame configuration (of all frames). Each register is named by a single character. All characters, including control and meta characters (but with the exception of `C-g`), can be used to name registers. Thus, there are 255 possible registers. A register is designated in Emacs Lisp by a character that is its name.

The functions in this section return unpredictable values unless otherwise stated.

register-alist   Variable
  This variable is an alist of elements of the form (*name . contents*). Normally, there is one element for each Emacs register that has been used.

  The object *name* is a character (an integer) identifying the register. The object *contents* is a string, marker, or list representing the register contents. A string represents text stored in the register. A marker represents a position. A list represents a rectangle; its elements are strings, one per line of the rectangle.

get-register *reg*   Function
  This function returns the contents of the register *reg*, or `nil` if it has no contents.

set-register *reg value*   Function
  This function sets the contents of register *reg* to *value*. A register can be set to any value, but the other register functions expect only certain data types. The return value is *value*.

view-register *reg*   Command
  This command displays what is contained in register *reg*.

insert-register *reg* &optional *beforep*   Command
  This command inserts contents of register *reg* into the current buffer.

  Normally, this command puts point before the inserted text, and the mark after it. However, if the optional second argument *beforep* is non-`nil`, it puts the mark before and point after. You can pass a non-`nil` second argument *beforep* to this function interactively by supplying any prefix argument.

If the register contains a rectangle, then the rectangle is inserted with its upper left corner at point. This means that text is inserted in the current line and underneath it on successive lines.

If the register contains something other than saved text (a string) or a rectangle (a list), currently useless things happen. This may be changed in the future.

29.21 Transposition of Text

This subroutine is used by the transposition commands.

transpose-regions *start1 end1 start2 end2* &optional   Function
      leave-markers
This function exchanges two nonoverlapping portions of the buffer. Arguments *start1* and *end1* specify the bounds of one portion and arguments *start2* and *end2* specify the bounds of the other portion.

Normally, `transpose-regions` relocates markers with the transposed text; a marker previously positioned within one of the two transposed portions moves along with that portion, thus remaining between the same two characters in their new position. However, if *leave-markers* is non-`nil`, `transpose-regions` does not do this—it leaves all markers unrelocated.

29.22 Change Hooks

These hook variables let you arrange to take notice of all changes in all buffers (or in a particular buffer, if you make them buffer-local). See also Section 29.18.4 [Special Properties], page 181, for how to detect changes to specific parts of the text.

The functions you use in these hooks should save and restore the match data if they do anything that uses regular expressions; otherwise, they will interfere in bizarre ways with the editing operations that call them.

before-change-functions   Variable
This variable holds a list of a functions to call before any buffer modification. Each function gets two arguments, the beginning and end of the region that is about to change, represented as integers. The buffer that is about to change is always the current buffer.

after-change-functions   Variable
This variable holds a list of a functions to call after any buffer modification. Each function receives three arguments: the beginning and end of the region just changed, and the length of the text that existed

before the change. (To get the current length, subtract the region beginning from the region end.) All three arguments are integers. The buffer that's about to change is always the current buffer.

before-change-function   Variable
This obsolete variable holds one function to call before any buffer modification (or `nil` for no function). It is called just like the functions in `before-change-functions`.

after-change-function   Variable
This obsolete variable holds one function to call after any buffer modification (or `nil` for no function). It is called just like the functions in `after-change-functions`.

The four variables above are temporarily bound to `nil` during the time that any of these functions is running. This means that if one of these functions changes the buffer, that change won't run these functions. If you do want a hook function to make changes that run these functions, make it bind these variables back to their usual values.

One inconvenient result of this protective feature is that you cannot have a function in `after-change-functions` or `before-change-functions` which changes the value of that variable. But that's not a real limitation. If you want those functions to change the list of functions to run, simply add one fixed function to the hook, and code that function to look in another variable for other functions to call. Here is an example:

```
(setq my-own-after-change-functions nil)
(defun indirect-after-change-function (beg end len)
  (let ((list my-own-after-change-functions))
    (while list
      (funcall (car list) beg end len)
      (setq list (cdr list)))))
(add-hooks 'after-change-functions
           'indirect-after-change-function)
```

first-change-hook   Variable
This variable is a normal hook that is run whenever a buffer is changed that was previously in the unmodified state.

30 Searching and Matching

GNU Emacs provides two ways to search through a buffer for specified text: exact string searches and regular expression searches. After a regular expression search, you can examine the *match data* to determine which text matched the whole regular expression or various portions of it.

The 'skip-chars...' functions also perform a kind of searching. See Section 27.2.7 [Skipping Characters], page 128.

30.1 Searching for Strings

These are the primitive functions for searching through the text in a buffer. They are meant for use in programs, but you may call them interactively. If you do so, they prompt for the search string; *limit* and *noerror* are set to `nil`, and *repeat* is set to 1.

search-forward *string* &optional *limit noerror repeat*   Command
This function searches forward from point for an exact match for *string*. If successful, it sets point to the end of the occurrence found, and returns the new value of point. If no match is found, the value and side effects depend on *noerror* (see below).

In the following example, point is initially at the beginning of the line. Then (search-forward "fox") moves point after the last letter of 'fox':

```
---------- Buffer: foo ----------
*The quick brown fox jumped over the lazy dog.
---------- Buffer: foo ----------

(search-forward "fox")
     ⇒ 20

---------- Buffer: foo ----------
The quick brown fox* jumped over the lazy dog.
---------- Buffer: foo ----------
```

The argument *limit* specifies the upper bound to the search. (It must be a position in the current buffer.) No match extending after that position is accepted. If *limit* is omitted or `nil`, it defaults to the end of the accessible portion of the buffer.

What happens when the search fails depends on the value of *noerror*. If *noerror* is `nil`, a `search-failed` error is signaled. If *noerror* is `t`, `search-forward` returns `nil` and does nothing. If *noerror* is neither `nil` nor `t`, then `search-forward` moves point to the upper bound and returns `nil`. (It would be more consistent now to return the new position of point in that case, but some programs may depend on a value of `nil`.)

If *repeat* is supplied (it must be a positive number), then the search is repeated that many times (each time starting at the end of the previous time's match). If these successive searches succeed, the function succeeds, moving point and returning its new value. Otherwise the search fails.

search-backward *string* &optional *limit noerror*   Command
    repeat

This function searches backward from point for *string*. It is just like `search-forward` except that it searches backwards and leaves point at the beginning of the match.

word-search-forward *string* &optional *limit noerror*   Command
    repeat

This function searches forward from point for a "word" match for *string*. If it finds a match, it sets point to the end of the match found, and returns the new value of point.

Word matching regards *string* as a sequence of words, disregarding punctuation that separates them. It searches the buffer for the same sequence of words. Each word must be distinct in the buffer (searching for the word 'ball' does not match the word 'balls'), but the details of punctuation and spacing are ignored (searching for 'ball boy' does match 'ball. Boy!').

In this example, point is initially at the beginning of the buffer; the search leaves it between the 'y' and the '!'.

```
---------- Buffer: foo ----------
*He said "Please!  Find
the ball boy!"
---------- Buffer: foo ----------

(word-search-forward "Please find the ball, boy.")
     ⇒ 35


---------- Buffer: foo ----------
He said "Please!  Find
the ball boy*!"
---------- Buffer: foo ----------
```

If *limit* is non-`nil` (it must be a position in the current buffer), then it is the upper bound to the search. The match found must not extend after that position.

If *noerror* is `nil`, then `word-search-forward` signals an error if the search fails. If *noerror* is `t`, then it returns `nil` instead of signaling an error. If *noerror* is neither `nil` nor `t`, it moves point to *limit* (or the end of the buffer) and returns `nil`.

If *repeat* is non-`nil`, then the search is repeated that many times. Point is positioned at the end of the last match.

word-search-backward *string* &optional *limit*   Command
          noerror repeat
This function searches backward from point for a word match to *string*. This function is just like `word-search-forward` except that it searches backward and normally leaves point at the beginning of the match.

30.2 Regular Expressions

A *regular expression* (*regexp*, for short) is a pattern that denotes a (possibly infinite) set of strings. Searching for matches for a regexp is a very powerful operation. This section explains how to write regexps; the following section says how to search for them.

30.2.1 Syntax of Regular Expressions

Regular expressions have a syntax in which a few characters are special constructs and the rest are *ordinary*. An ordinary character is a simple regular expression that matches that character and nothing else. The special characters are '.', '*', '+', '?', '[', ']', '^', '$', and '\'; no new special characters will be defined in the future. Any other character appearing in a regular expression is ordinary, unless a '\' precedes it.

For example, 'f' is not a special character, so it is ordinary, and therefore 'f' is a regular expression that matches the string 'f' and no other string. (It does *not* match the string 'ff'.) Likewise, 'o' is a regular expression that matches only 'o'.

Any two regular expressions *a* and *b* can be concatenated. The result is a regular expression that matches a string if *a* matches some amount of the beginning of that string and *b* matches the rest of the string.

As a simple example, we can concatenate the regular expressions 'f' and 'o' to get the regular expression 'fo', which matches only the string 'fo'. Still trivial. To do something more powerful, you need to use one of the special characters. Here is a list of them:

. (Period)   is a special character that matches any single character except a newline. Using concatenation, we can make regular expressions like 'a.b', which matches any three-character string that begins with 'a' and ends with 'b'.

*   is not a construct by itself; it is a suffix operator that means to repeat the preceding regular expression as many times as possible. In 'fo*', the '*' applies to the 'o', so 'fo*' matches one 'f' followed by any number of 'o's. The case of zero 'o's is allowed: 'fo*' does match 'f'.

'*' always applies to the *smallest* possible preceding expression. Thus, 'fo*' has a repeating 'o', not a repeating 'fo'.

The matcher processes a '*' construct by matching, immediately, as many repetitions as can be found. Then it continues with the rest of the pattern. If that fails, backtracking occurs, discarding some of the matches of the '*'-modified construct in case that makes it possible to match the rest of the pattern. For example, in matching 'ca*ar' against the string 'caaar', the 'a*' first tries to match all three 'a's; but the rest of the pattern is 'ar' and there is only 'r' left to match, so this try fails. The next alternative is for 'a*' to match only two 'a's. With this choice, the rest of the regexp matches successfully.

Nested repetition operators can be extremely slow if they specify backtracking loops. For example, it could take hours for the regular expression '\(x+y*\)*a' to match the sequence 'xxxxxxxxxxxxxxxxxxxxxxxxxxxxxxxxxxxz'. The slowness is because Emacs must try each imaginable way of grouping the 35 'x''s before concluding that none of them can work. To make sure your regular expressions run fast, check nested repetitions carefully.

+   is a suffix operator similar to '*' except that the preceding expression must match at least once. So, for example, 'ca+r' matches the strings 'car' and 'caaaar' but not the string 'cr', whereas 'ca*r' matches all three strings.

?   is a suffix operator similar to '*' except that the preceding expression can match either once or not at all. For example, 'ca?r' matches 'car' or 'cr', but does not match anything else.

[...]   '[' begins a *character set*, which is terminated by a ']'. In the simplest case, the characters between the two brackets form the set. Thus, '[ad]' matches either one 'a' or one 'd', and '[ad]*' matches any string composed of just 'a's and 'd's (including the empty string), from which it follows that 'c[ad]*r' matches 'cr', 'car', 'cdr', 'caddaar', etc.

The usual regular expression special characters are not special inside a character set. A completely different set of special characters exists inside character sets: ']', '-' and '^'.

'-' is used for ranges of characters. To write a range, write two characters with a '-' between them. Thus, '[a-z]' matches any lower case letter. Ranges may be intermixed freely with individual characters, as in '[a-z$%.]', which matches any lower case letter or '$', '%', or a period.

To include a ']' in a character set, make it the first character. For example, '[]a]' matches ']' or 'a'. To include a '-', write '-' as the first character in the set, or put it immediately after a range. (You can replace one individual character *c* with the range '*c-c*' to make a place to put the '-'.) There is no way to write a set containing just '-' and ']'.

To include '^' in a set, put it anywhere but at the beginning of the set.

[^ ...] '[^' begins a *complement character set*, which matches any character except the ones specified. Thus, '[^a-z0-9A-Z]' matches all characters *except* letters and digits.

'^' is not special in a character set unless it is the first character. The character following the '^' is treated as if it were first (thus, '-' and ']' are not special there).

Note that a complement character set can match a newline, unless newline is mentioned as one of the characters not to match.

^ is a special character that matches the empty string, but only at the beginning of a line in the text being matched. Otherwise it fails to match anything. Thus, '^foo' matches a 'foo' that occurs at the beginning of a line.

When matching a string instead of a buffer, '^' matches at the beginning of the string or after a newline character '\n'.

$ is similar to '^' but matches only at the end of a line. Thus, 'x+$' matches a string of one 'x' or more at the end of a line.

When matching a string instead of a buffer, '$' matches at the end of the string or before a newline character '\n'.

\ has two functions: it quotes the special characters (including '\'), and it introduces additional special constructs.

Because '\' quotes special characters, '\$' is a regular expression that matches only '$', and '\[' is a regular expression that matches only '[', and so on.

Note that '\' also has special meaning in the read syntax of Lisp strings (see Section 2.3.8 [String Type], page 27, vol. 1), and must be quoted with '\'. For example, the regular expression that matches the '\' character is '\\'. To write a Lisp string that contains the characters '\\', Lisp syntax requires you to quote each '\' with another '\'. Therefore, the read syntax for a regular expression matching '\' is "\\\\".

Please note: For historical compatibility, special characters are treated as ordinary ones if they are in contexts where their special meanings make no sense. For example, '*foo' treats '*' as ordinary since there is no preceding expression on which the '*' can act. It is poor practice to depend on this behavior; quote the special character anyway, regardless of where it appears.

For the most part, '\' followed by any character matches only that character. However, there are several exceptions: characters that, when preceded by '\', are special constructs. Such characters are always ordinary when encountered on their own. Here is a table of '\' constructs:

\| specifies an alternative. Two regular expressions a and b with '\|' in between form an expression that matches anything that either a or b matches.

Thus, 'foo\|bar' matches either 'foo' or 'bar' but no other string.

'\|' applies to the largest possible surrounding expressions. Only a surrounding '\(... \)' grouping can limit the grouping power of '\|'.

Full backtracking capability exists to handle multiple uses of '\|'.

\(... \)   is a grouping construct that serves three purposes:

1. To enclose a set of '\|' alternatives for other operations. Thus, '\(foo\|bar\)x' matches either 'foox' or 'barx'.

2. To enclose an expression for a suffix operator such as '*' to act on. Thus, 'ba\(na\)*' matches 'bananana', etc., with any (zero or more) number of 'na' strings.

3. To record a matched substring for future reference.

This last application is not a consequence of the idea of a parenthetical grouping; it is a separate feature that happens to be assigned as a second meaning to the same '\(... \)' construct because there is no conflict in practice between the two meanings. Here is an explanation of this feature:

\digit   matches the same text that matched the digitth occurrence of a '\(... \)' construct.

In other words, after the end of a '\(... \)' construct. the matcher remembers the beginning and end of the text matched by that construct. Then, later on in the regular expression, you can use '\' followed by *digit* to match that same text, whatever it may have been.

The strings matching the first nine '\(... \)' constructs appearing in a regular expression are assigned numbers 1 through 9 in the order that the open parentheses appear in the regular expression. So you can use '\1' through '\9' to refer to the text matched by the corresponding '\(... \)' constructs.

For example, '\(.*\)\1' matches any newline-free string that is composed of two identical halves. The '\(.*\)' matches the first half, which may be anything, but the '\1' that follows must match the same exact text.

\w   matches any word-constituent character. The editor syntax table determines which characters these are. See Chapter 31 [Syntax Tables], page 211.

\W   matches any character that is not a word constituent.

\s*code*   matches any character whose syntax is *code*. Here *code* is a character that represents a syntax code: thus, 'w' for word constituent, '-' for whitespace, '(' for open parenthesis, etc. See Chapter 31 [Syntax Tables], page 211, for a list of syntax codes and the characters that stand for them.

\S*code*   matches any character whose syntax is not *code*.

The following regular expression constructs match the empty string—that is, they don't use up any characters—but whether they match depends on the context.

\`   matches the empty string, but only at the beginning of the buffer or string being matched against.

\'   matches the empty string, but only at the end of the buffer or string being matched against.

\=   matches the empty string, but only at point. (This construct is not defined when matching against a string.)

\b   matches the empty string, but only at the beginning or end of a word. Thus, '\bfoo\b' matches any occurrence of 'foo' as a separate word. '\bballs?\b' matches 'ball' or 'balls' as a separate word.

\B   matches the empty string, but *not* at the beginning or end of a word.

\<   matches the empty string, but only at the beginning of a word.

\>   matches the empty string, but only at the end of a word.

Not every string is a valid regular expression. For example, a string with unbalanced square brackets is invalid (with a few exceptions, such as '[]]'), and so is a string that ends with a single '\'. If an invalid regular expression is passed to any of the search functions, an `invalid-regexp` error is signaled.

regexp-quote *string*   Function
> This function returns a regular expression string that matches exactly *string* and nothing else. This allows you to request an exact string match when calling a function that wants a regular expression.
>
> ```
> (regexp-quote "^The cat$")
>      ⇒ "\\^The cat\\$"
> ```

One use of `regexp-quote` is to combine an exact string match with context described as a regular expression. For example, this searches for the string that is the value of `string`, surrounded by whitespace:

```
(re-search-forward
 (concat "\\s-" (regexp-quote string) "\\s-"))
```

30.2.2 Complex Regexp Example

Here is a complicated regexp, used by Emacs to recognize the end of a sentence together with any whitespace that follows. It is the value of the variable `sentence-end`.

First, we show the regexp as a string in Lisp syntax to distinguish spaces from tab characters. The string constant begins and ends with a double-quote. '\"' stands for a double-quote as part of the string, '\\' for a backslash as part of the string, '\t' for a tab and '\n' for a newline.

```
"[.?!][]\"')}]*\\($\\| $\\|\t\\|  \\)[ \t\n]*"
```

In contrast, if you evaluate the variable `sentence-end`, you will see the following:

```
sentence-end
⇒
"[.?!][]\"')}]*\\($\\| $\\|  \\|  \\)[
]*"
```

In this output, tab and newline appear as themselves.

This regular expression contains four parts in succession and can be deciphered as follows:

[.?!]   The first part of the pattern is a character set that matches any one of three characters: period, question mark, and exclamation mark. The match must begin with one of these three characters.

`[]\"')}]*`
> The second part of the pattern matches any closing braces and
> quotation marks, zero or more of them, that may follow the
> period, question mark or exclamation mark. The `\"` is Lisp
> syntax for a double-quote in a string. The '`*`' at the end indicates
> that the immediately preceding regular expression (a character
> set, in this case) may be repeated zero or more times.

`\\($\\| $\\|\t\\|  \\)`
> The third part of the pattern matches the whitespace that fol-
> lows the end of a sentence: the end of a line, or a tab, or two
> spaces. The double backslashes mark the parentheses and ver-
> tical bars as regular expression syntax; the parentheses delimit
> a group and the vertical bars separate alternatives. The dollar
> sign is used to match the end of a line.

`[ \t\n]*`   Finally, the last part of the pattern matches any additional
> whitespace beyond the minimum needed to end a sentence.

30.3 Regular Expression Searching

In GNU Emacs, you can search for the next match for a regexp either
incrementally or not. For incremental search commands, see section "Regular Expression Search" in *The GNU Emacs Manual*. Here we describe only
the search functions useful in programs. The principal one is `re-search-`
`forward`.

re-search-forward *regexp* &optional *limit noerror*   Command
> *repeat*
> This function searches forward in the current buffer for a string of text
> that is matched by the regular expression *regexp*. The function skips
> over any amount of text that is not matched by *regexp*, and leaves
> point at the end of the first match found. It returns the new value of
> point.
>
> If *limit* is non-`nil` (it must be a position in the current buffer), then
> it is the upper bound to the search. No match extending after that
> position is accepted.
>
> What happens when the search fails depends on the value of *noerror*.
> If *noerror* is `nil`, a `search-failed` error is signaled. If *noerror* is
> `t`, `re-search-forward` does nothing and returns `nil`. If *noerror* is
> neither `nil` nor `t`, then `re-search-forward` moves point to *limit* (or
> the end of the buffer) and returns `nil`.
>
> If *repeat* is supplied (it must be a positive number), then the search
> is repeated that many times (each time starting at the end of the pre-
> vious time's match). If these successive searches succeed, the function

succeeds, moving point and returning its new value. Otherwise the search fails.

In the following example, point is initially before the 'T'. Evaluating the search call moves point to the end of that line (between the 't' of 'hat' and the newline).

```
---------- Buffer: foo ----------
I read "*The cat in the hat
comes back" twice.
---------- Buffer: foo ----------

(re-search-forward "[a-z]+" nil t 5)
     ⇒ 27


---------- Buffer: foo ----------
I read "The cat in the hat*
comes back" twice.
---------- Buffer: foo ----------
```

re-search-backward *regexp* &optional *limit noerror*   Command
          repeat
This function searches backward in the current buffer for a string of text that is matched by the regular expression *regexp*, leaving point at the beginning of the first text found.

This function is analogous to `re-search-forward`, but they are not simple mirror images. `re-search-forward` finds the match whose beginning is as close as possible to the starting point. If `re-search-backward` were a perfect mirror image, it would find the match whose end is as close as possible. However, in fact it finds the match whose beginning is as close as possible. The reason is that matching a regular expression at a given spot always works from beginning to end, and starts at a specified beginning position.

A true mirror-image of `re-search-forward` would require a special feature for matching regexps from end to beginning. It's not worth the trouble of implementing that.

string-match *regexp string* &optional *start*   Function
This function returns the index of the start of the first match for the regular expression *regexp* in *string*, or `nil` if there is no match. If *start* is non-`nil`, the search starts at that index in *string*.

For example,

```
(string-match
 "quick" "The quick brown fox jumped quickly.")
     ⇒ 4
```

```
(string-match
 "quick" "The quick brown fox jumped quickly." 8)
     ⇒ 27
```

The index of the first character of the string is 0, the index of the
second character is 1, and so on.

After this function returns, the index of the first character beyond the
match is available as (match-end 0). See Section 30.6 [Match Data],
page 204.

```
(string-match
 "quick" "The quick brown fox jumped quickly." 8)
     ⇒ 27

(match-end 0)
     ⇒ 32
```

looking-at *regexp*   Function
This function determines whether the text in the current buffer directly
following point matches the regular expression *regexp*. "Directly following" means precisely that: the search is "anchored" and it can
succeed only starting with the first character following point. The
result is t if so, nil otherwise.

This function does not move point, but it updates the match data,
which you can access using match-beginning and match-end. See
Section 30.6 [Match Data], page 204.

In this example, point is located directly before the 'T'. If it were
anywhere else, the result would be nil.

```
---------- Buffer: foo ----------
I read "⋆The cat in the hat
comes back" twice.
---------- Buffer: foo ----------

(looking-at "The cat in the hat$")
     ⇒ t
```

30.4 POSIX Regular Expression Searching

The usual regular expression functions do backtracking when necessary
to handle the '\|' and repetition constructs, but they continue this only until
they find *some* match. Then they succeed and report the first match found.

This section describes alternative search functions which perform the full
backtracking specified by the POSIX standard for regular expression matching. They continue backtracking until they have tried all possibilities and

found all matches, so they can report the longest match, as required by POSIX. This is much slower, so use these functions only when you really need the longest match.

In Emacs versions prior to 19.29, these functions did not exist, and the functions described above implemented full POSIX backtracking.

posix-search-forward *regexp* &optional *limit noerror*   Function
         repeat
This is like `re-search-forward` except that it performs the full backtracking specified by the POSIX standard for regular expression matching.

posix-search-backward *regexp* &optional *limit*   Function
         noerror repeat
This is like `re-search-backward` except that it performs the full backtracking specified by the POSIX standard for regular expression matching.

posix-looking-at *regexp*   Function
This is like `looking-at` except that it performs the full backtracking specified by the POSIX standard for regular expression matching.

posix-string-match *regexp string* &optional *start*   Function
This is like `string-match` except that it performs the full backtracking specified by the POSIX standard for regular expression matching.

30.5 Search and Replace

perform-replace *from-string replacements query-flag*   Function
         regexp-flag delimited-flag &optional *repeat-count map*
This function is the guts of `query-replace` and related commands. It searches for occurrences of *from-string* and replaces some or all of them. If *query-flag* is `nil`, it replaces all occurrences; otherwise, it asks the user what to do about each one.

If *regexp-flag* is non-`nil`, then *from-string* is considered a regular expression; otherwise, it must match literally. If *delimited-flag* is non-`nil`, then only replacements surrounded by word boundaries are considered.

The argument *replacements* specifies what to replace occurrences with. If it is a string, that string is used. It can also be a list of strings, to be used in cyclic order.

If *repeat-count* is non-`nil`, it should be an integer. Then it specifies how many times to use each of the strings in the *replacements* list before advancing cyclicly to the next one.

Normally, the keymap `query-replace-map` defines the possible user responses for queries. The argument *map*, if non-`nil`, is a keymap to use instead of `query-replace-map`.

query-replace-map   *Variable*
   This variable holds a special keymap that defines the valid user responses for `query-replace` and related functions, as well as `y-or-n-p` and `map-y-or-n-p`. It is unusual in two ways:

   - The "key bindings" are not commands, just symbols that are meaningful to the functions that use this map.
   - Prefix keys are not supported; each key binding must be for a single event key sequence. This is because the functions don't use read key sequence to get the input; instead, they read a single event and look it up "by hand."

Here are the meaningful "bindings" for `query-replace-map`. Several of them are meaningful only for `query-replace` and friends.

`act`   Do take the action being considered—in other words, "yes."

`skip`   Do not take action for this question—in other words, "no."

`exit`   Answer this question "no," and give up on the entire series of questions, assuming that the answers will be "no."

`act-and-exit`
             Answer this question "yes," and give up on the entire series of questions, assuming that subsequent answers will be "no."

`act-and-show`
             Answer this question "yes," but show the results—don't advance yet to the next question.

`automatic`
             Answer this question and all subsequent questions in the series with "yes," without further user interaction.

`backup`   Move back to the previous place that a question was asked about.

`edit`   Enter a recursive edit to deal with this question—instead of any other action that would normally be taken.

`delete-and-edit`
             Delete the text being considered, then enter a recursive edit to replace it.

`recenter`   Redisplay and center the window, then ask the same question again.

`quit`   Perform a quit right away. Only `y-or-n-p` and related functions use this answer.

`help`   Display some help, then ask again.

30.6 The Match Data

Emacs keeps track of the positions of the start and end of segments of text found during a regular expression search. This means, for example, that you can search for a complex pattern, such as a date in an Rmail message, and then extract parts of the match under control of the pattern.

Because the match data normally describe the most recent search only, you must be careful not to do another search inadvertently between the search you wish to refer back to and the use of the match data. If you can't avoid another intervening search, you must save and restore the match data around it, to prevent it from being overwritten.

30.6.1 Simple Match Data Access

This section explains how to use the match data to find out what was matched by the last search or match operation.

You can ask about the entire matching text, or about a particular parenthetical subexpression of a regular expression. The *count* argument in the functions below specifies which. If *count* is zero, you are asking about the entire match. If *count* is positive, it specifies which subexpression you want.

Recall that the subexpressions of a regular expression are those expressions grouped with escaped parentheses, '`\(`...`\)`'. The *count*th subexpression is found by counting occurrences of '`\(`' from the beginning of the whole regular expression. The first subexpression is numbered 1, the second 2, and so on. Only regular expressions can have subexpressions—after a simple string search, the only information available is about the entire match.

match-string *count* &optional *in-string*   Function
    This function returns, as a string, the text matched in the last search or match operation. It returns the entire text if *count* is zero, or just the portion corresponding to the *count*th parenthetical subexpression, if *count* is positive. If *count* is out of range, or if that subexpression didn't match anything, the value is `nil`.

    If the last such operation was done against a string with `string-match`, then you should pass the same string as the argument *in-string*. Otherwise, after a buffer search or match, you should omit *in-string* or pass `nil` for it; but you should make sure that the current buffer when you call `match-string` is the one in which you did the searching or matching.

match-beginning *count*   Function
   This function returns the position of the start of text matched by the
   last regular expression searched for, or a subexpression of it.

   If *count* is zero, then the value is the position of the start of the
   entire match. Otherwise, *count* specifies a subexpression in the regular
   expresion, and the value of the function is the starting position of the
   match for that subexpression.

   The value is `nil` for a subexpression inside a '\|' alternative that
   wasn't used in the match.

match-end *count*   Function
   This function is like `match-beginning` except that it returns the position of the end of the match, rather than the position of the beginning.

   Here is an example of using the match data, with a comment showing
the positions within the text:

```
(string-match "\\(qu\\)\\(ick\\)"
              "The quick fox jumped quickly.")
              ;0123456789
   ⇒ 4

(match-string 0 "The quick fox jumped quickly.")
   ⇒ "quick"
(match-string 1 "The quick fox jumped quickly.")
   ⇒ "qu"
(match-string 2 "The quick fox jumped quickly.")
   ⇒ "ick"

(match-beginning 1)            ; The beginning of the match
   ⇒ 4                         ;    with 'qu' is at index 4.

(match-beginning 2)            ; The beginning of the match
   ⇒ 6                         ;    with 'ick' is at index 6.

(match-end 1)                  ; The end of the match
   ⇒ 6                         ;    with 'qu' is at index 6.

(match-end 2)                  ; The end of the match
   ⇒ 9                         ;    with 'ick' is at index 9.
```

   Here is another example. Point is initially located at the beginning of
the line. Searching moves point to between the space and the word 'in'.
The beginning of the entire match is at the 9th character of the buffer ('T'),
and the beginning of the match for the first subexpression is at the 13th
character ('c').

```
(list
  (re-search-forward "The \\(cat \\)")
  (match-beginning 0)
  (match-beginning 1))
     ⇒ (9 9 13)
---------- Buffer: foo ----------
I read "The cat *in the hat comes back" twice.
               ^   ^

          9   13
---------- Buffer: foo ----------
```

(In this case, the index returned is a buffer position; the first character of
the buffer counts as 1.)

30.6.2 Replacing the Text That Matched

This function replaces the text matched by the last search with *replace-ment*.

replace-match *replacement* &optional *fixedcase literal*   Function
            string

This function replaces the text in the buffer (or in *string*) that was
matched by the last search. It replaces that text with *replacement*.

If you did the last search in a buffer, you should specify `nil` for *string*.
Then `replace-match` does the replacement by editing the buffer; it
leaves point at the end of the replacement text, and returns `t`.

If you did the search in a string, pass the same string as *string*. Then
`replace-match` does the replacement by constructing and returning a
new string.

If *fixedcase* is non-`nil`, then the case of the replacement text is not
changed; otherwise, the replacement text is converted to a different
case depending upon the capitalization of the text to be replaced. If
the original text is all upper case, the replacement text is converted to
upper case. If the first word of the original text is capitalized, then the
first word of the replacement text is capitalized. If the original text
contains just one word, and that word is a capital letter, `replace-
match` considers this a capitalized first word rather than all upper
case.

If `case-replace` is `nil`, then case conversion is not done, regardless of the value of *fixed-case*. See Section 30.7 [Searching and Case],
page 208.

If *literal* is non-`nil`, then *replacement* is inserted exactly as it is, the
only alterations being case changes as needed. If it is `nil` (the de-

fault), then the character '\' is treated specially. If a '\' appears in *replacement*, then it must be part of one of the following sequences:

'\&'   '\&' stands for the entire text being replaced.

'\n'   '\n', where *n* is a digit, stands for the text that matched
              the *n*th subexpression in the original regexp. Subexpres-
              sions are those expressions grouped inside '\(...\)'.

'\\'   '\\' stands for a single '\' in the replacement text.

30.6.3 Accessing the Entire Match Data

The functions `match-data` and `set-match-data` read or write the entire match data, all at once.

match-data   *Function*

This function returns a newly constructed list containing all the information on what text the last search matched. Element zero is the
position of the beginning of the match for the whole expression; element one is the position of the end of the match for the expression.
The next two elements are the positions of the beginning and end of
the match for the first subexpression, and so on. In general, element
number $2n$ corresponds to (`match-beginning` *n*); and element number $2n + 1$ corresponds to (`match-end` *n*).

All the elements are markers or `nil` if matching was done on a buffer,
and all are integers or `nil` if matching was done on a string with
`string-match`. (In Emacs 18 and earlier versions, markers were used
even for matching on a string, except in the case of the integer 0.)

As always, there must be no possibility of intervening searches between
the call to a search function and the call to `match-data` that is intended
to access the match data for that search.

```
    (match-data)
        ⇒   (#<marker at 9 in foo>
             #<marker at 17 in foo>
             #<marker at 13 in foo>
             #<marker at 17 in foo>)
```

set-match-data *match-list*   *Function*

This function sets the match data from the elements of *match-list*,
which should be a list that was the value of a previous call to `match-
data`.

If *match-list* refers to a buffer that doesn't exist, you don't get an
error; that sets the match data in a meaningless but harmless way.

`store-match-data` is an alias for `set-match-data`.

30.6.4 Saving and Restoring the Match Data

When you call a function that may do a search, you may need to save and restore the match data around that call, if you want to preserve the match data from an earlier search for later use. Here is an example that shows the problem that arises if you fail to save the match data:

```
(re-search-forward "The \\(cat \\)")
     ⇒ 48
(foo)                            ; Perhaps foo does
                                 ;   more searching.
(match-end 0)
     ⇒ 61                        ; Unexpected result—not 48!
```

You can save and restore the match data with `save-match-data`:

save-match-data *body...*   Macro
This special form executes *body*, saving and restoring the match data around it.

You can use `set-match-data` together with `match-data` to imitate the effect of the special form `save-match-data`. This is useful for writing code that can run in Emacs 18. Here is how:

```
(let ((data (match-data)))
   (unwind-protect
       ...    ; May change the original match data.
     (set-match-data data)))
```

Emacs automatically saves and restores the match data when it runs process filter functions (see Section 33.9.2 [Filter Functions], page 242) and process sentinels (see Section 33.10 [Sentinels], page 245).

30.7 Searching and Case

By default, searches in Emacs ignore the case of the text they are searching through; if you specify searching for 'FOO', then 'Foo' or 'foo' is also considered a match. Regexps, and in particular character sets, are included: thus, '[aB]' would match 'a' or 'A' or 'b' or 'B'.

If you do not want this feature, set the variable `case-fold-search` to `nil`. Then all letters must match exactly, including case. This is a buffer-local variable; altering the variable affects only the current buffer. (See Section 10.9.1 [Intro to Buffer-Local], page 151, vol. 1.) Alternatively, you may change the value of `default-case-fold-search`, which is the default value of `case-fold-search` for buffers that do not override it.

Note that the user-level incremental search feature handles case distinctions differently. When given a lower case letter, it looks for a match of either case, but when given an upper case letter, it looks for an upper case letter only. But this has nothing to do with the searching functions Lisp functions use.

case-replace   User Option

This variable determines whether the replacement functions should preserve case. If the variable is `nil`, that means to use the replacement text verbatim. A non-`nil` value means to convert the case of the replacement text according to the text being replaced.

The function `replace-match` is where this variable actually has its effect. See Section 30.6.2 [Replacing Match], page 206.

case-fold-search   User Option

This buffer-local variable determines whether searches should ignore case. If the variable is `nil` they do not ignore case; otherwise they do ignore case.

default-case-fold-search   Variable

The value of this variable is the default value for `case-fold-search` in buffers that do not override it. This is the same as (`default-value` `'case-fold-search`).

30.8 Standard Regular Expressions Used in Editing

This section describes some variables that hold regular expressions used for certain purposes in editing:

page-delimiter   Variable

This is the regexp describing line-beginnings that separate pages. The default value is `"^\014"` (i.e., `"^^L"` or `"^\C-l"`); this matches a line that starts with a formfeed character.

The following two regular expressions should *not* assume the match always starts at the beginning of a line; they should not use '`^`' to anchor the match. Most often, the paragraph commands do check for a match only at the beginning of a line, which means that '`^`' would be superfluous. When there is a nonzero left margin, they accept matches that start after the left margin. In that case, a '`^`' would be incorrect. However, a '`^`' is harmless in modes where a left margin is never used.

paragraph-separate   Variable

This is the regular expression for recognizing the beginning of a line that separates paragraphs. (If you change this, you may have to change `paragraph-start` also.) The default value is `"[ \t\f]*$"`, which matches a line that consists entirely of spaces, tabs, and form feeds (after its left margin).

paragraph-start   *Variable*
This is the regular expression for recognizing the beginning of a line
that starts *or* separates paragraphs. The default value is "[\t\n\f]",
which matches a line starting with a space, tab, newline, or form feed
(after its left margin).

sentence-end   *Variable*
This is the regular expression describing the end of a sentence. (All
paragraph boundaries also end sentences, regardless.) The default
value is:

```
"[.?!][]\"')}]*\\($\\| $\\|\t\\| \\)[ \t\n]*"
```

This means a period, question mark or exclamation mark, followed
optionally by a closing parenthetical character, followed by tabs, spaces
or new lines.

For a detailed explanation of this regular expression, see Section 30.2.2
[Regexp Example], page 198.

31 Syntax Tables

A *syntax table* specifies the syntactic textual function of each character. This information is used by the parsing commands, the complex movement commands, and others to determine where words, symbols, and other syntactic constructs begin and end. The current syntax table controls the meaning of the word motion functions (see Section 27.2.2 [Word Motion], page 121) and the list motion functions (see Section 27.2.6 [List Motion], page 126) as well as the functions in this chapter.

31.1 Syntax Table Concepts

A syntax table is a vector of 256 elements; it contains one entry for each of the 256 possible characters in an 8-bit byte. Each element is an integer that encodes the syntax of the character in question.

Syntax tables are used only for moving across text, not for the Emacs Lisp reader. Emacs Lisp uses built-in syntactic rules when reading Lisp expressions, and these rules cannot be changed.

Each buffer has its own major mode, and each major mode has its own idea of the syntactic class of various characters. For example, in Lisp mode, the character ';' begins a comment, but in C mode, it terminates a statement. To support these variations, Emacs makes the choice of syntax table local to each buffer. Typically, each major mode has its own syntax table and installs that table in each buffer that uses that mode. Changing this table alters the syntax in all those buffers as well as in any buffers subsequently put in that mode. Occasionally several similar modes share one syntax table. See Section 20.1.2 [Example Major Modes], page 344, vol. 1, for an example of how to set up a syntax table.

A syntax table can inherit the data for some characters from the standard syntax table, while specifying other characters itself. The "inherit" syntax class means "inherit this character's syntax from the standard syntax table." Most major modes' syntax tables inherit the syntax of character codes 0 through 31 and 128 through 255. This is useful with character sets such as ISO Latin-1 that have additional alphabetic characters in the range 128 to 255. Just changing the standard syntax for these characters affects all major modes.

syntax-table-p *object*   Function
    This function returns t if *object* is a vector of length 256 elements. This means that the vector may be a syntax table. However, according to this test, any vector of length 256 is considered to be a syntax table, no matter what its contents.

31.2 Syntax Descriptors

This section describes the syntax classes and flags that denote the syntax of a character, and how they are represented as a *syntax descriptor*, which is a Lisp string that you pass to `modify-syntax-entry` to specify the desired syntax.

Emacs defines a number of *syntax classes*. Each syntax table puts each character into one class. There is no necessary relationship between the class of a character in one syntax table and its class in any other table.

Each class is designated by a mnemonic character, which serves as the name of the class when you need to specify a class. Usually the designator character is one that is frequently in that class; however, its meaning as a designator is unvarying and independent of what syntax that character currently has.

A syntax descriptor is a Lisp string that specifies a syntax class, a matching character (used only for the parenthesis classes) and flags. The first character is the designator for a syntax class. The second character is the character to match; if it is unused, put a space there. Then come the characters for any desired flags. If no matching character or flags are needed, one character is sufficient.

For example, the descriptor for the character '*' in C mode is '. 23' (i.e., punctuation, matching character slot unused, second character of a comment-starter, first character of an comment-ender), and the entry for '/' is '. 14' (i.e., punctuation, matching character slot unused, first character of a comment-starter, second character of a comment-ender).

31.2.1 Table of Syntax Classes

Here is a table of syntax classes, the characters that stand for them, their meanings, and examples of their use.

whitespace character   Syntax class

   Whitespace characters (designated with ' ' or '-') separate symbols and words from each other. Typically, whitespace characters have no other syntactic significance, and multiple whitespace characters are syntactically equivalent to a single one. Space, tab, newline and form-feed are almost always classified as whitespace.

word constituent   Syntax class

   Word constituents (designated with 'w') are parts of normal English words and are typically used in variable and command names in programs. All upper- and lower-case letters, and the digits, are typically word constituents.

symbol constituent   Syntax class

Symbol constituents (designated with '_') are the extra characters that
are used in variable and command names along with word constituents.
For example, the symbol constituents class is used in Lisp mode to indicate that certain characters may be part of symbol names even though
they are not part of English words. These characters are '$&*+-_<>'.
In standard C, the only non-word-constituent character that is valid
in symbols is underscore ('_').

punctuation character   Syntax class

Punctuation characters ('.') are those characters that are used as
punctuation in English, or are used in some way in a programming
language to separate symbols from one another. Most programming
language modes, including Emacs Lisp mode, have no characters in
this class since the few characters that are not symbol or word constituents all have other uses.

open parenthesis character   Syntax class
close parenthesis character   Syntax class

Open and close *parenthesis characters* are characters used in dissimi-
lar pairs to surround sentences or expressions. Such a grouping is be-
gun with an open parenthesis character and terminated with a close.
Each open parenthesis character matches a particular close parenthesis
character, and vice versa. Normally, Emacs indicates momentarily the
matching open parenthesis when you insert a close parenthesis. See
Section 35.11 [Blinking], page 291.

The class of open parentheses is designated with '(', and that of close
parentheses with ')'.

In English text, and in C code, the parenthesis pairs are '()', '[]', and
'{}'. In Emacs Lisp, the delimiters for lists and vectors ('()' and '[]')
are classified as parenthesis characters.

string quote   Syntax class

String quote characters (designated with '"') are used in many languages, including Lisp and C, to delimit string constants. The same
string quote character appears at the beginning and the end of a string.
Such quoted strings do not nest.

The parsing facilities of Emacs consider a string as a single token. The
usual syntactic meanings of the characters in the string are suppressed.

The Lisp modes have two string quote characters: double-quote ('"')
and vertical bar ('|'). '|' is not used in Emacs Lisp, but it is used in
Common Lisp. C also has two string quote characters: double-quote
for strings, and single-quote (''') for character constants.

English text has no string quote characters because English is not a programming language. Although quotation marks are used in English, we do not want them to turn off the usual syntactic properties of other characters in the quotation.

escape   Syntax class

An *escape character* (designated with '\') starts an escape sequence such as is used in C string and character constants. The character '\' belongs to this class in both C and Lisp. (In C, it is used thus only inside strings, but it turns out to cause no trouble to treat it this way throughout C code.)

Characters in this class count as part of words if `words-include-escapes` is non-`nil`. See Section 27.2.2 [Word Motion], page 121.

character quote   Syntax class

A *character quote character* (designated with '/') quotes the following character so that it loses its normal syntactic meaning. This differs from an escape character in that only the character immediately following is ever affected.

Characters in this class count as part of words if `words-include-escapes` is non-`nil`. See Section 27.2.2 [Word Motion], page 121.

This class is used for backslash in TeX mode.

paired delimiter   Syntax class

Paired delimiter characters (designated with '$') are like string quote characters except that the syntactic properties of the characters between the delimiters are not suppressed. Only TeX mode uses a paired delimiter presently—the '$' that both enters and leaves math mode.

expression prefix   Syntax class

An *expression prefix operator* (designated with ' ') is used for syntactic operators that are part of an expression if they appear next to one. These characters in Lisp include the apostrophe, ' ' (used for quoting), the comma, ',' (used in macros), and '#' (used in the read syntax for certain data types).

comment starter   Syntax class
comment ender   Syntax class

The *comment starter* and *comment ender* characters are used in various languages to delimit comments. These classes are designated with '<' and '>', respectively.

English text has no comment characters. In Lisp, the semicolon (';') starts a comment and a newline or formfeed ends one.

inherit   Syntax class
 This syntax class does not specify a syntax. It says to look in the standard syntax table to find the syntax of this character. The designator
 for this syntax code is '@'.

31.2.2 Syntax Flags

In addition to the classes, entries for characters in a syntax table can
include flags. There are six possible flags, represented by the characters '1',
'2', '3', '4', 'b' and 'p'.

All the flags except 'p' are used to describe multi-character comment
delimiters. The digit flags indicate that a character can *also* be part of a
comment sequence, in addition to the syntactic properties associated with
its character class. The flags are independent of the class and each other
for the sake of characters such as '*' in C mode, which is a punctuation
character, *and* the second character of a start-of-comment sequence ('/*'),
and the first character of an end-of-comment sequence ('*/').

The flags for a character c are:

- '1' means c is the start of a two-character comment-start sequence.

- '2' means c is the second character of such a sequence.

- '3' means c is the start of a two-character comment-end sequence.

- '4' means c is the second character of such a sequence.

- 'b' means that c as a comment delimiter belongs to the alternative "b"
  comment style.

  Emacs supports two comment styles simultaneously in any one syntax
  table. This is for the sake of C++. Each style of comment syntax has
  its own comment-start sequence and its own comment-end sequence.
  Each comment must stick to one style or the other; thus, if it starts
  with the comment-start sequence of style "b", it must also end with the
  comment-end sequence of style "b".

  The two comment-start sequences must begin with the same character;
  only the second character may differ. Mark the second character of the
  "b"-style comment-start sequence with the 'b' flag.

  A comment-end sequence (one or two characters) applies to the "b"
  style if its first character has the 'b' flag set; otherwise, it applies to the
  "a" style.

  The appropriate comment syntax settings for C++ are as follows:

  '/'   '124b'

  '*'   '23'

  newline   '>b'

This defines four comment-delimiting sequences:

'/*'   This is a comment-start sequence for "a" style because the
            second character, '*', does not have the 'b' flag.

'//'   This is a comment-start sequence for "b" style because the
            second character, '/', does have the 'b' flag.

'*/'   This is a comment-end sequence for "a" style because the
            first character, '*', does not have the 'b' flag

newline   This is a comment-end sequence for "b" style, because the
            newline character has the 'b' flag.

- 'p' identifies an additional "prefix character" for Lisp syntax. These
  characters are treated as whitespace when they appear between expressions. When they appear within an expression, they are handled
  according to their usual syntax codes.

  The function `backward-prefix-chars` moves back over these characters, as well as over characters whose primary syntax class is prefix (' ').
  See Section 31.4 [Motion and Syntax], page 218.

31.3 Syntax Table Functions

In this section we describe functions for creating, accessing and altering
syntax tables.

make-syntax-table   Function
    This function creates a new syntax table. Character codes 0 through
    31 and 128 through 255 are set up to inherit from the standard syntax
    table. The other character codes are set up by copying what the
    standard syntax table says about them.

    Most major mode syntax tables are created in this way.

copy-syntax-table &optional *table*   Function
    This function constructs a copy of *table* and returns it. If *table* is
    not supplied (or is `nil`), it returns a copy of the current syntax table.
    Otherwise, an error is signaled if *table* is not a syntax table.

modify-syntax-entry *char syntax-descriptor*   Command
            &optional *table*
    This function sets the syntax entry for *char* according to *syntax-
    descriptor*. The syntax is changed only for *table*, which defaults to
    the current buffer's syntax table, and not in any other syntax table.
    The argument *syntax-descriptor* specifies the desired syntax; this is
    a string beginning with a class designator character, and optionally
    containing a matching character and flags as well. See Section 31.2
    [Syntax Descriptors], page 212.

This function always returns `nil`. The old syntax information in the table for this character is discarded.

An error is signaled if the first character of the syntax descriptor is not one of the twelve syntax class designator characters. An error is also signaled if *char* is not a character.

Examples:

```
;; Put the space character in class whitespace.
(modify-syntax-entry ?\  " ")
     ⇒ nil

;; Make '$' an open parenthesis character,
;;    with '^' as its matching close.
(modify-syntax-entry ?$ "(^")
     ⇒ nil

;; Make '^' a close parenthesis character,
;;    with '$' as its matching open.
(modify-syntax-entry ?^ ")$")
     ⇒ nil

;; Make '/' a punctuation character,
;;    the first character of a start-comment sequence,
;;    and the second character of an end-comment sequence.
;;    This is used in C mode.
(modify-syntax-entry ?/ ". 14")
     ⇒ nil
```

char-syntax *character*   Function

This function returns the syntax class of *character*, represented by its mnemonic designator character. This *only* returns the class, not any matching parenthesis or flags.

An error is signaled if *char* is not a character.

The following examples apply to C mode. The first example shows that the syntax class of space is whitespace (represented by a space). The second example shows that the syntax of '/' is punctuation. This does not show the fact that it is also part of comment-start and -end sequences. The third example shows that open parenthesis is in the class of open parentheses. This does not show the fact that it has a matching character, ')'.

```
(char-to-string (char-syntax ?\ ))
     ⇒ " "

(char-to-string (char-syntax ?/))
     ⇒ "."
```

```
(char-to-string (char-syntax ?\())
    ⇒ "("
```

set-syntax-table *table*   Function
This function makes *table* the syntax table for the current buffer. It
returns *table*.

syntax-table   Function
This function returns the current syntax table, which is the table for
the current buffer.

31.4 Motion and Syntax

This section describes functions for moving across characters in certain
syntax classes. None of these functions exists in Emacs version 18 or earlier.

skip-syntax-forward *syntaxes* &optional *limit*   Function
This function moves point forward across characters having syntax
classes mentioned in *syntaxes*. It stops when it encounters the end
of the buffer, or position *limit* (if specified), or a character it is not
supposed to skip.

skip-syntax-backward *syntaxes* &optional *limit*   Function
This function moves point backward across characters whose syntax
classes are mentioned in *syntaxes*. It stops when it encounters the
beginning of the buffer, or position *limit* (if specified), or a character
it is not supposed to skip.

backward-prefix-chars   Function
This function moves point backward over any number of characters
with expression prefix syntax. This includes both characters in the
expression prefix syntax class, and characters with the 'p' flag.

31.5 Parsing Balanced Expressions

Here are several functions for parsing and scanning balanced expressions,
also known as *sexps*, in which parentheses match in pairs. The syntax table controls the interpretation of characters, so these functions can be used
for Lisp expressions when in Lisp mode and for C expressions when in C
mode. See Section 27.2.6 [List Motion], page 126, for convenient higher-level
functions for moving over balanced expressions.

parse-partial-sexp *start limit* &optional *target-depth*   Function
        stop-before state stop-comment
This function parses a sexp in the current buffer starting at *start*, not
scanning past *limit*. It stops at position *limit* or when certain criteria

described below are met, and sets point to the location where parsing stops. It returns a value describing the status of the parse at the point where it stops.

If *state* is nil, *start* is assumed to be at the top level of parenthesis structure, such as the beginning of a function definition. Alternatively, you might wish to resume parsing in the middle of the structure. To do this, you must provide a *state* argument that describes the initial status of parsing.

If the third argument *target-depth* is non-nil, parsing stops if the depth in parentheses becomes equal to *target-depth*. The depth starts at 0, or at whatever is given in *state*.

If the fourth argument *stop-before* is non-nil, parsing stops when it comes to any character that starts a sexp. If *stop-comment* is non-nil, parsing stops when it comes to the start of a comment.

The fifth argument *state* is an eight-element list of the same form as the value of this function, described below. The return value of one call may be used to initialize the state of the parse on another call to `parse-partial-sexp`.

The result is a list of eight elements describing the final state of the parse:

0. The depth in parentheses, counting from 0.

1. The character position of the start of the innermost parenthetical grouping containing the stopping point; nil if none.

2. The character position of the start of the last complete subexpression terminated; nil if none.

3. Non-nil if inside a string. More precisely, this is the character that will terminate the string.

4. t if inside a comment (of either style).

5. t if point is just after a quote character.

6. The minimum parenthesis depth encountered during this scan.

7. t if inside a comment of style "b".

Elements 0, 3, 4, 5 and 7 are significant in the argument *state*.

This function is most often used to compute indentation for languages that have nested parentheses.

scan-lists *from count depth*   Function
   This function scans forward *count* balanced parenthetical groupings from character number *from*. It returns the character position where the scan stops.

   If *depth* is nonzero, parenthesis depth counting begins from that value. The only candidates for stopping are places where the depth in parentheses becomes zero; `scan-lists` counts *count* such places and then stops. Thus, a positive value for *depth* means go out *depth* levels of parenthesis.

Scanning ignores comments if `parse-sexp-ignore-comments` is non-`nil`.

If the scan reaches the beginning or end of the buffer (or its accessible portion), and the depth is not zero, an error is signaled. If the depth is zero but the count is not used up, `nil` is returned.

scan-sexps *from count*   Function
    This function scans forward *count* sexps from character position *from*. It returns the character position where the scan stops.

    Scanning ignores comments if `parse-sexp-ignore-comments` is non-`nil`.

    If the scan reaches the beginning or end of (the accessible part of) the buffer in the middle of a parenthetical grouping, an error is signaled. If it reaches the beginning or end between groupings but before count is used up, `nil` is returned.

parse-sexp-ignore-comments   Variable
    If the value is non-`nil`, then comments are treated as whitespace by the functions in this section and by `forward-sexp`.

    In older Emacs versions, this feature worked only when the comment terminator is something like '`*/`', and appears only to end a comment. In languages where newlines terminate comments, it was necessary make this variable `nil`, since not every newline is the end of a comment. This limitation no longer exists.

You can use `forward-comment` to move forward or backward over one comment or several comments.

forward-comment *count*   Function
    This function moves point forward across *count* comments (backward, if *count* is negative). If it finds anything other than a comment or whitespace, it stops, leaving point at the place where it stopped. It also stops after satisfying *count*.

To move forward over all comments and whitespace following point, use `(forward-comment (buffer-size))`. `(buffer-size)` is a good argument to use, because the number of comments in the buffer cannot exceed that many.

31.6 Some Standard Syntax Tables

Most of the major modes in Emacs have their own syntax tables. Here are several of them:

standard-syntax-table   Function
> This function returns the standard syntax table, which is the syntax table used in Fundamental mode.

text-mode-syntax-table   Variable
> The value of this variable is the syntax table used in Text mode.

c-mode-syntax-table   Variable
> The value of this variable is the syntax table for C-mode buffers.

emacs-lisp-mode-syntax-table   Variable
> The value of this variable is the syntax table used in Emacs Lisp mode by editing commands. (It has no effect on the Lisp `read` function.)

31.7 Syntax Table Internals

Each element of a syntax table is an integer that encodes the syntax of one character: the syntax class, possible matching character, and flags. Lisp programs don't usually work with the elements directly; the Lisp-level syntax table functions usually work with syntax descriptors (see Section 31.2 [Syntax Descriptors], page 212).

The low 8 bits of each element of a syntax table indicate the syntax class.

Integer	Class
0	whitespace
1	punctuation
2	word
3	symbol
4	open parenthesis
5	close parenthesis
6	expression prefix
7	string quote
8	paired delimiter
9	escape
10	character quote

11   comment-start

12   comment-end

13   inherit

The next 8 bits are the matching opposite parenthesis (if the character has parenthesis syntax); otherwise, they are not meaningful. The next 6 bits are the flags.

32 Abbrevs And Abbrev Expansion

An abbreviation or *abbrev* is a string of characters that may be expanded to a longer string. The user can insert the abbrev string and find it replaced automatically with the expansion of the abbrev. This saves typing.

The set of abbrevs currently in effect is recorded in an *abbrev table*. Each buffer has a local abbrev table, but normally all buffers in the same major mode share one abbrev table. There is also a global abbrev table. Normally both are used.

An abbrev table is represented as an obarray containing a symbol for each abbreviation. The symbol's name is the abbreviation; its value is the expansion; its function definition is the hook function to do the expansion (see Section 32.3 [Defining Abbrevs], page 224); its property list cell contains the use count, the number of times the abbreviation has been expanded. Because these symbols are not interned in the usual obarray, they will never appear as the result of reading a Lisp expression; in fact, normally they are never used except by the code that handles abbrevs. Therefore, it is safe to use them in an extremely nonstandard way. See Section 7.3 [Creating Symbols], page 101, vol. 1.

For the user-level commands for abbrevs, see section "Abbrev Mode" in *The GNU Emacs Manual*.

32.1 Setting Up Abbrev Mode

Abbrev mode is a minor mode controlled by the value of the variable `abbrev-mode`.

abbrev-mode   *Variable*
> A non-`nil` value of this variable turns on the automatic expansion of abbrevs when their abbreviations are inserted into a buffer. If the value is `nil`, abbrevs may be defined, but they are not expanded automatically.
>
> This variable automatically becomes local when set in any fashion.

default-abbrev-mode   *Variable*
> This is the value of `abbrev-mode` for buffers that do not override it. This is the same as (default-value 'abbrev-mode).

32.2 Abbrev Tables

This section describes how to create and manipulate abbrev tables.

make-abbrev-table   Function

This function creates and returns a new, empty abbrev table—an obar-ray containing no symbols. It is a vector filled with zeros.

clear-abbrev-table *table*   Function

This function undefines all the abbrevs in abbrev table *table*, leaving it empty. The function returns `nil`.

define-abbrev-table *tabname definitions*   Function

This function defines *tabname* (a symbol) as an abbrev table name, i.e., as a variable whose value is an abbrev table. It defines abbrevs in the table according to *definitions*, a list of elements of the form (*abbrevname expansion hook usecount*). The value is always `nil`.

abbrev-table-name-list   Variable

This is a list of symbols whose values are abbrev tables. `define-abbrev-table` adds the new abbrev table name to this list.

insert-abbrev-table-description *name* &optional   Function
    human

This function inserts before point a description of the abbrev table named *name*. The argument *name* is a symbol whose value is an abbrev table. The value is always `nil`.

If *human* is non-`nil`, the description is human-oriented. Otherwise the description is a Lisp expression—a call to `define-abbrev-table` that would define *name* exactly as it is currently defined.

32.3 Defining Abbrevs

These functions define an abbrev in a specified abbrev table. `define-abbrev` is the low-level basic function, while `add-abbrev` is used by commands that ask for information from the user.

add-abbrev *table type arg*   Function

This function adds an abbreviation to abbrev table *table* based on information from the user. The argument *type* is a string describing in English the kind of abbrev this will be (typically, `"global"` or `"mode-specific"`); this is used in prompting the user. The argument *arg* is the number of words in the expansion.

The return value is the symbol that internally represents the new abbrev, or `nil` if the user declines to confirm redefining an existing abbrev.

define-abbrev *table name expansion hook*   Function
This function defines an abbrev in *table* named *name*, to expand to
expansion, and call *hook*. The return value is an uninterned symbol
that represents the abbrev inside Emacs; its name is *name*.

The argument *name* should be a string. The argument *expansion*
should be a string, or `nil` to undefine the abbrev.

The argument *hook* is a function or `nil`. If *hook* is non-`nil`, then it is
called with no arguments after the abbrev is replaced with *expansion*;
point is located at the end of *expansion* when *hook* is called.

The use count of the abbrev is initialized to zero.

only-global-abbrevs   User Option
If this variable is non-`nil`, it means that the user plans to use global
abbrevs only. This tells the commands that define mode-specific abbrevs to define global ones instead. This variable does not alter the
behavior of the functions in this section; it is examined by their callers.

32.4 Saving Abbrevs in Files

A file of saved abbrev definitions is actually a file of Lisp code. The
abbrevs are saved in the form of a Lisp program to define the same abbrev
tables with the same contents. Therefore, you can load the file with `load`
(see Section 13.1 [How Programs Do Loading], page 183, vol. 1). However,
the function `quietly-read-abbrev-file` is provided as a more convenient
interface.

User-level facilities such as `save-some-buffers` can save abbrevs in a file
automatically, under the control of variables described here.

abbrev-file-name   User Option
This is the default file name for reading and saving abbrevs.

quietly-read-abbrev-file *filename*   Function
This function reads abbrev definitions from a file named *filename*, previously written with `write-abbrev-file`. If *filename* is `nil`, the file
specified in `abbrev-file-name` is used. `save-abbrevs` is set to `t` so
that changes will be saved.

This function does not display any messages. It returns `nil`.

save-abbrevs   User Option
A non-`nil` value for `save-abbrev` means that Emacs should save abbrevs when files are saved. `abbrev-file-name` specifies the file to save
the abbrevs in.

abbrevs-changed   Variable

This variable is set non-`nil` by defining or altering any abbrevs. This serves as a flag for various Emacs commands to offer to save your abbrevs.

write-abbrev-file *filename*   Command

Save all abbrev definitions, in all abbrev tables, in the file *filename*, in the form of a Lisp program that when loaded will define the same abbrevs. This function returns `nil`.

32.5 Looking Up and Expanding Abbreviations

Abbrevs are usually expanded by commands for interactive use, including `self-insert-command`. This section describes the subroutines used in writing such functions, as well as the variables they use for communication.

abbrev-symbol *abbrev* &optional *table*   Function

This function returns the symbol representing the abbrev named *abbrev*. The value returned is `nil` if that abbrev is not defined. The optional second argument *table* is the abbrev table to look it up in. If *table* is `nil`, this function tries first the current buffer's local abbrev table, and second the global abbrev table.

abbrev-expansion *abbrev* &optional *table*   Function

This function returns the string that *abbrev* would expand into (as defined by the abbrev tables used for the current buffer). The optional argument *table* specifies the abbrev table to use, as in `abbrev-symbol`.

expand-abbrev   Command

This command expands the abbrev before point, if any. If point does not follow an abbrev, this command does nothing. The command returns `t` if it did expansion, `nil` otherwise.

abbrev-prefix-mark &optional *arg*   Command

Mark current point as the beginning of an abbrev. The next call to `expand-abbrev` will use the text from here to point (where it is then) as the abbrev to expand, rather than using the previous word as usual.

abbrev-all-caps   User Option

When this is set non-`nil`, an abbrev entered entirely in upper case is expanded using all upper case. Otherwise, an abbrev entered entirely in upper case is expanded by capitalizing each word of the expansion.

abbrev-start-location   Variable

This is the buffer position for `expand-abbrev` to use as the start of the next abbrev to be expanded. (`nil` means use the word before point instead.) `abbrev-start-location` is set to `nil` each time `expand-abbrev` is called. This variable is also set by `abbrev-prefix-mark`.

abbrev-start-location-buffer   Variable
The value of this variable is the buffer for which `abbrev-start-location` has been set. Trying to expand an abbrev in any other buffer clears `abbrev-start-location`. This variable is set by `abbrev-prefix-mark`.

last-abbrev   Variable
This is the `abbrev-symbol` of the last abbrev expanded. This information is left by `expand-abbrev` for the sake of the `unexpand-abbrev` command.

last-abbrev-location   Variable
This is the location of the last abbrev expanded. This contains information left by `expand-abbrev` for the sake of the `unexpand-abbrev` command.

last-abbrev-text   Variable
This is the exact expansion text of the last abbrev expanded, after case conversion (if any). Its value is `nil` if the abbrev has already been unexpanded. This contains information left by `expand-abbrev` for the sake of the `unexpand-abbrev` command.

pre-abbrev-expand-hook   Variable
This is a normal hook whose functions are executed, in sequence, just before any expansion of an abbrev. See Section 20.4 [Hooks], page 360, vol. 1. Since it is a normal hook, the hook functions receive no arguments. However, they can find the abbrev to be expanded by looking in the buffer before point.

The following sample code shows a simple use of `pre-abbrev-expand-hook`. If the user terminates an abbrev with a punctuation character, the hook function asks for confirmation. Thus, this hook allows the user to decide whether to expand the abbrev, and aborts expansion if it is not confirmed.

```
(add-hook 'pre-abbrev-expand-hook 'query-if-not-space)

;; This is the function invoked by pre-abbrev-expand-hook.

;; If the user terminated the abbrev with a space, the function does
;; nothing (that is, it returns so that the abbrev can expand).  If the
;; user entered some other character, this function asks whether
;; expansion should continue.

;; If the user answers the prompt with y, the function returns
;; nil (because of the not function), but that is
;; acceptable; the return value has no effect on expansion.
```

```
(defun query-if-not-space ()
  (if (/= ?\  (preceding-char))
      (if (not (y-or-n-p "Do you want to expand this abbrev? "))
          (error "Not expanding this abbrev"))))
```

32.6 Standard Abbrev Tables

Here we list the variables that hold the abbrev tables for the preloaded major modes of Emacs.

global-abbrev-table   Variable
This is the abbrev table for mode-independent abbrevs. The abbrevs defined in it apply to all buffers. Each buffer may also have a local abbrev table, whose abbrev definitions take precedence over those in the global table.

local-abbrev-table   Variable
The value of this buffer-local variable is the (mode-specific) abbreviation table of the current buffer.

fundamental-mode-abbrev-table   Variable
This is the local abbrev table used in Fundamental mode; in other words, it is the local abbrev table in all buffers in Fundamental mode.

text-mode-abbrev-table   Variable
This is the local abbrev table used in Text mode.

c-mode-abbrev-table   Variable
This is the local abbrev table used in C mode.

lisp-mode-abbrev-table   Variable
This is the local abbrev table used in Lisp mode and Emacs Lisp mode.

33 Processes

In the terminology of operating systems, a *process* is a space in which a program can execute. Emacs runs in a process. Emacs Lisp programs can invoke other programs in processes of their own. These are called *subprocesses* or *child processes* of the Emacs process, which is their *parent process*.

A subprocess of Emacs may be *synchronous* or *asynchronous*, depending on how it is created. When you create a synchronous subprocess, the Lisp program waits for the subprocess to terminate before continuing execution. When you create an asynchronous subprocess, it can run in parallel with the Lisp program. This kind of subprocess is represented within Emacs by a Lisp object which is also called a "process". Lisp programs can use this object to communicate with the subprocess or to control it. For example, you can send signals, obtain status information, receive output from the process, or send input to it.

processp *object*   Function
    This function returns t if *object* is a process, nil otherwise.

33.1 Functions that Create Subprocesses

There are three functions that create a new subprocess in which to run a program. One of them, `start-process`, creates an asynchronous process and returns a process object (see Section 33.4 [Asynchronous Processes], page 234). The other two, `call-process` and `call-process-region`, create a synchronous process and do not return a process object (see Section 33.2 [Synchronous Processes], page 230).

Synchronous and asynchronous processes are explained in following sections. Since the three functions are all called in a similar fashion, their common arguments are described here.

In all cases, the function's *program* argument specifies the program to be run. An error is signaled if the file is not found or cannot be executed. If the file name is relative, the variable `exec-path` contains a list of directories to search. Emacs initializes `exec-path` when it starts up, based on the value of the environment variable PATH. The standard file name constructs, '~', '.', and '..', are interpreted as usual in `exec-path`, but environment variable substitutions ('$HOME', etc.) are not recognized; use `substitute-in-file-name` to perform them (see Section 22.8.4 [File Name Expansion], page 32).

Each of the subprocess-creating functions has a *buffer-or-name* argument which specifies where the standard output from the program will go. If *buffer-or-name* is nil, that says to discard the output unless a filter function handles it. (See Section 33.9.2 [Filter Functions], page 242, and Chapter 16 [Read and Print], page 241, vol. 1.) Normally, you should avoid having multiple processes send output to the same buffer because their output would be intermixed randomly.

All three of the subprocess-creating functions have a &rest argument, *args*. The *args* must all be strings, and they are supplied to *program* as separate command line arguments. Wildcard characters and other shell constructs are not allowed in these strings, since they are passed directly to the specified program.

Please note: The argument *program* contains only the name of the program; it may not contain any command-line arguments. You must use *args* to provide those.

The subprocess gets its current directory from the value of default-directory (see Section 22.8.4 [File Name Expansion], page 32).

The subprocess inherits its environment from Emacs; but you can specify overrides for it with process-environment. See Section 34.3 [System Environment], page 256.

exec-directory   *Variable*
> The value of this variable is the name of a directory (a string) that contains programs that come with GNU Emacs, that are intended for Emacs to invoke. The program wakeup is an example of such a program; the display-time command uses it to get a reminder once per minute.

exec-path   *User Option*
> The value of this variable is a list of directories to search for programs to run in subprocesses. Each element is either the name of a directory (i.e., a string), or nil, which stands for the default directory (which is the value of default-directory).
>
> The value of exec-path is used by call-process and start-process when the *program* argument is not an absolute file name.

33.2 Creating a Synchronous Process

After a *synchronous process* is created, Emacs waits for the process to terminate before continuing. Starting Dired is an example of this: it runs ls in a synchronous process, then modifies the output slightly. Because the process is synchronous, the entire directory listing arrives in the buffer before Emacs tries to do anything with it.

While Emacs waits for the synchronous subprocess to terminate, the user can quit by typing C-g. The first C-g tries to kill the subprocess with a SIGINT signal; but it waits until the subprocess actually terminates before quitting. If during that time the user types another C-g, that kills the subprocess instantly with SIGKILL and quits immediately. See Section 18.8 [Quitting], page 305, vol. 1.

The synchronous subprocess functions returned nil in version 18. In version 19, they return an indication of how the process terminated.

call-process *program* &optional *infile destination display*   Function
            &rest *args*

This function calls *program* in a separate process and waits for it to finish.

The standard input for the process comes from file *infile* if *infile* is not nil and from '/dev/null' otherwise. The argument *destination* says where to put the process output. Here are the possibilities:

a buffer   Insert the output in that buffer, before point. This includes both the standard output stream and the standard error stream of the process.

a string   Find or create a buffer with that name, then insert the output in that buffer, before point.

t   Insert the output in the current buffer, before point.

nil   Discard the output.

0   Discard the output, and return immediately without waiting for the subprocess to finish.

            In this case, the process is not truly synchronous, since it can run in parallel with Emacs; but you can think of it as synchronous in that Emacs is essentially finished with the subprocess as soon as this function returns.

(*real-destination error-destination*)

            Keep the standard output stream separate from the standard error stream; deal with the ordinary output as specified by *real-destination*, and dispose of the error output according to *error-destination*. The value nil means discard it, t means mix it with the ordinary output, and a string specifies a file name to redirect error output into.

            You can't directly specify a buffer to put the error output in; that is too difficult to implement. But you can achieve this result by sending the error output to a temporary file and then inserting the file into a buffer.

If *display* is non-nil, then call-process redisplays the buffer as output is inserted. Otherwise the function does no redisplay, and the results become visible on the screen only when Emacs redisplays that buffer in the normal course of events.

The remaining arguments, *args*, are strings that specify command line arguments for the program.

The value returned by `call-process` (unless you told it not to wait) indicates the reason for process termination. A number gives the exit status of the subprocess; 0 means success, and any other value means failure. If the process terminated with a signal, `call-process` returns a string describing the signal.

In the examples below, the buffer 'foo' is current.

```
(call-process "pwd" nil t)
     ⇒ nil

---------- Buffer: foo ----------
/usr/user/lewis/manual
---------- Buffer: foo ----------

(call-process "grep" nil "bar" nil "lewis" "/etc/passwd")
     ⇒ nil

---------- Buffer: bar ----------
lewis:5LTsHm66CSWKg:398:21:Bil Lewis:/user/lewis:/bin/csh

---------- Buffer: bar ----------
```

The `insert-directory` function contains a good example of the use of `call-process`:

```
(call-process insert-directory-program nil t nil switches
              (if full-directory-p
                  (concat (file-name-as-directory file) ".")
                file))
```

call-process-region *start end program* &optional *delete*   Function
       destination display &rest *args*

This function sends the text between *start* to *end* as standard input to a process running *program*. It deletes the text sent if *delete* is non-nil; this is useful when *buffer* is t, to insert the output in the current buffer.

The arguments *destination* and *display* control what to do with the output from the subprocess, and whether to update the display as it comes in. For details, see the description of `call-process`, above. If *destination* is the integer 0, `call-process-region` discards the output and returns `nil` immediately, without waiting for the subprocess to finish.

The remaining arguments, *args*, are strings that specify command line arguments for the program.

The return value of `call-process-region` is just like that of `call-process`: `nil` if you told it to return without waiting; otherwise, a number or string which indicates how the subprocess terminated.

In the following example, we use `call-process-region` to run the `cat` utility, with standard input being the first five characters in buffer 'foo' (the word 'input'). `cat` copies its standard input into its standard output. Since the argument *destination* is `t`, this output is inserted in the current buffer.

```
---------- Buffer: foo ----------
input⋆
---------- Buffer: foo ----------

(call-process-region 1 6 "cat" nil t)
     ⇒ nil

---------- Buffer: foo ----------
inputinput⋆
---------- Buffer: foo ----------
```

The `shell-command-on-region` command uses `call-process-region` like this:

```
(call-process-region
 start end
 shell-file-name        ; Name of program.
 nil                    ; Do not delete region.
 buffer                 ; Send output to buffer.
 nil                    ; No redisplay during output.
 "-c" command)          ; Arguments for the shell.
```

33.3 MS-DOS Subprocesses

On MS-DOS, you must indicate whether the data going to and from a synchronous subprocess are text or binary. Text data requires translation between the end-of-line convention used within Emacs (a single newline character) and the convention used outside Emacs (the two-character sequence, CRLF).

The variable `binary-process-input` applies to input sent to the subprocess, and `binary-process-output` applies to output received from it. A non-nil value means the data is non-text; `nil` means the data is text, and calls for conversion.

binary-process-input   Variable

If this variable is `nil`, convert newlines to CRLF sequences in the input to a synchronous subprocess.

binary-process-output   Variable

If this variable is `nil`, convert CRLF sequences to newlines in the output from a synchronous subprocess.

See Section 22.13 [Files and MS-DOS], page 42, for related information.

33.4 Creating an Asynchronous Process

After an *asynchronous process* is created, Emacs and the Lisp program both continue running immediately. The process may thereafter run in parallel with Emacs, and the two may communicate with each other using the functions described in following sections. Here we describe how to create an asynchronous process with `start-process`.

start-process *name buffer-or-name program* &rest *args*   Function

This function creates a new asynchronous subprocess and starts the program *program* running in it. It returns a process object that stands for the new subprocess in Lisp. The argument *name* specifies the name for the process object; if a process with this name already exists, then *name* is modified (by adding '<1>', etc.) to be unique. The buffer *buffer-or-name* is the buffer to associate with the process.

The remaining arguments, *args*, are strings that specify command line arguments for the program.

In the example below, the first process is started and runs (rather, sleeps) for 100 seconds. Meanwhile, the second process is started, and given the name 'my-process<1>' for the sake of uniqueness. It inserts the directory listing at the end of the buffer 'foo', before the first process finishes. Then it finishes, and a message to that effect is inserted in the buffer. Much later, the first process finishes, and another message is inserted in the buffer for it.

```
(start-process "my-process" "foo" "sleep" "100")
    ⇒ #<process my-process>

(start-process "my-process" "foo" "ls" "-l" "/user/lewis/bin")
    ⇒ #<process my-process<1>>

---------- Buffer: foo ----------
total 2
lrwxrwxrwx  1 lewis      14 Jul 22 10:12 gnuemacs --> /emacs
-rwxrwxrwx  1 lewis      19 Jul 30 21:02 lemon

Process my-process<1> finished

Process my-process finished
---------- Buffer: foo ----------
```

start-process-shell-command *name buffer-or-name*   Function
        command &rest *command-args*

This function is like `start-process` except that it uses a shell to execute the specified command. The argument *command* is a shell command name, and *command-args* are the arguments for the shell command.

process-connection-type   *Variable*

This variable controls the type of device used to communicate with asynchronous subprocesses. If it is non-`nil`, then PTYs are used, when available. Otherwise, pipes are used.

PTYs are usually preferable for processes visible to the user, as in Shell mode, because they allow job control (`C-c`, `C-z`, etc.) to work between the process and its children whereas pipes do not. For subprocesses used for internal purposes by programs, it is often better to use a pipe, because they are more efficient. In addition, the total number of PTYs is limited on many systems and it is good not to waste them.

The value `process-connection-type` is used when `start-process` is called. So you can specify how to communicate with one subprocess by binding the variable around the call to `start-process`.

```
(let ((process-connection-type nil))   ; Use a pipe.
   (start-process ...))
```

To determine whether a given subprocess actually got a pipe or a PTY, use the function `process-tty-name` (see Section 33.6 [Process Information], page 236).

33.5 Deleting Processes

Deleting a process disconnects Emacs immediately from the subprocess, and removes it from the list of active processes. It sends a signal to the subprocess to make the subprocess terminate, but this is not guaranteed to happen immediately. The process object itself continues to exist as long as other Lisp objects point to it.

You can delete a process explicitly at any time. Processes are deleted automatically after they terminate, but not necessarily right away. If you delete a terminated process explicitly before it is deleted automatically, no harm results.

delete-exited-processes   *Variable*

This variable controls automatic deletion of processes that have terminated (due to calling `exit` or to a signal). If it is `nil`, then they continue to exist until the user runs `list-processes`. Otherwise, they are deleted immediately after they exit.

delete-process *name*   *Function*

This function deletes the process associated with *name*, killing it with a `SIGHUP` signal. The argument *name* may be a process, the name of a process, a buffer, or the name of a buffer.

```
(delete-process "*shell*")
     ⇒ nil
```

process-kill-without-query *process*   Function
    This function declares that Emacs need not query the user if *process*
    is still running when Emacs is exited. The process will be deleted
    silently. The value is t.

```
(process-kill-without-query (get-process "shell"))
     ⇒ t
```

33.6 Process Information

    Several functions return information about processes. `list-processes`
is provided for interactive use.

list-processes   Command
    This command displays a listing of all living processes. In addition, it
    finally deletes any process whose status was 'Exited' or 'Signaled'.
    It returns nil.

process-list   Function
    This function returns a list of all processes that have not been deleted.

```
(process-list)
     ⇒ (#<process display-time> #<process shell>)
```

get-process *name*   Function
    This function returns the process named *name*, or nil if there is none.
    An error is signaled if *name* is not a string.

```
(get-process "shell")
     ⇒ #<process shell>
```

process-command *process*   Function
    This function returns the command that was executed to start *process*.
    This is a list of strings, the first string being the program executed
    and the rest of the strings being the arguments that were given to the
    program.

```
(process-command (get-process "shell"))
     ⇒ ("/bin/csh" "-i")
```

process-id *process*   Function
    This function returns the PID of *process*. This is an integer that dis-
    tinguishes the process *process* from all other processes running on the
    same computer at the current time. The PID of a process is chosen by
    the operating system kernel when the process is started and remains
    constant as long as the process exists.

process-name *process*   Function
    This function returns the name of *process*.

process-status *process-name*   Function

This function returns the status of *process-name* as a symbol. The argument *process-name* must be a process, a buffer, a process name (string) or a buffer name (string).

The possible values for an actual subprocess are:

run   for a process that is running.

stop   for a process that is stopped but continuable.

exit   for a process that has exited.

signal   for a process that has received a fatal signal.

open   for a network connection that is open.

closed   for a network connection that is closed. Once a connection is closed, you cannot reopen it, though you might be able to open a new connection to the same place.

nil   if *process-name* is not the name of an existing process.

```
(process-status "shell")
     ⇒ run
(process-status (get-buffer "*shell*"))
     ⇒ run
x
     ⇒ #<process xx<1>>
(process-status x)
     ⇒ exit
```

For a network connection, `process-status` returns one of the symbols `open` or `closed`. The latter means that the other side closed the connection, or Emacs did `delete-process`.

In earlier Emacs versions (prior to version 19), the status of a network connection was `run` if open, and `exit` if closed.

process-exit-status *process*   Function

This function returns the exit status of *process* or the signal number that killed it. (Use the result of `process-status` to determine which of those it is.) If *process* has not yet terminated, the value is 0.

process-tty-name *process*   Function

This function returns the terminal name that *process* is using for its communication with Emacs—or `nil` if it is using pipes instead of a terminal (see `process-connection-type` in Section 33.4 [Asynchronous Processes], page 234).

33.7 Sending Input to Processes

Asynchronous subprocesses receive input when it is sent to them by Emacs, which is done with the functions in this section. You must specify the process to send input to, and the input data to send. The data appears on the "standard input" of the subprocess.

Some operating systems have limited space for buffered input in a PTY. On these systems, Emacs sends an EOF periodically amidst the other characters, to force them through. For most programs, these EOFs do no harm.

process-send-string *process-name string*   Function

This function sends *process-name* the contents of *string* as standard input. The argument *process-name* must be a process or the name of a process. If it is **nil**, the current buffer's process is used.

The function returns **nil**.

```
(process-send-string "shell<1>" "ls\n")
     ⇒ nil


---------- Buffer: *shell* ----------
...
introduction.texi           syntax-tables.texi~
introduction.texi~          text.texi
introduction.txt            text.texi~
...
---------- Buffer: *shell* ----------
```

process-send-region *process-name start end*   Command

This function sends the text in the region defined by *start* and *end* as standard input to *process-name*, which is a process or a process name. (If it is **nil**, the current buffer's process is used.)

An error is signaled unless both *start* and *end* are integers or markers that indicate positions in the current buffer. (It is unimportant which number is larger.)

process-send-eof &optional *process-name*   Function

This function makes *process-name* see an end-of-file in its input. The EOF comes after any text already sent to it.

If *process-name* is not supplied, or if it is **nil**, then this function sends the EOF to the current buffer's process. An error is signaled if the current buffer has no process.

The function returns *process-name*.

```
(process-send-eof "shell")
     ⇒ "shell"
```

33.8 Sending Signals to Processes

Sending a signal to a subprocess is a way of interrupting its activities. There are several different signals, each with its own meaning. The set of signals and their names is defined by the operating system. For example, the signal SIGINT means that the user has typed C-c, or that some analogous thing has happened.

Each signal has a standard effect on the subprocess. Most signals kill the subprocess, but some stop or resume execution instead. Most signals can optionally be handled by programs; if the program handles the signal, then we can say nothing in general about its effects.

You can send signals explicitly by calling the functions in this section. Emacs also sends signals automatically at certain times: killing a buffer sends a SIGHUP signal to all its associated processes; killing Emacs sends a SIGHUP signal to all remaining processes. (SIGHUP is a signal that usually indicates that the user hung up the phone.)

Each of the signal-sending functions takes two optional arguments: *process-name* and *current-group*.

The argument *process-name* must be either a process, the name of one, or nil. If it is nil, the process defaults to the process associated with the current buffer. An error is signaled if *process-name* does not identify a process.

The argument *current-group* is a flag that makes a difference when you are running a job-control shell as an Emacs subprocess. If it is non-nil, then the signal is sent to the current process-group of the terminal that Emacs uses to communicate with the subprocess. If the process is a job-control shell, this means the shell's current subjob. If it is nil, the signal is sent to the process group of the immediate subprocess of Emacs. If the subprocess is a job-control shell, this is the shell itself.

The flag *current-group* has no effect when a pipe is used to communicate with the subprocess, because the operating system does not support the distinction in the case of pipes. For the same reason, job-control shells won't work when a pipe is used. See process-connection-type in Section 33.4 [Asynchronous Processes], page 234.

interrupt-process &optional *process-name*   Function
   current-group
  This function interrupts the process *process-name* by sending the signal SIGINT. Outside of Emacs, typing the "interrupt character" (normally C-c on some systems, and DEL on others) sends this signal. When the argument *current-group* is non-nil, you can think of this function as "typing C-c" on the terminal by which Emacs talks to the subprocess.

kill-process &optional *process-name current-group*   Function

This function kills the process *process-name* by sending the signal SIGKILL. This signal kills the subprocess immediately, and cannot be handled by the subprocess.

quit-process &optional *process-name current-group*   Function

This function sends the signal SIGQUIT to the process *process-name*. This signal is the one sent by the "quit character" (usually C-b or C-\) when you are not inside Emacs.

stop-process &optional *process-name current-group*   Function

This function stops the process *process-name* by sending the signal SIGTSTP. Use continue-process to resume its execution.

On systems with job control, the "stop character" (usually C-z) sends this signal (outside of Emacs). When *current-group* is non-nil, you can think of this function as "typing C-z" on the terminal Emacs uses to communicate with the subprocess.

continue-process &optional *process-name*   Function
    current-group

This function resumes execution of the process *process* by sending it the signal SIGCONT. This presumes that *process-name* was stopped previously.

signal-process *pid signal*   Function

This function sends a signal to process *pid*, which need not be a child of Emacs. The argument *signal* specifies which signal to send; it should be an integer.

33.9 Receiving Output from Processes

There are two ways to receive the output that a subprocess writes to its standard output stream. The output can be inserted in a buffer, which is called the associated buffer of the process, or a function called the *filter function* can be called to act on the output. If the process has no buffer and no filter function, its output is discarded.

33.9.1 Process Buffers

A process can (and usually does) have an *associated buffer*, which is an ordinary Emacs buffer that is used for two purposes: storing the output from the process, and deciding when to kill the process. You can also use the buffer to identify a process to operate on, since in normal practice only one process is associated with any given buffer. Many applications of processes also use the buffer for editing input to be sent to the process, but this is not built into Emacs Lisp.

Unless the process has a filter function (see Section 33.9.2 [Filter Functions], page 242), its output is inserted in the associated buffer. The position to insert the output is determined by the `process-mark`, which is then updated to point to the end of the text just inserted. Usually, but not always, the `process-mark` is at the end of the buffer.

process-buffer *process*   Function
> This function returns the associated buffer of the process *process*.
>
> ```
> (process-buffer (get-process "shell"))
>     ⇒ #<buffer *shell*>
> ```

process-mark *process*   Function
> This function returns the process marker for *process*, which is the marker that says where to insert output from the process.
>
> If *process* does not have a buffer, `process-mark` returns a marker that points nowhere.
>
> Insertion of process output in a buffer uses this marker to decide where to insert, and updates it to point after the inserted text. That is why successive batches of output are inserted consecutively.
>
> Filter functions normally should use this marker in the same fashion as is done by direct insertion of output in the buffer. A good example of a filter function that uses `process-mark` is found at the end of the following section.
>
> When the user is expected to enter input in the process buffer for transmission to the process, the process marker is useful for distinguishing the new input from previous output.

set-process-buffer *process buffer*   Function
> This function sets the buffer associated with *process* to *buffer*. If *buffer* is `nil`, the process becomes associated with no buffer.

get-buffer-process *buffer-or-name*   Function
> This function returns the process associated with *buffer-or-name*. If there are several processes associated with it, then one is chosen. (Presently, the one chosen is the one most recently created.) It is usually a bad idea to have more than one process associated with the same buffer.
>
> ```
> (get-buffer-process "*shell*")
>     ⇒ #<process shell>
> ```

Killing the process's buffer deletes the process, which kills the subprocess with a `SIGHUP` signal (see Section 33.8 [Signals to Processes], page 239).

33.9.2 Process Filter Functions

A process *filter function* is a function that receives the standard output from the associated process. If a process has a filter, then *all* output from that process is passed to the filter. The process buffer is used directly for output from the process only when there is no filter.

A filter function must accept two arguments: the associated process and a string, which is the output. The function is then free to do whatever it chooses with the output.

A filter function runs only while Emacs is waiting (e.g., for terminal input, or for time to elapse, or for process output). This avoids the timing errors that could result from running filters at random places in the middle of other Lisp programs. You may explicitly cause Emacs to wait, so that filter functions will run, by calling `sit-for` or `sleep-for` (see Section 18.7 [Waiting], page 303, vol. 1), or `accept-process-output` (see Section 33.9.3 [Accepting Output], page 244). Emacs is also waiting when the command loop is reading input.

Quitting is normally inhibited within a filter function—otherwise, the effect of typing `C-g` at command level or to quit a user command would be unpredictable. If you want to permit quitting inside a filter function, bind `inhibit-quit` to `nil`. See Section 18.8 [Quitting], page 305, vol. 1.

If an error happens during execution of a filter function, it is caught automatically, so that it doesn't stop the execution of whatever program was running when the filter function was started. However, if `debug-on-error` is non-`nil`, the error-catching is turned off. This makes it possible to use the Lisp debugger to debug the filter function. See Section 15.1 [Debugger], page 205, vol. 1.

Many filter functions sometimes or always insert the text in the process's buffer, mimicking the actions of Emacs when there is no filter. Such filter functions need to use `set-buffer` in order to be sure to insert in that buffer. To avoid setting the current buffer semipermanently, these filter functions must use `unwind-protect` to make sure to restore the previous current buffer. They should also update the process marker, and in some cases update the value of point. Here is how to do these things:

```
(defun ordinary-insertion-filter (proc string)
  (let ((old-buffer (current-buffer)))
    (unwind-protect
        (let (moving)
          (set-buffer (process-buffer proc))
          (setq moving (= (point) (process-mark proc)))
```

```
              (save-excursion
                ;; Insert the text, moving the process-marker.
                (goto-char (process-mark proc))
                (insert string)
                (set-marker (process-mark proc) (point)))
            (if moving (goto-char (process-mark proc))))
        (set-buffer old-buffer)))))
```

The reason to use an explicit `unwind-protect` rather than letting `save-excursion` restore the current buffer is so as to preserve the change in point made by `goto-char`.

To make the filter force the process buffer to be visible whenever new text arrives, insert the following line just before the `unwind-protect`:

```
(display-buffer (process-buffer proc))
```

To force point to move to the end of the new output no matter where it was previously, eliminate the variable `moving` and call `goto-char` unconditionally.

In earlier Emacs versions, every filter function that did regexp searching or matching had to explicitly save and restore the match data. Now Emacs does this automatically; filter functions never need to do it explicitly. See Section 30.6 [Match Data], page 204.

A filter function that writes the output into the buffer of the process should check whether the buffer is still alive. If it tries to insert into a dead buffer, it will get an error. If the buffer is dead, `(buffer-name (process-buffer` *process*`))` returns `nil`.

The output to the function may come in chunks of any size. A program that produces the same output twice in a row may send it as one batch of 200 characters one time, and five batches of 40 characters the next.

set-process-filter *process filter*   Function
> This function gives *process* the filter function *filter*. If *filter* is `nil`, it gives the process no filter.

process-filter *process*   Function
> This function returns the filter function of *process*, or `nil` if it has none.

> Here is an example of use of a filter function:
> ```
> (defun keep-output (process output)
>   (setq kept (cons output kept)))
>      ⇒ keep-output
> (setq kept nil)
>      ⇒ nil
> (set-process-filter (get-process "shell") 'keep-output)
>      ⇒ keep-output
> ```

```
(process-send-string "shell" "ls ~/other\n")
     ⇒ nil
kept
     ⇒ ("lewis@slug[8] % "
"FINAL-W87-SHORT.MSS    backup.otl          kolstad.mss~
address.txt            backup.psf          kolstad.psf
backup.bib~            david.mss           resume-Dec-86.mss~
backup.err             david.psf           resume-Dec.psf
backup.mss             dland               syllabus.mss
"
"#backups.mss#          backup.mss~         kolstad.mss
")
```

33.9.3 Accepting Output from Processes

Output from asynchronous subprocesses normally arrives only while
Emacs is waiting for some sort of external event, such as elapsed time or
terminal input. Occasionally it is useful in a Lisp program to explicitly permit output to arrive at a specific point, or even to wait until output arrives
from a process.

accept-process-output &optional *process seconds*   Function
        millisec
    This function allows Emacs to read pending output from processes.
    The output is inserted in the associated buffers or given to their filter
    functions. If *process* is non-`nil` then this function does not return
    until some output has been received from *process*.

    The arguments *seconds* and *millisec* let you specify timeout periods.
    The former specifies a period measured in seconds and the latter speci-
    fies one measured in milliseconds. The two time periods thus specified
    are added together, and `accept-process-output` returns after that
    much time whether or not there has been any subprocess output.

    The argument *seconds* need not be an integer. If it is a floating point
    number, this function waits for a fractional number of seconds. Some
    systems support only a whole number of seconds; on these systems,
    seconds is rounded down. If the system doesn't support waiting frac-
    tions of a second, you get an error if you specify nonzero *millisec*.

    Not all operating systems support waiting periods other than multiples
    of a second; on those that do not, you get an error if you specify nonzero
    millisec.

    The function `accept-process-output` returns non-`nil` if it did get
    some output, or `nil` if the timeout expired before output arrived.

33.10 Sentinels: Detecting Process Status Changes

A *process sentinel* is a function that is called whenever the associated process changes status for any reason, including signals (whether sent by Emacs or caused by the process's own actions) that terminate, stop, or continue the process. The process sentinel is also called if the process exits. The sentinel receives two arguments: the process for which the event occurred, and a string describing the type of event.

The string describing the event looks like one of the following:

- `"finished\n"`.
- `"exited abnormally with code` *exitcode*`\n"`.
- `"`*name-of-signal*`\n"`.
- `"`*name-of-signal* `(core dumped)\n"`.

A sentinel runs only while Emacs is waiting (e.g., for terminal input, or for time to elapse, or for process output). This avoids the timing errors that could result from running them at random places in the middle of other Lisp programs. A program can wait, so that sentinels will run, by calling `sit-for` or `sleep-for` (see Section 18.7 [Waiting], page 303, vol. 1), or `accept-process-output` (see Section 33.9.3 [Accepting Output], page 244). Emacs is also waiting when the command loop is reading input.

Quitting is normally inhibited within a sentinel—otherwise, the effect of typing `C-g` at command level or to quit a user command would be unpredictable. If you want to permit quitting inside a sentinel, bind `inhibit-quit` to `nil`. See Section 18.8 [Quitting], page 305, vol. 1.

A sentinel that writes the output into the buffer of the process should check whether the buffer is still alive. If it tries to insert into a dead buffer, it will get an error. If the buffer is dead, `(buffer-name (process-buffer` *process*`))` returns `nil`.

If an error happens during execution of a sentinel, it is caught automatically, so that it doesn't stop the execution of whatever programs was running when the sentinel was started. However, if `debug-on-error` is non-`nil`, the error-catching is turned off. This makes it possible to use the Lisp debugger to debug the sentinel. See Section 15.1 [Debugger], page 205, vol. 1.

In earlier Emacs versions, every sentinel that did regexp searching or matching had to explicitly save and restore the match data. Now Emacs does this automatically; sentinels never need to do it explicitly. See Section 30.6 [Match Data], page 204.

set-process-sentinel *process sentinel*   Function
   This function associates *sentinel* with *process*. If *sentinel* is `nil`, then the process will have no sentinel. The default behavior when there is no sentinel is to insert a message in the process's buffer when the process status changes.

```
(defun msg-me (process event)
   (princ
     (format "Process: %s had the event '%s'" process event)))
(set-process-sentinel (get-process "shell") 'msg-me)
      ⇒ msg-me
(kill-process (get-process "shell"))
         ⊣ Process: #<process shell> had the event 'killed'
         ⇒ #<process shell>
```

process-sentinel *process*   Function
    This function returns the sentinel of *process*, or `nil` if it has none.

waiting-for-user-input-p   Function
    While a sentinel or filter function is running, this function returns non-`nil` if Emacs was waiting for keyboard input from the user at the time the sentinel or filter function was called, `nil` if it was not.

33.11 Transaction Queues

You can use a *transaction queue* for more convenient communication with subprocesses using transactions. First use `tq-create` to create a transaction queue communicating with a specified process. Then you can call `tq-enqueue` to send a transaction.

tq-create *process*   Function
    This function creates and returns a transaction queue communicating with *process*. The argument *process* should be a subprocess capable of sending and receiving streams of bytes. It may be a child process, or it may be a TCP connection to a server, possibly on another machine.

tq-enqueue *queue question regexp closure fn*   Function
    This function sends a transaction to queue *queue*. Specifying the queue has the effect of specifying the subprocess to talk to.

    The argument *question* is the outgoing message that starts the transaction. The argument *fn* is the function to call when the corresponding answer comes back; it is called with two arguments: *closure*, and the answer received.

    The argument *regexp* is a regular expression that should match the entire answer, but nothing less; that's how `tq-enqueue` determines where the answer ends.

    The return value of `tq-enqueue` itself is not meaningful.

tq-close *queue*   Function
    Shut down transaction queue *queue*, waiting for all pending transactions to complete, and then terminate the connection or child process.

Transaction queues are implemented by means of a filter function. See Section 33.9.2 [Filter Functions], page 242.

33.12 Network Connections

Emacs Lisp programs can open TCP network connections to other processes on the same machine or other machines. A network connection is handled by Lisp much like a subprocess, and is represented by a process object. However, the process you are communicating with is not a child of the Emacs process, so you can't kill it or send it signals. All you can do is send and receive data. `delete-process` closes the connection, but does not kill the process at the other end; that process must decide what to do about closure of the connection.

You can distinguish process objects representing network connections from those representing subprocesses with the `process-status` function. It always returns either `open` or `closed` for a network connection, and it never returns either of those values for a real subprocess. See Section 33.6 [Process Information], page 236.

open-network-stream *name buffer-or-name host*   Function
        service

This function opens a TCP connection for a service to a host. It returns a process object to represent the connection.

The *name* argument specifies the name for the process object. It is modified as necessary to make it unique.

The *buffer-or-name* argument is the buffer to associate with the connection. Output from the connection is inserted in the buffer, unless you specify a filter function to handle the output. If *buffer-or-name* is `nil`, it means that the connection is not associated with any buffer.

The arguments *host* and *service* specify where to connect to; *host* is the host name (a string), and *service* is the name of a defined network service (a string) or a port number (an integer).

34 Operating System Interface

This chapter is about starting and getting out of Emacs, access to values in the operating system environment, and terminal input, output, and flow control.

See Section B.1 [Building Emacs], page 323, for related information. See also Chapter 35 [Display], page 275, for additional operating system status information pertaining to the terminal and the screen.

34.1 Starting Up Emacs

This section describes what Emacs does when it is started, and how you can customize these actions.

34.1.1 Summary: Sequence of Actions at Start Up

The order of operations performed (in 'startup.el') by Emacs when it is started up is as follows:

1. It loads the initialization library for the window system, if you are using a window system. This library's name is 'term/*windowsystem*-win.el'.

2. It processes the initial options. (Some of them are handled even earlier than this.)

3. It initializes the X window frame and faces, if appropriate.

4. It runs the normal hook before-init-hook.

5. It loads the library 'site-start', unless the option '-no-site-file' was specified. The library's file name is usually 'site-start.el'.

6. It loads the file '~/.emacs' unless '-q' was specified on the command line. (This is not done in '-batch' mode.) The '-u' option can specify the user name whose home directory should be used instead of '~'.

7. It loads the library 'default' unless inhibit-default-init is non-nil. (This is not done in '-batch' mode or if '-q' was specified on the command line.) The library's file name is usually 'default.el'.

8. It runs the normal hook after-init-hook.

9. It sets the major mode according to initial-major-mode, provided the buffer '*scratch*' is still current and still in Fundamental mode.

10. It loads the terminal-specific Lisp file, if any, except when in batch mode or using a window system.

11. It displays the initial echo area message, unless you have suppressed that with inhibit-startup-echo-area-message.

12. It processes the action arguments from the command line.

13. It runs `term-setup-hook`.

14. It calls `frame-notice-user-settings`, which modifies the parameters of the selected frame according to whatever the init files specify.

15. It runs `window-setup-hook`. See Section 35.16 [Window Systems], page 297.

16. It displays copyleft, nonwarranty, and basic use information, provided there were no remaining command line arguments (a few steps above) and the value of `inhibit-startup-message` is `nil`.

inhibit-startup-message   User Option

This variable inhibits the initial startup messages (the nonwarranty, etc.). If it is non-`nil`, then the messages are not printed.

This variable exists so you can set it in your personal init file, once you are familiar with the contents of the startup message. Do not set this variable in the init file of a new user, or in a way that affects more than one user, because that would prevent new users from receiving the information they are supposed to see.

inhibit-startup-echo-area-message   User Option

This variable controls the display of the startup echo area message. You can suppress the startup echo area message by adding text with this form to your '.emacs' file:

```
(setq inhibit-startup-echo-area-message
      "your-login-name")
```

Simply setting `inhibit-startup-echo-area-message` to your login name is not sufficient to inhibit the message; Emacs explicitly checks whether '.emacs' contains an expression as shown above. Your login name must appear in the expression as a Lisp string constant.

This way, you can easily inhibit the message for yourself if you wish, but thoughtless copying of your '.emacs' file will not inhibit the message for someone else.

34.1.2 The Init File: '.emacs'

When you start Emacs, it normally attempts to load the file '.emacs' from your home directory. This file, if it exists, must contain Lisp code. It is called your *init file*. The command line switches '-q' and '-u' affect the use of the init file; '-q' says not to load an init file, and '-u' says to load a specified user's init file instead of yours. See section "Entering Emacs" in *The GNU Emacs Manual*.

A site may have a *default init file*, which is the library named 'default.el'. Emacs finds the 'default.el' file through the standard search path for libraries (see Section 13.1 [How Programs Do Loading], page 183, vol. 1). The Emacs distribution does not come with this file; sites may provide one for local customizations. If the default init file exists, it is loaded whenever you start Emacs, except in batch mode or if '-q' is specified. But your own personal init file, if any, is loaded first; if it sets `inhibit-default-init` to a non-`nil` value, then Emacs does not subsequently load the 'default.el' file.

Another file for site-customization is 'site-start.el'. Emacs loads this *before* the user's init file. You can inhibit the loading of this file with the option '-no-site-file'.

site-run-file   *Variable*
> This variable specifies the site-customization file to load before the user's init file. Its normal value is `"site-start"`.

If there is a great deal of code in your '.emacs' file, you should move it into another file named '*something*.el', byte-compile it (see Chapter 14 [Byte Compilation], page 193, vol. 1), and make your '.emacs' file load the other file using `load` (see Chapter 13 [Loading], page 183, vol. 1).

See section "Init File Examples" in *The GNU Emacs Manual*, for examples of how to make various commonly desired customizations in your '.emacs' file.

inhibit-default-init   *User Option*
> This variable prevents Emacs from loading the default initialization library file for your session of Emacs. If its value is non-`nil`, then the default library is not loaded. The default value is `nil`.

before-init-hook   *Variable*
after-init-hook   *Variable*
> These two normal hooks are run just before, and just after, loading of the user's init file, 'default.el', and/or 'site-start.el'.

34.1.3 Terminal-Specific Initialization

Each terminal type can have its own Lisp library that Emacs loads when run on that type of terminal. For a terminal type named *termtype*, the library is called '`term/`*termtype*'. Emacs finds the file by searching the `load-path` directories as it does for other files, and trying the '.elc' and '.el' suffixes. Normally, terminal-specific Lisp library is located in 'emacs/lisp/term', a subdirectory of the 'emacs/lisp' directory in which most Emacs Lisp libraries are kept.

The library's name is constructed by concatenating the value of the variable `term-file-prefix` and the terminal type. Normally, `term-file-prefix` has the value `"term/"`; changing this is not recommended.

252   GNU Emacs Lisp Reference Manual: Volume 2

The usual function of a terminal-specific library is to enable special keys to send sequences that Emacs can recognize. It may also need to set or add to `function-key-map` if the Termcap entry does not specify all the terminal's function keys. See Section 34.8 [Terminal Input], page 265.

When the name of the terminal type contains a hyphen, only the part of the name before the first hyphen is significant in choosing the library name. Thus, terminal types 'aaa-48' and 'aaa-30-rv' both use the 'term/aaa' library. If necessary, the library can evaluate (`getenv "TERM"`) to find the full name of the terminal type.

Your '.emacs' file can prevent the loading of the terminal-specific library by setting the variable `term-file-prefix` to `nil`. This feature is useful when experimenting with your own peculiar customizations.

You can also arrange to override some of the actions of the terminal-specific library by setting the variable `term-setup-hook`. This is a normal hook which Emacs runs using `run-hooks` at the end of Emacs initialization, after loading both your '.emacs' file and any terminal-specific libraries. You can use this variable to define initializations for terminals that do not have their own libraries. See Section 20.4 [Hooks], page 360, vol. 1.

term-file-prefix   Variable
> If the `term-file-prefix` variable is non-`nil`, Emacs loads a terminal-specific initialization file as follows:
>
>   (load (concat term-file-prefix (getenv "TERM")))
>
> You may set the `term-file-prefix` variable to `nil` in your '.emacs' file if you do not wish to load the terminal-initialization file. To do this, put the following in your '.emacs' file: (`setq term-file-prefix nil`).

term-setup-hook   Variable
> This variable is a normal hook that Emacs runs after loading your '.emacs' file, the default initialization file (if any) and the terminal-specific Lisp file.
>
> You can use `term-setup-hook` to override the definitions made by a terminal-specific file.

See `window-setup-hook` in Section 35.16 [Window Systems], page 297, for a related feature.

34.1.4 Command Line Arguments

You can use command line arguments to request various actions when you start Emacs. Since you do not need to start Emacs more than once per day, and will often leave your Emacs session running longer than that, command line arguments are hardly ever used. As a practical matter, it is best to avoid making the habit of using them, since this habit would encourage you to kill and restart Emacs unnecessarily often. These options exist for two reasons: to be compatible with other editors (for invocation by other programs) and to enable shell scripts to run specific Lisp programs.

This section describes how Emacs processes command line arguments, and how you can customize them.

command-line   Function

This function parses the command line that Emacs was called with, processes it, loads the user's '.emacs' file and displays the startup messages.

command-line-processed   Variable

The value of this variable is t once the command line has been processed.

If you redump Emacs by calling dump-emacs, you may wish to set this variable to nil first in order to cause the new dumped Emacs to process its new command line arguments.

command-switch-alist   Variable

The value of this variable is an alist of user-defined command-line options and associated handler functions. This variable exists so you can add elements to it.

A *command line option* is an argument on the command line of the form:

    -option

The elements of the command-switch-alist look like this:

    (*option* . *handler-function*)

The *handler-function* is called to handle *option* and receives the option name as its sole argument.

In some cases, the option is followed in the command line by an argument. In these cases, the *handler-function* can find all the remaining command-line arguments in the variable command-line-args-left. (The entire list of command-line arguments is in command-line-args.)

The command line arguments are parsed by the command-line-1 function in the 'startup.el' file. See also section "Command Line Switches and Arguments" in *The GNU Emacs Manual*.

command-line-args   Variable

The value of this variable is the list of command line arguments passed to Emacs.

command-line-functions Variable

This variable's value is a list of functions for handling an unrecognized command-line argument. Each time the next argument to be processed has no special meaning, the functions in this list are called, in order of appearance, until one of them returns a non-`nil` value.

These functions are called with no arguments. They can access the command-line argument under consideration through the variable `argi`. The remaining arguments (not including the current one) are in the variable `command-line-args-left`.

When a function recognizes and processes the argument in `argi`, it should return a non-`nil` value to say it has dealt with that argument. If it has also dealt with some of the following arguments, it can indicate that by deleting them from `command-line-args-left`.

If all of these functions return `nil`, then the argument is used as a file name to visit.

34.2 Getting Out of Emacs

There are two ways to get out of Emacs: you can kill the Emacs job, which exits permanently, or you can suspend it, which permits you to reenter the Emacs process later. As a practical matter, you seldom kill Emacs—only when you are about to log out. Suspending is much more common.

34.2.1 Killing Emacs

Killing Emacs means ending the execution of the Emacs process. The parent process normally resumes control. The low-level primitive for killing Emacs is `kill-emacs`.

kill-emacs &optional *exit-data* Function

This function exits the Emacs process and kills it.

If *exit-data* is an integer, then it is used as the exit status of the Emacs process. (This is useful primarily in batch operation; see Section 34.12 [Batch Mode], page 272.)

If *exit-data* is a string, its contents are stuffed into the terminal input buffer so that the shell (or whatever program next reads input) can read them.

All the information in the Emacs process, aside from files that have been saved, is lost when the Emacs is killed. Because killing Emacs inadvertently can lose a lot of work, Emacs queries for confirmation before actually terminating if you have buffers that need saving or subprocesses that are running. This is done in the function `save-buffers-kill-emacs`.

kill-emacs-query-functions   Variable

> After asking the standard questions, `save-buffers-kill-emacs` calls
> the functions in the list `kill-buffer-query-functions`, in order of
> appearance, with no arguments. These functions can ask for additional
> confirmation from the user. If any of them returns non-`nil`, Emacs is
> not killed.

kill-emacs-hook   Variable

> This variable is a normal hook; once `save-buffers-kill-emacs` is
> finished with all file saving and confirmation, it runs the functions in
> this hook.

34.2.2 Suspending Emacs

Suspending Emacs means stopping Emacs temporarily and returning control to its superior process, which is usually the shell. This allows you to resume editing later in the same Emacs process, with the same buffers, the same kill ring, the same undo history, and so on. To resume Emacs, use the appropriate command in the parent shell—most likely `fg`.

Some operating systems do not support suspension of jobs; on these systems, "suspension" actually creates a new shell temporarily as a subprocess of Emacs. Then you would exit the shell to return to Emacs.

Suspension is not useful with window systems such as X, because the Emacs job may not have a parent that can resume it again, and in any case you can give input to some other job such as a shell merely by moving to a different window. Therefore, suspending is not allowed when Emacs is an X client.

suspend-emacs *string*   Function

> This function stops Emacs and returns control to the superior process.
> If and when the superior process resumes Emacs, `suspend-emacs` re-
> turns `nil` to its caller in Lisp.
>
> If *string* is non-`nil`, its characters are sent to be read as terminal input
> by Emacs's superior shell. The characters in *string* are not echoed by
> the superior shell; only the results appear.
>
> Before suspending, `suspend-emacs` runs the normal hook `suspend-hook`. In Emacs version 18, `suspend-hook` was not a normal hook; its
> value was a single function, and if its value was non-`nil`, then `suspend-emacs` returned immediately without actually suspending anything.
>
> After the user resumes Emacs, `suspend-emacs` runs the normal hook
> `suspend-resume-hook`. See Section 20.4 [Hooks], page 360, vol. 1.
>
> The next redisplay after resumption will redraw the entire screen, un-
> less the variable `no-redraw-on-reenter` is non-`nil` (see Section 35.1
> [Refresh Screen], page 275).

In the following example, note that 'pwd' is not echoed after Emacs is
suspended. But it is read and executed by the shell.

```
(suspend-emacs)
     ⇒ nil

(add-hook 'suspend-hook
          (function (lambda ()
                         (or (y-or-n-p
                              "Really suspend? ")
                             (error "Suspend cancelled")))))
     ⇒ (lambda nil
         (or (y-or-n-p "Really suspend? ")
             (error "Suspend cancelled")))
(add-hook 'suspend-resume-hook
          (function (lambda () (message "Resumed!"))))
     ⇒ (lambda nil (message "Resumed!"))
(suspend-emacs "pwd")
     ⇒ nil
---------- Buffer: Minibuffer ----------
Really suspend? y
---------- Buffer: Minibuffer ----------

---------- Parent Shell ----------
lewis@slug[23] % /user/lewis/manual
lewis@slug[24] % fg

---------- Echo Area ----------
Resumed!
```

suspend-hook   Variable
    This variable is a normal hook run before suspending.

suspend-resume-hook   Variable
    This variable is a normal hook run after suspending.

34.3 Operating System Environment

Emacs provides access to variables in the operating system environment
through various functions. These variables include the name of the system,
the user's UID, and so on.

system-type   Variable
    The value of this variable is a symbol indicating the type of operating
    system Emacs is operating on. Here is a table of the possible values:

    aix-v3   AIX.

    berkeley-unix
                Berkeley BSD.

    dgux   Data General DGUX operating system.

    gnu   A GNU system using the GNU HURD and Mach.

hpux   Hewlett-Packard HPUX operating system.

irix   Silicon Graphics Irix system.

linux   A GNU system using the Linux kernel.

ms-dos   Microsoft MS-DOS "operating system."

next-mach
            NeXT Mach-based system.

rtu   Masscomp RTU, UCB universe.

unisoft-unix
            UniSoft UniPlus.

usg-unix-v
            AT&T System V.

vax-vms   VAX VMS.

windows-nt
            Microsoft windows NT.

xenix   SCO Xenix 386.

We do not wish to add new symbols to make finer distinctions unless it
is absolutely necessary! In fact, we hope to eliminate some of these alternatives in the future. We recommend using `system-configuration`
to distinguish between different operating systems.

system-configuration   Variable
   This variable holds the three-part configuration name for the hard-
   ware/software configuration of your system, as a string. The convenient way to test parts of this string is with `string-match`.

system-name   Function
   This function returns the name of the machine you are running on.

```
(system-name)
   ⇒ "prep.ai.mit.edu"
```

   The symbol `system-name` is a variable as well as a function. In fact, the
function returns whatever value the variable `system-name` currently holds.
Thus, you can set the variable `system-name` in case Emacs is confused about
the name of your system. The variable is also useful for constructing frame
titles (see Section 26.4 [Frame Titles], page 105).

mail-host-address   Variable
   If this variable is non-`nil`, it is used instead of `system-name` for purposes of generating email addresses. For example, it is used when constructing the default value of `user-mail-address`. See Section 34.4

[User Identification], page 259. (Since this is done when Emacs starts up, the value actually used is the one saved when Emacs was dumped. See Section B.1 [Building Emacs], page 323.)

getenv *var*   Function

This function returns the value of the environment variable *var*, as a string. Within Emacs, the environment variable values are kept in the Lisp variable `process-environment`.

```
(getenv "USER")
     ⇒ "lewis"

lewis@slug[10] % printenv
PATH=.:/user/lewis/bin:/usr/bin:/usr/local/bin
USER=lewis
TERM=ibmapa16
SHELL=/bin/csh
HOME=/user/lewis
```

setenv *variable value*   Command

This command sets the value of the environment variable named *variable* to *value*. Both arguments should be strings. This function works by modifying `process-environment`; binding that variable with `let` is also reasonable practice.

process-environment   Variable

This variable is a list of strings, each describing one environment variable. The functions `getenv` and `setenv` work by means of this variable.

```
process-environment
⇒ ("l=/usr/stanford/lib/gnuemacs/lisp"
    "PATH=.:/user/lewis/bin:/usr/class:/nfsusr/local/bin"
    "USER=lewis"
    "TERM=ibmapa16"
    "SHELL=/bin/csh"
    "HOME=/user/lewis")
```

path-separator   Variable

This variable holds a string which says which character separates directories in a search path (as found in an environment variable). Its value is `":"` for Unix and GNU systems, and `";"` for MS-DOS and Windows NT.

invocation-name   Variable

This variable holds the program name under which Emacs was invoked. The value is a string, and does not include a directory name.

invocation-directory   Variable

This variable holds the directory from which the Emacs executable was invoked, or perhaps `nil` if that directory cannot be determined.

installation-directory   *Variable*
If non-`nil`, this is a directory within which to look for the 'lib-src'
and 'etc' subdirectories. This is non-`nil` when Emacs can't find those
directories in their standard installed locations, but can find them in a
directory related somehow to the one containing the Emacs executable.

load-average   *Function*
This function returns the current 1-minute, 5-minute and 15-minute
load averages in a list. The values are integers that are 100 times
the system load averages. (The load averages indicate the number of
processes trying to run.)

```
(load-average)
     ⇒ (169 48 36)

lewis@rocky[5] % uptime
 11:55am  up 1 day, 19:37,  3 users,
 load average: 1.69, 0.48, 0.36
```

emacs-pid   *Function*
This function returns the process ID of the Emacs process.

setprv *privilege-name* &optional *setp getprv*   *Function*
This function sets or resets a VMS privilege. (It does not exist on
Unix.) The first arg is the privilege name, as a string. The second
argument, *setp*, is `t` or `nil`, indicating whether the privilege is to be
turned on or off. Its default is `nil`. The function returns `t` if successful,
`nil` otherwise.

If the third argument, *getprv*, is non-`nil`, `setprv` does not change
the privilege, but returns `t` or `nil` indicating whether the privilege is
currently enabled.

34.4 User Identification

user-mail-address   *Variable*
This holds the nominal email address of the user who is using Emacs.
When Emacs starts up, it computes a default value that is usually
right, but users often set this themselves when the default value is not
right.

user-login-name &optional *uid*   *Function*
If you don't specify *uid*, this function returns the name under which
the user is logged in. If the environment variable `LOGNAME` is set, that
value is used. Otherwise, if the environment variable `USER` is set, that
value is used. Otherwise, the value is based on the effective UID, not
the real UID.

If you specify *uid*, the value is the user name that corresponds to *uid* (which should be an integer).

```
(user-login-name)
    ⇒ "lewis"
```

user-real-login-name   Function
This function returns the user name corresponding to Emacs's real UID. This ignores the effective UID and ignores the environment variables LOGNAME and USER.

user-full-name   Function
This function returns the full name of the user.

```
(user-full-name)
    ⇒ "Bil Lewis"
```

The symbols `user-login-name`, `user-real-login-name` and `user-full-name` are variables as well as functions. The functions return the same values that the variables hold. These variables allow you to "fake out" Emacs by telling the functions what to return. The variables are also useful for constructing frame titles (see Section 26.4 [Frame Titles], page 105).

user-real-uid   Function
This function returns the real UID of the user.

```
(user-real-uid)
    ⇒ 19
```

user-uid   Function
This function returns the effective UID of the user.

34.5 Time of Day

This section explains how to determine the current time and the time zone.

current-time-string &optional *time-value*   Function
This function returns the current time and date as a humanly-readable string. The format of the string is unvarying; the number of characters used for each part is always the same, so you can reliably use `substring` to extract pieces of it. It is wise to count the characters from the beginning of the string rather than from the end, as additional information may be added at the end.

The argument *time-value*, if given, specifies a time to format instead of the current time. The argument should be a list whose first two elements are integers. Thus, you can use times obtained from `current-`

time (see below) and from `file-attributes` (see Section 22.6.4 [File
Attributes], page 23).

>   (current-time-string)
>   ⇒ "Wed Oct 14 22:21:05 1987"

current-time   *Function*

This function returns the system's time value as a list of three integers:
(*high low microsec*). The integers *high* and *low* combine to give the
number of seconds since 0:00 January 1, 1970, which is $high*2^{16}+low$.

The third element, *microsec*, gives the microseconds since the start
of the current second (or 0 for systems that return time only on the
resolution of a second).

The first two elements can be compared with file time values such as
you get with the function `file-attributes`. See Section 22.6.4 [File
Attributes], page 23.

current-time-zone &optional *time-value*   *Function*

This function returns a list describing the time zone that the user is
in.

The value has the form (*offset name*). Here *offset* is an integer giving
the number of seconds ahead of UTC (east of Greenwich). A negative
value means west of Greenwich. The second element, *name* is a string
giving the name of the time zone. Both elements change when daylight
savings time begins or ends; if the user has specified a time zone that
does not use a seasonal time adjustment, then the value is constant
through time.

If the operating system doesn't supply all the information necessary
to compute the value, both elements of the list are `nil`.

The argument *time-value*, if given, specifies a time to analyze instead
of the current time. The argument should be a cons cell containing
two integers, or a list whose first two elements are integers. Thus,
you can use times obtained from `current-time` (see above) and from
`file-attributes` (see Section 22.6.4 [File Attributes], page 23).

34.6 Time Conversion

These functions convert time values (lists of two or three integers) to
strings or to calendrical information. There is also a function to convert
calendrical information to a time value. You can get time values from the
functions `current-time` (see Section 34.5 [Time of Day], page 260) and
`file-attributes` (see Section 22.6.4 [File Attributes], page 23).

format-time-string *format-string time*   Function
This function converts *time* to a string according to *format-string*.
The argument *format-string* may contain '%'-sequences which say to
substitute parts of the time. Here is a table of what the '%'-sequences
mean:

'%a'   This stands for the abbreviated name of the day of week.

'%A'   This stands for the full name of the day of week.

'%b'   This stands for the abbreviated name of the month.

'%B'   This stands for the full name of the month.

'%c'   This is a synonym for '%x %X'.

'%C'   This has a locale-specific meaning. In the default locale
              (named C), it is equivalent to '%A, %B %e, %Y'.

'%d'   This stands for the day of month, zero-padded.

'%D'   This is a synonym for '%m/%d/%y'.

'%e'   This stands for the day of month, blank-padded.

'%h'   This is a synonym for '%b'.

'%H'   This stands for the hour (00-23).

'%I'   This stands for the hour (00-12).

'%j'   This stands for the day of the year (001-366).

'%k'   This stands for the hour (0-23), blank padded.

'%l'   This stands for the hour (1-12), blank padded.

'%m'   This stands for the month (01-12).

'%M'   This stands for the minute (00-59).

'%n'   This stands for a newline.

'%p'   This stands for 'AM' or 'PM', as appropriate.

'%r'   This is a synonym for '%I:%M:%S %p'.

'%R'   This is a synonym for '%H:%M'.

'%S'   This stands for the seconds (00-60).

'%t'   This stands for a tab character.

'%T'   This is a synonym for '%H:%M:%S'.

'%U'   This stands for the week of the year (01-52), assuming
              that weeks start on Sunday.

'%w'   This stands for the numeric day of week (0-6). Sunday is
            day 0.

'%W'   This stands for the week of the year (01-52), assuming
            that weeks start on Monday.

'%x'   This has a locale-specific meaning. In the default locale
            (named C), it is equivalent to '%D'.

'%X'   This has a locale-specific meaning. In the default locale
            (named C), it is equivalent to '%T'.

'%y'   This stands for the year without century (00-99).

'%Y'   This stands for the year with century.

'%Z'   This stands for the time zone abbreviation.

decode-time *time*   Function
This function converts a time value into calendrical information. The
return value is a list of nine elements, as follows:

> (*seconds minutes hour day month year dow dst zone*)

Here is what the elements mean:

sec   The number of seconds past the minute, as an integer
            between 0 and 59.

minute   The number of minutes past the hour, as an integer be-
            tween 0 and 59.

hour   The hour of the day, as an integer between 0 and 23.

day   The day of the month, as an integer between 1 and 31.

month   The month of the year, as an integer between 1 and 12.

year   The year, an integer typically greater than 1900.

dow   The day of week, as an integer between 0 and 6, where 0
            stands for Sunday.

dst   t if daylight savings time is effect, otherwise `nil`.

zone   An integer indicating the time zone, as the number of sec-
            onds east of Greenwich.

Note that Common Lisp has different meanings for *dow* and *zone*.

encode-time *seconds minutes hour day month year*   Function
            &optional *zone*
This function is the inverse of `decode-time`. It converts seven items of
calendrical data into a time value. For the meanings of the arguments,
see the table above under `decode-time`.

Year numbers less than 100 are treated just like other year numbers. If you want them to stand for years above 1900, you must alter them yourself before you call `encode-time`.

The optional argument *zone* defaults to the current time zone and its daylight savings time rules. If specified, it can be either a list (as you would get from `current-time-zone`) or an integer (as you would get from `decode-time`). The specified zone is used without any further alteration for daylight savings time.

34.7 Timers for Delayed Execution

You can set up a timer to call a function at a specified future time.

run-at-time *time repeat function* &rest *args*   Function
This function arranges to call *function* with arguments *args* at time *time*. The argument *function* is a function to call later, and *args* are the arguments to give it when it is called. The time *time* is specified as a string.

Absolute times may be specified in a wide variety of formats; The form '*hour*:*min*:*sec timezone month*/*day*/*year*', where all fields are numbers, works; the format that `current-time-string` returns is also allowed.

To specify a relative time, use numbers followed by units. For example:

'1 min'   denotes 1 minute from now.

'1 min 5 sec'
             denotes 65 seconds from now.

'1 min 2 sec 3 hour 4 day 5 week 6 fortnight 7 month 8 year'
             denotes exactly 103 months, 123 days, and 10862 seconds from now.

If *time* is an integer, that specifies a relative time measured in seconds.

The argument *repeat* specifies how often to repeat the call. If *repeat* is `nil`, there are no repetitions; *function* is called just once, at *time*. If *repeat* is an integer, it specifies a repetition period measured in seconds. In any case, *repeat* has no effect on when *first* call takes place—*time* specifies that.

The function `run-at-time` returns a timer value that identifies the particular scheduled future action. You can use this value to call `cancel-timer`.

cancel-timer *timer*   Function
Cancel the requested action for *timer*, which should be a value previously returned by `run-at-time`. This cancels the effect of that call to

`run-at-time`; the arrival of the specified time will not cause anything special to happen.

34.8 Terminal Input

This section describes functions and variables for recording or manipulating terminal input. See Chapter 35 [Display], page 275, for related functions.

34.8.1 Input Modes

set-input-mode *interrupt flow meta quit-char*   Function
This function sets the mode for reading keyboard input. If *interrupt* is non-null, then Emacs uses input interrupts. If it is `nil`, then it uses CBREAK mode. When Emacs communicates directly with X, it ignores this argument and uses interrupts if that is the way it knows how to communicate.

If *flow* is non-`nil`, then Emacs uses XON/XOFF (`C-q`, `C-s`) flow control for output to the terminal. This has no effect except in CBREAK mode. See Section 34.11 [Flow Control], page 271.

The default setting is system dependent. Some systems always use CBREAK mode regardless of what is specified.

The argument *meta* controls support for input character codes above 127. If *meta* is `t`, Emacs converts characters with the 8th bit set into Meta characters. If *meta* is `nil`, Emacs disregards the 8th bit; this is necessary when the terminal uses it as a parity bit. If *meta* is neither `t` nor `nil`, Emacs uses all 8 bits of input unchanged. This is good for terminals using European 8-bit character sets.

If *quit-char* is non-`nil`, it specifies the character to use for quitting. Normally this character is `C-g`. See Section 18.8 [Quitting], page 305, vol. 1.

The `current-input-mode` function returns the input mode settings Emacs is currently using.

current-input-mode   Function
This function returns current mode for reading keyboard input. It returns a list, corresponding to the arguments of `set-input-mode`, of the form (*interrupt flow meta quit*) in which:

interrupt   is non-`nil` when Emacs is using interrupt-driven input. If `nil`, Emacs is using CBREAK mode.

flow   is non-`nil` if Emacs uses XON/XOFF (`C-q`, `C-s`) flow control for output to the terminal. This value has no effect unless *interrupt* is non-`nil`.

meta   is t if Emacs treats the eighth bit of input characters as
the meta bit; nil means Emacs clears the eighth bit of
every input character; any other value means Emacs uses
all eight bits as the basic character code.

quit   is the character Emacs currently uses for quitting, usually
C-g.

34.8.2 Translating Input Events

This section describes features for translating input events into other
input events before they become part of key sequences.

extra-keyboard-modifiers   Variable
This variable lets Lisp programs "press" the modifier keys on the keyboard. The value is a bit mask:

1   The SHIFT key.

2   The LOCK key.

4   The CTL key.

8   The META key.

Each time the user types a keyboard key, it is altered as if the modifier
keys specified in the bit mask were held down.

When using X windows, the program can "press" any of the modifier keys in this way. Otherwise, only the CTL and META keys can be
virtually pressed.

keyboard-translate-table   Variable
This variable is the translate table for keyboard characters. It lets you
reshuffle the keys on the keyboard without changing any command
bindings. Its value must be a string or nil.

If keyboard-translate-table is a string, then each character read
from the keyboard is looked up in this string and the character in the
string is used instead. If the string is of length n, character codes n
and up are untranslated.

In the example below, we set keyboard-translate-table to a string
of 128 characters. Then we fill it in to swap the characters C-s and
C-\ and the characters C-q and C-^. Subsequently, typing C-\ has
all the usual effects of typing C-s, and vice versa. (See Section 34.11
[Flow Control], page 271 for more information on this subject.)

```
(defun evade-flow-control ()
  "Replace C-s with C-\ and C-q with C-^."
  (interactive)
```

```
(let ((the-table (make-string 128 0)))
  (let ((i 0))
    (while (< i 128)
      (aset the-table i i)
      (setq i (1+ i))))
  ;; Swap C-s and C-\.
  (aset the-table ?\034 ?\^s)
  (aset the-table ?\^s ?\034)
  ;; Swap C-q and C-^.
  (aset the-table ?\036 ?\^q)
  (aset the-table ?\^q ?\036)
  (setq keyboard-translate-table the-table)))
```

Note that this translation is the first thing that happens to a character after it is read from the terminal. Record-keeping features such as `recent-keys` and dribble files record the characters after translation.

keyboard-translate *from to*   Function

This function modifies `keyboard-translate-table` to translate character code *from* into character code *to*. It creates or enlarges the translate table if necessary.

function-key-map   Variable

This variable holds a keymap that describes the character sequences sent by function keys on an ordinary character terminal. This keymap uses the same data structure as other keymaps, but is used differently: it specifies translations to make while reading events.

If `function-key-map` "binds" a key sequence *k* to a vector *v*, then when *k* appears as a subsequence *anywhere* in a key sequence, it is replaced with the events in *v*.

For example, VT100 terminals send ESC O P when the keypad PF1 key is pressed. Therefore, we want Emacs to translate that sequence of events into the single event pf1. We accomplish this by "binding" ESC O P to [pf1] in `function-key-map`, when using a VT100.

Thus, typing C-c PF1 sends the character sequence C-c ESC O P; later the function `read-key-sequence` translates this back into C-c PF1, which it returns as the vector [?\C-c pf1].

Entries in `function-key-map` are ignored if they conflict with bindings made in the minor mode, local, or global keymaps. The intent is that the character sequences that function keys send should not have command bindings in their own right.

The value of `function-key-map` is usually set up automatically according to the terminal's Terminfo or Termcap entry, but sometimes those need help from terminal-specific Lisp files. Emacs comes with terminal-specific files for many common terminals; their main purpose is to make entries in `function-key-map` beyond those that can be deduced from Termcap and Terminfo. See Section 34.1.3 [Terminal-Specific], page 251.

Emacs versions 18 and earlier used totally different means of detecting the character sequences that represent function keys.

key-translation-map   *Variable*
This variable is another keymap used just like `function-key-map` to translate input events into other events. It differs from `function-key-map` in two ways:

- `key-translation-map` goes to work after `function-key-map` is finished; it receives the results of translation by `function-key-map`.

- `key-translation-map` overrides actual key bindings.

The intent of `key-translation-map` is for users to map one character set to another, including ordinary characters normally bound to `self-insert-command`.

You can use `function-key-map` or `key-translation-map` for more than simple aliases, by using a function, instead of a key sequence, as the "translation" of a key. Then this function is called to compute the translation of that key.

The key translation function receives one argument, which is the prompt that was specified in `read-key-sequence`—or `nil` if the key sequence is being read by the editor command loop. In most cases you can ignore the prompt value.

If the function reads input itself, it can have the effect of altering the event that follows. For example, here's how to define C-c h to turn the character that follows into a Hyper character:

```
(defun hyperify (prompt)
  (let ((e (read-event)))
    (vector (if (numberp e)
                (logior (lsh 1 20) e)
              (if (memq 'hyper (event-modifiers e))
                  e
                (add-event-modifier "H-" e))))))

(defun add-event-modifier (string e)
  (let ((symbol (if (symbolp e) e (car e))))
    (setq symbol (intern (concat string
                                 (symbol-name symbol))))
```

```
(if (symbolp e)
    symbol
  (cons symbol (cdr e)))))
```

```
(define-key function-key-map "\C-ch" 'hyperify)
```

The 'iso-transl' library uses this feature to provide a way of inputting non-ASCII Latin-1 characters.

34.8.3 Recording Input

recent-keys   Function

This function returns a vector containing the last 100 input events from the keyboard or mouse. All input events are included, whether or not they were used as parts of key sequences. Thus, you always get the last 100 inputs, not counting keyboard macros. (Events from keyboard macros are excluded because they are less interesting for debugging; it should be enough to see the events that invoked the macros.)

open-dribble-file *filename*   Command

This function opens a *dribble file* named *filename*. When a dribble file is open, each input event from the keyboard or mouse (but not those from keyboard macros) is written in that file. A non-character event is expressed using its printed representation surrounded by '<...>'.

You close the dribble file by calling this function with an argument of `nil`.

This function is normally used to record the input necessary to trigger an Emacs bug, for the sake of a bug report.

```
(open-dribble-file "~/dribble")
    ⇒ nil
```

See also the `open-termscript` function (see Section 34.9 [Terminal Output], page 269).

34.9 Terminal Output

The terminal output functions send output to the terminal or keep track of output sent to the terminal. The variable `baud-rate` tells you what Emacs thinks is the output speed of the terminal.

baud-rate   Variable

This variable's value is the output speed of the terminal, as far as Emacs knows. Setting this variable does not change the speed of actual data transmission, but the value is used for calculations such as padding. It also affects decisions about whether to scroll part of the screen or repaint—even when using a window system. (We designed it this way despite the fact that a window system has no true "output speed", to give you a way to tune these decisions.)

The value is measured in baud.

If you are running across a network, and different parts of the network work at different baud rates, the value returned by Emacs may be different from the value used by your local terminal. Some network protocols communicate the local terminal speed to the remote machine, so that Emacs and other programs can get the proper value, but others do not. If Emacs has the wrong value, it makes decisions that are less than optimal. To fix the problem, set `baud-rate`.

baud-rate   Function

This function returns the value of the variable `baud-rate`. In Emacs versions 18 and earlier, this was the only way to find out the terminal speed.

send-string-to-terminal *string*   Function

This function sends *string* to the terminal without alteration. Control characters in *string* have terminal-dependent effects.

One use of this function is to define function keys on terminals that have downloadable function key definitions. For example, this is how on certain terminals to define function key 4 to move forward four characters (by transmitting the characters C-u C-f to the computer):

```
(send-string-to-terminal "\eF4\^U\^F")
     ⇒ nil
```

open-termscript *filename*   Command

This function is used to open a *termscript file* that will record all the characters sent by Emacs to the terminal. It returns `nil`. Termscript files are useful for investigating problems where Emacs garbles the screen, problems that are due to incorrect Termcap entries or to undesirable settings of terminal options more often than to actual Emacs bugs. Once you are certain which characters were actually output, you can determine reliably whether they correspond to the Termcap specifications in use.

See also `open-dribble-file` in Section 34.8 [Terminal Input], page 265.

```
(open-termscript "../junk/termscript")
     ⇒ nil
```

34.10 System-Specific X11 Keysyms

To define system-specific X11 keysyms, set the variable `system-key-alist`.

system-key-alist   *Variable*
This variable's value should be an alist with one element for each system-specific keysym. An element has this form: (*code* . *symbol*), where *code* is the numeric keysym code (not including the "vendor specific" bit, 1 << 28), and *symbol* is the name for the function key.

For example (`168` . `mute-acute`) defines a system-specific key used by HP X servers whose numeric code is (1 << 28) + 168.

It is not a problem if the alist defines keysyms for other X servers, as long as they don't conflict with the ones used by the X server actually in use.

The variable is always local to the current X terminal and cannot be buffer-local. See Section 26.2 [Multiple Displays], page 98.

34.11 Flow Control

This section attempts to answer the question "Why does Emacs choose to use flow-control characters in its command character set?" For a second view on this issue, read the comments on flow control in the 'emacs/INSTALL' file from the distribution; for help with Termcap entries and DEC terminal concentrators, see 'emacs/etc/TERMS'.

At one time, most terminals did not need flow control, and none used C-s and C-q for flow control. Therefore, the choice of C-s and C-q as command characters was uncontroversial. Emacs, for economy of keystrokes and portability, used nearly all the ASCII control characters, with mnemonic meanings when possible; thus, C-s for search and C-q for quote.

Later, some terminals were introduced which required these characters for flow control. They were not very good terminals for full-screen editing, so Emacs maintainers did not pay attention. In later years, flow control with C-s and C-q became widespread among terminals, but by this time it was usually an option. And the majority of users, who can turn flow control off, were unwilling to switch to less mnemonic key bindings for the sake of flow control.

So which usage is "right", Emacs's or that of some terminal and concentrator manufacturers? This question has no simple answer.

One reason why we are reluctant to cater to the problems caused by C-s and C-q is that they are gratuitous. There are other techniques (albeit less common in practice) for flow control that preserve transparency of the character stream. Note also that their use for flow control is not an official standard. Interestingly, on the model 33 teletype with a paper tape punch (which is very old), `C-s` and `C-q` were sent by the computer to turn the punch on and off!

As X servers and other window systems replace character-only terminals, this problem is gradually being cured. For the mean time, Emacs provides a convenient way of enabling flow control if you want it: call the function `enable-flow-control`.

enable-flow-control   Function

> This function enables use of `C-s` and `C-q` for output flow control, and provides the characters `C-\` and `C-^` as aliases for them using `keyboard-translate-table` (see Section 34.8.2 [Translating Input], page 266).

You can use the function `enable-flow-control-on` in your '.emacs' file to enable flow control automatically on certain terminal types.

enable-flow-control-on &rest *termtypes*   Function

> This function enables flow control, and the aliases `C-\` and `C-^`, if the terminal type is one of *termtypes*. For example:
>
>   (enable-flow-control-on "vt200" "vt300" "vt101" "vt131")

Here is how `enable-flow-control` does its job:

1. It sets CBREAK mode for terminal input, and tells the operating system to handle flow control, with `(set-input-mode nil t)`.

2. It sets up `keyboard-translate-table` to translate `C-\` and `C-^` into `C-s` and `C-q`. Except at its very lowest level, Emacs never knows that the characters typed were anything but `C-s` and `C-q`, so you can in effect type them as `C-\` and `C-^` even when they are input for other commands. See Section 34.8.2 [Translating Input], page 266.

If the terminal is the source of the flow control characters, then once you enable kernel flow control handling, you probably can make do with less padding than normal for that terminal. You can reduce the amount of padding by customizing the Termcap entry. You can also reduce it by setting `baud-rate` to a smaller value so that Emacs uses a smaller speed when calculating the padding needed. See Section 34.9 [Terminal Output], page 269.

34.12 Batch Mode

The command line option '-batch' causes Emacs to run noninteractively. In this mode, Emacs does not read commands from the terminal, it does not alter the terminal modes, and it does not expect to be outputting to an erasable screen. The idea is that you specify Lisp programs to run; when they are finished, Emacs should exit. The way to specify the programs to run is with '-l *file*', which loads the library named *file*, and '-f *function*', which calls *function* with no arguments.

Any Lisp program output that would normally go to the echo area, either using `message` or using `prin1`, etc., with `t` as the stream, goes instead to Emacs's standard error descriptor when in batch mode. Thus, Emacs behaves much like a noninteractive application program. (The echo area output that Emacs itself normally generates, such as command echoing, is suppressed entirely.)

noninteractive *Variable*
  This variable is non-`nil` when Emacs is running in batch mode.

35 Emacs Display

This chapter describes a number of features related to the display that Emacs presents to the user.

35.1 Refreshing the Screen

The function `redraw-frame` redisplays the entire contents of a given frame. See Chapter 26 [Frames], page 97.

redraw-frame *frame*   Function
    This function clears and redisplays frame *frame*.

Even more powerful is `redraw-display`:

redraw-display   Command
    This function clears and redisplays all visible frames.

Processing user input takes absolute priority over redisplay. If you call these functions when input is available, they do nothing immediately, but a full redisplay does happen eventually—after all the input has been processed.

Normally, suspending and resuming Emacs also refreshes the screen. Some terminal emulators record separate contents for display-oriented programs such as Emacs and for ordinary sequential display. If you are using such a terminal, you might want to inhibit the redisplay on resumption.

no-redraw-on-reenter   Variable
    This variable controls whether Emacs redraws the entire screen after it has been suspended and resumed. Non-`nil` means yes, `nil` means no.

35.2 Screen Size

The screen size functions access or specify the height or width of the terminal. When you are using multiple frames, they apply to the selected frame (see Chapter 26 [Frames], page 97).

screen-height   Function
    This function returns the number of lines on the screen that are available for display.

```
(screen-height)
     ⇒  50
```

screen-width   Function

This function returns the number of columns on the screen that are available for display.

```
(screen-width)
     ⇒ 80
```

set-screen-height *lines* &optional *not-actual-size*   Function

This function declares that the terminal can display *lines* lines. The sizes of existing windows are altered proportionally to fit.

If *not-actual-size* is non-nil, then Emacs displays *lines* lines of output, but does not change its value for the actual height of the screen. (Knowing the correct actual size may be necessary for correct cursor positioning.) Using a smaller height than the terminal actually implements may be useful to reproduce behavior observed on a smaller screen, or if the terminal malfunctions when using its whole screen.

If *lines* is different from what it was previously, then the entire screen is cleared and redisplayed using the new size.

This function returns nil.

set-screen-width *columns* &optional *not-actual-size*   Function

This function declares that the terminal can display *columns* columns. The details are as in set-screen-height.

35.3 Truncation

When a line of text extends beyond the right edge of a window, the line can either be continued on the next screen line, or truncated to one screen line. The additional screen lines used to display a long text line are called *continuation* lines. Normally, a '$' in the rightmost column of the window indicates truncation; a '\' on the rightmost column indicates a line that "wraps" or is continued onto the next line. (The display table can specify alternative indicators; see Section 35.14 [Display Tables], page 294.)

Note that continuation is different from filling; continuation happens on the screen only, not in the buffer contents, and it breaks a line precisely at the right margin, not at a word boundary. See Section 29.11 [Filling], page 160.

truncate-lines   User Option

This buffer-local variable controls how Emacs displays lines that extend beyond the right edge of the window. The default is nil, which specifies continuation. If the value is non-nil, then these lines are truncated.

If the variable `truncate-partial-width-windows` is non-`nil`, then truncation is always used for side-by-side windows (within one frame) regardless of the value of `truncate-lines`.

default-truncate-lines   User Option

This variable is the default value for `truncate-lines`, for buffers that do not have local values for it.

truncate-partial-width-windows   User Option

This variable controls display of lines that extend beyond the right edge of the window, in side-by-side windows (see Section 25.2 [Splitting Windows], page 70). If it is non-`nil`, these lines are truncated; otherwise, `truncate-lines` says what to do with them.

You can override the images that indicate continuation or truncation with the display table; see Section 35.14 [Display Tables], page 294.

If your buffer contains **very** long lines, and you use continuation to display them, just thinking about them can make Emacs redisplay slow. The column computation and indentation functions also become slow. Then you might find it advisable to set `cache-long-line-scans` to `t`.

cache-long-line-scans   Variable

If this variable is non-`nil`, various indentation and motion functions, and Emacs redisplay, cache the results of scanning the buffer, and consult the cache to avoid rescanning regions of the buffer unless they are modified.

Turning on the cache slows down processing of short lines somewhat.

This variable is automatically local in every buffer.

35.4 The Echo Area

The *echo area* is used for displaying messages made with the `message` primitive, and for echoing keystrokes. It is not the same as the minibuffer, despite the fact that the minibuffer appears (when active) in the same place on the screen as the echo area. The *GNU Emacs Manual* specifies the rules for resolving conflicts between the echo area and the minibuffer for use of that screen space (see section "The Minibuffer" in *The GNU Emacs Manual*). Error messages appear in the echo area; see Section 9.5.3 [Errors], page 128, vol. 1.

You can write output in the echo area by using the Lisp printing functions with `t` as the stream (see Section 16.5 [Output Functions], page 247, vol. 1), or as follows:

message *string* &rest *arguments*   Function
    This function displays a one-line message in the echo area. The argument *string* is similar to a C language `printf` control string. See `format` in Section 4.5 [String Conversion], page 62, vol. 1, for the details on the conversion specifications. `message` returns the constructed string.

    In batch mode, `message` prints the message text on the standard error stream, followed by a newline.

    If *string* is `nil`, `message` clears the echo area. If the minibuffer is active, this brings the minibuffer contents back onto the screen immediately.

```
(message "Minibuffer depth is %d."
         (minibuffer-depth))
 ⊣ Minibuffer depth is 0.
 ⇒ "Minibuffer depth is 0."

---------- Echo Area ----------
Minibuffer depth is 0.
---------- Echo Area ----------
```

    Almost all the messages displayed in the echo area are also recorded in the '`*Messages*`' buffer.

message-log-max   User Option
    This variable specifies how many lines to keep in the '`*Messages*`' buffer. The value `t` means there is no limit on how many lines to keep. The value `nil` disables message logging entirely. Here's how to display a message and prevent it from being logged:

```
(let (message-log-max)
  (message ...))
```

echo-keystrokes   Variable
    This variable determines how much time should elapse before command characters echo. Its value must be an integer, which specifies the number of seconds to wait before echoing. If the user types a prefix key (such as `C-x`) and then delays this many seconds before continuing, the prefix key is echoed in the echo area. Any subsequent characters in the same command will be echoed as well.

    If the value is zero, then command input is not echoed.

cursor-in-echo-area   Variable
    This variable controls where the cursor appears when a message is displayed in the echo area. If it is non-`nil`, then the cursor appears at the end of the message. Otherwise, the cursor appears at point—not in the echo area at all.

The value is normally `nil`; Lisp programs bind it to `t` for brief periods
of time.

35.5 Invisible Text

You can make characters *invisible*, so that they do not appear on the
screen, with the `invisible` property. This can be either a text property or
a property of an overlay.

In the simplest case, any non-`nil` `invisible` property makes a character invisible. This is the default case—if you don't alter the default value of
`buffer-invisibility-spec`, this is how the `invisibility` property works.
This feature is much like selective display (see Section 35.6 [Selective Dis-
play], page 280), but more general and cleaner.

More generally, you can use the variable `buffer-invisibility-spec` to
control which values of the `invisible` property make text invisible. This
permits you to classify the text into different subsets in advance, by giving
them different `invisible` values, and subsequently make various subsets
visible or invisible by changing the value of `buffer-invisibility-spec`.

Controlling visibility with `buffer-invisibility-spec` is especially useful in a program to display the list of entries in a data base. It permits the
implementation of convenient filtering commands to view just a part of the
entries in the data base. Setting this variable is very fast, much faster than
scanning all the text in the buffer looking for properties to change.

buffer-invisibility-spec   *Variable*
  This variable specifies which kinds of `invisible` properties actually
  make a character invisible.

  t   A character is invisible if its `invisible` property is non-
             `nil`. This is the default.

  a list   Each element of the list makes certain characters invisible.
             Ultimately, a character is invisible if any of the elements
             of this list applies to it. The list can have two kinds of
             elements:

             atom   A character is invisible if its `invisible` prop-
                             ery value is *atom* or if it is a list with *atom* as
                             a member.

             (*atom* . t)
                             A character is invisible if its `invisible` prop-
                             ery value is *atom* or if it is a list with *atom*
                             as a member. Moreover, if this character is at
                             the end of a line and is followed by a visible
                             newline, it displays an ellipsis.

Ordinarily, commands that operate on text or move point do not care whether the text is invisible. However, the user-level line motion commands explicitly ignore invisible newlines.

35.6 Selective Display

Selective display is a pair of features that hide certain lines on the screen.

The first variant, explicit selective display, is designed for use in a Lisp program. The program controls which lines are hidden by altering the text. Outline mode has traditionally used this variant. It has been partially replaced by the invisible text feature (see Section 35.5 [Invisible Text], page 279); there is a new version of Outline mode which uses that instead.

In the second variant, the choice of lines to hide is made automatically based on indentation. This variant is designed to be a user-level feature.

The way you control explicit selective display is by replacing a newline (control-j) with a carriage return (control-m). The text that was formerly a line following that newline is now invisible. Strictly speaking, it is temporarily no longer a line at all, since only newlines can separate lines; it is now part of the previous line.

Selective display does not directly affect editing commands. For example, `C-f` (`forward-char`) moves point unhesitatingly into invisible text. However, the replacement of newline characters with carriage return characters affects some editing commands. For example, `next-line` skips invisible lines, since it searches only for newlines. Modes that use selective display can also define commands that take account of the newlines, or that make parts of the text visible or invisible.

When you write a selectively displayed buffer into a file, all the control-m's are output as newlines. This means that when you next read in the file, it looks OK, with nothing invisible. The selective display effect is seen only within Emacs.

selective-display   *Variable*
  This buffer-local variable enables selective display. This means that lines, or portions of lines, may be made invisible.

  - If the value of `selective-display` is t, then any portion of a line that follows a control-m is not displayed.

  - If the value of `selective-display` is a positive integer, then lines that start with more than that many columns of indentation are not displayed.

When some portion of a buffer is invisible, the vertical movement commands operate as if that portion did not exist, allowing a single `next-line` command to skip any number of invisible lines. However, character movement commands (such as `forward-char`) do not skip the invisible portion, and it is possible (if tricky) to insert or delete text in an invisible portion.

In the examples below, we show the *display appearance* of the buffer foo, which changes with the value of `selective-display`. The *contents* of the buffer do not change.

```
(setq selective-display nil)
     ⇒ nil


---------- Buffer: foo ----------
1 on this column
 2on this column
   3n this column
   3n this column
 2on this column
1 on this column
---------- Buffer: foo ----------

(setq selective-display 2)
     ⇒ 2


---------- Buffer: foo ----------
1 on this column
 2on this column
 2on this column
1 on this column
---------- Buffer: foo ----------
```

selective-display-ellipses   *Variable*

If this buffer-local variable is non-nil, then Emacs displays '...' at the end of a line that is followed by invisible text. This example is a continuation of the previous one.

```
(setq selective-display-ellipses t)
     ⇒ t


---------- Buffer: foo ----------
1 on this column
 2on this column ...
 2on this column
1 on this column
---------- Buffer: foo ----------
```

You can use a display table to substitute other text for the ellipsis ('...'). See Section 35.14 [Display Tables], page 294.

35.7 The Overlay Arrow

The *overlay arrow* is useful for directing the user's attention to a particular line in a buffer. For example, in the modes used for interface to debuggers, the overlay arrow indicates the line of code about to be executed.

overlay-arrow-string   Variable

This variable holds the string to display to call attention to a particular line, or `nil` if the arrow feature is not in use.

overlay-arrow-position   Variable

This variable holds a marker that indicates where to display the overlay arrow. It should point at the beginning of a line. The arrow text appears at the beginning of that line, overlaying any text that would otherwise appear. Since the arrow is usually short, and the line usually begins with indentation, normally nothing significant is overwritten.

The overlay string is displayed only in the buffer that this marker points into. Thus, only one buffer can have an overlay arrow at any given time.

You can do the same job by creating an overlay with a `before-string` property. See Section 35.9.1 [Overlay Properties], page 284.

35.8 Temporary Displays

Temporary displays are used by commands to put output into a buffer and then present it to the user for perusal rather than for editing. Many of the help commands use this feature.

with-output-to-temp-buffer *buffer-name*   Special Form
                forms...

This function executes *forms* while arranging to insert any output they print into the buffer named *buffer-name*. The buffer is then shown in some window for viewing, displayed but not selected.

The string *buffer-name* specifies the temporary buffer, which need not already exist. The argument must be a string, not a buffer. The buffer is erased initially (with no questions asked), and it is marked as unmodified after `with-output-to-temp-buffer` exits.

`with-output-to-temp-buffer` binds `standard-output` to the temporary buffer, then it evaluates the forms in *forms*. Output using the Lisp output functions within *forms* goes by default to that buffer (but screen display and messages in the echo area, although they are "output" in the general sense of the word, are not affected). See Section 16.5 [Output Functions], page 247, vol. 1.

The value of the last form in *forms* is returned.

```
---------- Buffer: foo ----------
 This is the contents of foo.
---------- Buffer: foo ----------

(with-output-to-temp-buffer "foo"
    (print 20)
    (print standard-output))
⇒ #<buffer foo>


---------- Buffer: foo ----------
20

#<buffer foo>

---------- Buffer: foo ----------
```

temp-buffer-show-function   *Variable*

If this variable is non-nil, with-output-to-temp-buffer calls it as a function to do the job of displaying a help buffer. The function gets one argument, which is the buffer it should display.

In Emacs versions 18 and earlier, this variable was called temp-buffer-show-hook.

momentary-string-display *string position* &optional   *Function*
char message

This function momentarily displays *string* in the current buffer at *position*. It has no effect on the undo list or on the buffer's modification status.

The momentary display remains until the next input event. If the next input event is *char*, momentary-string-display ignores it and returns. Otherwise, that event remains buffered for subsequent use as input. Thus, typing *char* will simply remove the string from the display, while typing (say) C-f will remove the string from the display and later (presumably) move point forward. The argument *char* is a space by default.

The return value of momentary-string-display is not meaningful.

If the string *string* does not contain control characters, you can do the same job in a more general way by creating an overlay with a before-string property. See Section 35.9.1 [Overlay Properties], page 284.

If *message* is non-nil, it is displayed in the echo area while *string* is displayed in the buffer. If it is nil, a default message says to type *char* to continue.

In this example, point is initially located at the beginning of the second line:

```
---------- Buffer: foo ----------
This is the contents of foo.
*Second line.
---------- Buffer: foo ----------

(momentary-string-display
  "**** Important Message! ****"
  (point) ?\r
  "Type RET when done reading")
⇒ t

---------- Buffer: foo ----------
This is the contents of foo.
**** Important Message! ****Second line.
---------- Buffer: foo ----------


---------- Echo Area ----------
Type RET when done reading
---------- Echo Area ----------
```

35.9 Overlays

You can use *overlays* to alter the appearance of a buffer's text on the screen, for the sake of presentation features. An overlay is an object that belongs to a particular buffer, and has a specified beginning and end. It also has properties that you can examine and set; these affect the display of the text within the overlay.

35.9.1 Overlay Properties

Overlay properties are like text properties in some respects, but the differences are more important than the similarities. Text properties are considered a part of the text; overlays are specifically considered not to be part of the text. Thus, copying text between various buffers and strings preserves text properties, but does not try to preserve overlays. Changing a buffer's text properties marks the buffer as modified, while moving an overlay or changing its properties does not. Unlike text propery changes, overlay changes are not recorded in the buffer's undo list.

priority   This property's value (which should be a nonnegative number) determines the priority of the overlay. The priority matters when two or more overlays cover the same character and both specify a face for display; the one whose `priority` value is larger takes priority over the other, and its face attributes override the face attributes of the lower priority overlay.

Currently, all overlays take priority over text properties. Please avoid using negative priority values, as we have not yet decided just what they should mean.

window   If the `window` property is non-`nil`, then the overlay applies only on that window.

category If an overlay has a `category` property, we call it the *category* of the overlay. It should be a symbol. The properties of the symbol serve as defaults for the properties of the overlay.

face   This property controls the font and color of text. Its value is a face name or a list of face names. See Section 35.10 [Faces], page 288, for more information. This feature may be temporary; in the future, we may replace it with other ways of specifying how to display text.

mouse-face

This property is used instead of `face` when the mouse is within the range of the overlay. This feature may be temporary, like `face`.

modification-hooks

This property's value is a list of functions to be called if any character within the overlay is changed or if text is inserted strictly within the overlay.

The hook functions are called both before and after each change. If the functions save the information they receive, and compare notes between calls, they can determine exactly what change has been made in the buffer text.

When called before a change, each function receives four arguments: the overlay, `nil`, and the beginning and end of the text range to be modified.

When called after a change, each function receives five arguments: the overlay, `t`, the beginning and end of the text range just modified, and the length of the pre-change text replaced by that range. (For an insertion, the pre-change length is zero; for a deletion, that length is the number of characters deleted, and the post-change beginning and end are equal.)

insert-in-front-hooks

This property's value is a list of functions to be called before and after inserting text right at the beginning of the overlay. The calling conventions are the same as for the `modification-hooks` functions.

insert-behind-hooks

This property's value is a list of functions to be called before and after inserting text right at the end of the overlay. The calling conventions are the same as for the `modification-hooks` functions.

`invisible`

The `invisible` property can make the text in the overlay invisible, which means that it does not appear on the screen. See Section 35.5 [Invisible Text], page 279, for details.

`intangible`

The `intangible` property on an overlay works just like the `intangible` text property. See Section 29.18.4 [Special Properties], page 181, for details.

`before-string`

This property's value is a string to add to the display at the beginning of the overlay. The string does not appear in the buffer in any sense—only on the screen. The string should contain only characters that display as a single column—control characters, including tabs or newlines, will give strange results.

`after-string`

This property's value is a string to add to the display at the end of the overlay. The string does not appear in the buffer in any sense—only on the screen. The string should contain only characters that display as a single column—control characters, including tabs or newlines, will give strange results.

`evaporate`

If this property is non-`nil`, the overlay is deleted automatically if it ever becomes empty (i.e., if it spans no characters).

These are the functions for reading and writing the properties of an overlay.

overlay-get *overlay prop*   Function

This function returns the value of property *prop* recorded in *overlay*, if any. If *overlay* does not record any value for that property, but it does have a `category` property which is a symbol, that symbol's *prop* property is used. Otherwise, the value is `nil`.

overlay-put *overlay prop value*   Function

This function sets the value of property *prop* recorded in *overlay* to *value*. It returns *value*.

See also the function `get-char-property` which checks both overlay properties and text properties for a given character. See Section 29.18.1 [Examining Properties], page 176.

35.9.2 Managing Overlays

This section describes the functions to create, delete and move overlays, and to examine their contents.

make-overlay *start end &optional buffer*   Function

This function creates and returns an overlay that belongs to *buffer* and ranges from *start* to *end*. Both *start* and *end* must specify buffer positions; they may be integers or markers. If *buffer* is omitted, the overlay is created in the current buffer.

overlay-start *overlay*   Function

This function returns the position at which *overlay* starts.

overlay-end *overlay*   Function

This function returns the position at which *overlay* ends.

overlay-buffer *overlay*   Function

This function returns the buffer that *overlay* belongs to.

delete-overlay *overlay*   Function

This function deletes *overlay*. The overlay continues to exist as a Lisp object, but ceases to be part of the buffer it belonged to, and ceases to have any effect on display.

move-overlay *overlay start end &optional buffer*   Function

This function moves *overlay* to *buffer*, and places its bounds at *start* and *end*. Both arguments *start* and *end* must specify buffer positions; they may be integers or markers. If *buffer* is omitted, the overlay stays in the same buffer.

The return value is *overlay*.

This is the only valid way to change the endpoints of an overlay. Do not try modifying the markers in the overlay by hand, as that fails to update other vital data structures and can cause some overlays to be "lost".

overlays-at *pos*   Function

This function returns a list of all the overlays that contain position *pos* in the current buffer. The list is in no particular order. An overlay contains position *pos* if it begins at or before *pos*, and ends after *pos*.

next-overlay-change *pos*   Function

This function returns the buffer position of the next beginning or end of an overlay, after *pos*.

previous-overlay-change *pos*   Function

This function returns the buffer position of the previous beginning or end of an overlay, before *pos*.

35.10 Faces

A *face* is a named collection of graphical attributes: font, foreground color, background color and optional underlining. Faces control the display of text on the screen.

Each face has its own *face id number* which distinguishes faces at low levels within Emacs. However, for most purposes, you can refer to faces in Lisp programs by their names.

facep *object*   Function
  This function returns t if *object* is a face name symbol (or if it is a vector of the kind used internally to record face data). It returns nil otherwise.

Each face name is meaningful for all frames, and by default it has the same meaning in all frames. But you can arrange to give a particular face name a special meaning in one frame if you wish.

35.10.1 Standard Faces

This table lists all the standard faces and their uses.

default   This face is used for ordinary text.

modeline   This face is used for mode lines and menu bars.

region   This face is used for highlighting the region in Transient Mark
           mode.

secondary-selection
           This face is used to show any secondary selection you have made.

highlight
           This face is meant to be used for highlighting for various pur-
           poses.

underline
           This face underlines text.

bold   This face uses a bold font, if possible. It uses the bold variant of
           the frame's font, if it has one. It's up to you to choose a default
           font that has a bold variant, if you want to use one.

italic   This face uses the italic variant of the frame's font, if it has one.

bold-italic
           This face uses the bold italic variant of the frame's font, if it has
           one.

35.10.2 Merging Faces for Display

Here are all the ways to specify which face to use for display of text:

- With defaults. Each frame has a *default face*, whose id number is zero, which is used for all text that doesn't somehow specify another face.
- With text properties. A character may have a `face` property; if so, it is displayed with that face. See Section 29.18.4 [Special Properties], page 181.

  If the character has a `mouse-face` property, that is used instead of the `face` property when the mouse is "near enough" to the character.
- With overlays. An overlay may have `face` and `mouse-face` properties too; they apply to all the text covered by the overlay.
- With a region that is active. In Transient Mark mode, the region is highlighted with a particular face (see `region-face`, below).
- With special glyphs. Each glyph can specify a particular face id number. See Section 35.14.3 [Glyphs], page 295.

If these various sources together specify more than one face for a particular character, Emacs merges the attributes of the various faces specified. The attributes of the faces of special glyphs come first; then comes the face for region highlighting, if appropriate; then come attributes of faces from overlays, followed by those from text properties, and last the default face.

When multiple overlays cover one character, an overlay with higher priority overrides those with lower priority. See Section 35.9 [Overlays], page 284.

If an attribute such as the font or a color is not specified in any of the above ways, the frame's own font or color is used.

35.10.3 Functions for Working with Faces

The attributes a face can specify include the font, the foreground color, the background color, and underlining. The face can also leave these unspecified by giving the value `nil` for them.

Here are the primitives for creating and changing faces.

make-face *name*   Function
This function defines a new face named *name*, initially with all attributes `nil`. It does nothing if there is already a face named *name*.

face-list   Function
This function returns a list of all defined face names.

copy-face *old-face new-name* &optional *frame new-frame*   Function
This function defines the face *new-name* as a copy of the existing face named *old-face*. It creates the face *new-name* if that doesn't already exist.

If the optional argument *frame* is given, this function applies only to that frame. Otherwise it applies to each frame individually, copying attributes from *old-face* in each frame to *new-face* in the same frame.

If the optional argument *new-frame* is given, then `copy-face` copies the attributes of *old-face* in *frame* to *new-name* in *new-frame*.

You can modify the attributes of an existing face with the following functions. If you specify *frame*, they affect just that frame; otherwise, they affect all frames as well as the defaults that apply to new frames.

set-face-foreground *face color* &optional *frame*   Function
set-face-background *face color* &optional *frame*   Function
These functions set the foreground (or background, respectively) color of face *face* to *color*. The argument *color* should be a string, the name of a color.

Certain shades of gray are implemented by stipple patterns on black-and-white screens.

set-face-stipple *face pattern* &optional *frame*   Function
This function sets the background stipple pattern of face *face* to *pattern*. The argument *pattern* should be the name of a stipple pattern defined by the X server, or `nil` meaning don't use stipple.

Normally there is no need to pay attention to stipple patterns, because they are used automatically to handle certain shades of gray.

set-face-font *face font* &optional *frame*   Function
This function sets the font of face *face*. The argument *font* should be a string.

set-face-underline-p *face underline-p* &optional *frame*   Function
This function sets the underline attribute of face *face*. Non-`nil` means do underline; `nil` means don't.

invert-face *face* &optional *frame*   Function
Swap the foreground and background colors of face *face*. If the face doesn't specify both foreground and background, then its foreground and background are set to the default background and foreground, respectively.

These functions examine the attributes of a face. If you don't specify *frame*, they refer to the default data for new frames.

face-foreground *face* &optional *frame*   Function
face-background *face* &optional *frame*   Function
These functions return the foreground color (or background color, respectively) of face *face*, as a string.

face-stipple *face* &optional *frame*   Function
This function returns the name of the background stipple pattern of
face *face*, or `nil` if it doesn't have one.

face-font *face* &optional *frame*   Function
This function returns the name of the font of face *face*.

face-underline-p *face* &optional *frame*   Function
This function returns the underline attribute of face *face*.

face-id *face*   Function
This function returns the face id number of face *face*.

face-equal *face1 face2* &optional *frame*   Function
This returns `t` if the faces *face1* and *face2* have the same attributes
for display.

face-differs-from-default-p *face* &optional *frame*   Function
This returns `t` if the face *face* displays differently from the default
face. A face is considered to be "the same" as the normal face if each
attribute is either the same as that of the default face or `nil` (meaning
to inherit from the default).

region-face   Variable
This variable's value specifies the face id to use to display characters
in the region when it is active (in Transient Mark mode only). The
face thus specified takes precedence over all faces that come from text
properties and overlays, for characters in the region. See Section 28.6
[The Mark], page 137, for more information about Transient Mark
mode.

Normally, the value is the id number of the face named `region`.

35.11 Blinking Parentheses

This section describes the mechanism by which Emacs shows a matching
open parenthesis when the user inserts a close parenthesis.

blink-paren-function   Variable
The value of this variable should be a function (of no arguments)
to be called whenever a character with close parenthesis syntax is
inserted. The value of `blink-paren-function` may be `nil`, in which
case nothing is done.

> **Please note:** This variable was named `blink-paren-hook`
> in older Emacs versions, but since it is not called with the
> standard convention for hooks, it was renamed to `blink-`
> `paren-function` in version 19.

blink-matching-paren   Variable
   If this variable is `nil`, then `blink-matching-open` does nothing.

blink-matching-paren-distance   Variable
   This variable specifies the maximum distance to scan for a matching
   parenthesis before giving up.

blink-matching-paren-delay   Variable
   This variable specifies the number of seconds for the cursor to remain
   at the matching parenthesis. A fraction of a second often gives good
   results, but the default is 1, which works on all systems.

blink-matching-open   Function
   This function is the default value of `blink-paren-function`. It assumes that point follows a character with close parenthesis syntax and
   moves the cursor momentarily to the matching opening character. If
   that character is not already on the screen, it displays the character's
   context in the echo area. To avoid long delays, this function does not
   search farther than `blink-matching-paren-distance` characters.

   Here is an example of calling this function explicitly.

```
(defun interactive-blink-matching-open ()
  "Indicate momentarily the start of sexp before point."
  (interactive)
  (let ((blink-matching-paren-distance
         (buffer-size))
        (blink-matching-paren t))
    (blink-matching-open)))
```

35.12 Inverse Video

inverse-video   User Option
   This variable controls whether Emacs uses inverse video for all text on
   the screen. Non-`nil` means yes, `nil` means no. The default is `nil`.

mode-line-inverse-video   User Option
   This variable controls the use of inverse video for mode lines. If it is
   non-`nil`, then mode lines are displayed in inverse video. Otherwise,
   mode lines are displayed normally, just like text. The default is `t`.

   For X window frames, this displays mode lines using the face named
   `modeline`, which is normally the inverse of the default face unless you
   change it.

35.13 Usual Display Conventions

The usual display conventions define how to display each character code. You can override these conventions by setting up a display table (see Section 35.14 [Display Tables], page 294). Here are the usual display conventions:

- Character codes 32 through 126 map to glyph codes 32 through 126. Normally this means they display as themselves.

- Character code 9 is a horizontal tab. It displays as whitespace up to a position determined by `tab-width`.

- Character code 10 is a newline.

- All other codes in the range 0 through 31, and code 127, display in one of two ways according to the value of `ctl-arrow`. If it is non-`nil`, these codes map to sequences of two glyphs, where the first glyph is the ASCII code for '^'. (A display table can specify a glyph to use instead of '^'.) Otherwise, these codes map just like the codes in the range 128 to 255.

- Character codes 128 through 255 map to sequences of four glyphs, where the first glyph is the ASCII code for '\', and the others are digit characters representing the code in octal. (A display table can specify a glyph to use instead of '\'.)

The usual display conventions apply even when there is a display table, for any character whose entry in the active display table is `nil`. Thus, when you set up a display table, you need only specify the characters for which you want unusual behavior.

These variables affect the way certain characters are displayed on the screen. Since they change the number of columns the characters occupy, they also affect the indentation functions.

ctl-arrow   User Option
This buffer-local variable controls how control characters are displayed. If it is non-`nil`, they are displayed as a caret followed by the character: '^A'. If it is `nil`, they are displayed as a backslash followed by three octal digits: '\001'.

default-ctl-arrow   Variable
The value of this variable is the default value for `ctl-arrow` in buffers that do not override it. See Section 10.9.3 [Default Value], page 155, vol. 1.

tab-width   User Option
The value of this variable is the spacing between tab stops used for displaying tab characters in Emacs buffers. The default is 8. Note that this feature is completely independent from the user-settable tab

stops used by the command `tab-to-tab-stop`. See Section 29.16.5
[Indent Tabs], page 174.

35.14 Display Tables

You can use the *display table* feature to control how all 256 possible
character codes display on the screen. This is useful for displaying European
languages that have letters not in the ASCII character set.

The display table maps each character code into a sequence of *glyphs*,
each glyph being an image that takes up one character position on the screen.
You can also define how to display each glyph on your terminal, using the
glyph table.

35.14.1 Display Table Format

A display table is actually an array of 262 elements.

make-display-table   Function
> This creates and returns a display table. The table initially has `nil`
> in all elements.

The first 256 elements correspond to character codes; the *n*th element says
how to display the character code *n*. The value should be `nil` or a vector of
glyph values (see Section 35.14.3 [Glyphs], page 295). If an element is `nil`,
it says to display that character according to the usual display conventions
(see Section 35.13 [Usual Display], page 293).

If you use the display table to change the display of newline characters,
the whole buffer will be displayed as one long "line."

The remaining six elements of a display table serve special purposes, and
`nil` means use the default stated below.

256   The glyph for the end of a truncated screen line (the default for
           this is '$'). See Section 35.14.3 [Glyphs], page 295.

257   The glyph for the end of a continued line (the default is '\').

258   The glyph for indicating a character displayed as an octal char-
           acter code (the default is '\').

259   The glyph for indicating a control character (the default is '^').

260   A vector of glyphs for indicating the presence of invisible lines
           (the default is '...'). See Section 35.6 [Selective Display],
           page 280.

261   The glyph used to draw the border between side-by-side win-
           dows (the default is '|'). See Section 25.2 [Splitting Windows],
           page 70.

For example, here is how to construct a display table that mimics the effect of setting `ctl-arrow` to a non-`nil` value:

```
(setq disptab (make-display-table))
(let ((i 0))
  (while (< i 32)
    (or (= i ?\t) (= i ?\n)
        (aset disptab i (vector ?^ (+ i 64))))
    (setq i (1+ i)))
  (aset disptab 127 (vector ?^ ??)))
```

35.14.2 Active Display Table

Each window can specify a display table, and so can each buffer. When a buffer *b* is displayed in window *w*, display uses the display table for window *w* if it has one; otherwise, the display table for buffer *b* if it has one; otherwise, the standard display table if any. The display table chosen is called the *active* display table.

window-display-table *window*   Function
  This function returns *window*'s display table, or `nil` if *window* does not have an assigned display table.

set-window-display-table *window table*   Function
  This function sets the display table of *window* to *table*. The argument *table* should be either a display table or `nil`.

buffer-display-table   Variable
  This variable is automatically local in all buffers; its value in a particular buffer is the display table for that buffer, or `nil` if the buffer does not have an assigned display table.

standard-display-table   Variable
  This variable's value is the default display table, used whenever a window has no display table and neither does the buffer displayed in that window. This variable is `nil` by default.

If there is no display table to use for a particular window—that is, if the window has none, its buffer has none, and `standard-display-table` has none—then Emacs uses the usual display conventions for all character codes in that window. See Section 35.13 [Usual Display], page 293.

35.14.3 Glyphs

A *glyph* is a generalization of a character; it stands for an image that takes up a single character position on the screen. Glyphs are represented in Lisp as integers, just as characters are.

The meaning of each integer, as a glyph, is defined by the glyph table, which is the value of the variable `glyph-table`.

glyph-table   *Variable*
   The value of this variable is the current glyph table. It should be a vector; the *g*th element defines glyph code *g*. If the value is `nil` instead of a vector, then all glyphs are simple (see below).

   Here are the possible types of elements in the glyph table:

string   Send the characters in *string* to the terminal to output this glyph. This alternative is available on character terminals, but not under X.

integer   Define this glyph code as an alias for code *integer*. You can use an alias to specify a face code for the glyph; see below.

`nil`   This glyph is simple. On an ordinary terminal, the glyph code mod 256 is the character to output. With X, the glyph code mod 256 is the character to output, and the glyph code divided by 256 specifies the *face id number* to use while outputting it. See Section 35.10 [Faces], page 288.

   If a glyph code is greater than or equal to the length of the glyph table, that code is automatically simple.

35.14.4 ISO Latin 1

   If you have a terminal that can handle the entire ISO Latin 1 character set, you can arrange to use that character set as follows:

```
(require 'disp-table)
;; Set char codes 160–255 to display as themselves.
;; (Codes 128–159 are the additional control characters.)
(standard-display-8bit 160 255)
```

   If you are editing buffers written in the ISO Latin 1 character set and your terminal doesn't handle anything but ASCII, you can load the file 'iso-ascii' to set up a display table that displays the other ISO characters as explanatory sequences of ASCII characters. For example, the character "o with umlaut" displays as '{"o}'.

   Some European countries have terminals that don't support ISO Latin 1 but do support the special characters for that country's language. You can define a display table to work one language using such terminals. For an example, see 'lisp/iso-swed.el', which handles certain Swedish terminals.

   You can load the appropriate display table for your terminal automatically by writing a terminal-specific Lisp file for the terminal type.

35.15 Beeping

You can make Emacs ring a bell (or blink the screen) to attract the user's attention. Be conservative about how often you do this; frequent bells can become irritating. Also be careful not to use beeping alone when signaling an error is appropriate. (See Section 9.5.3 [Errors], page 128, vol. 1.)

ding &optional *dont-terminate*   Function
   This function beeps, or flashes the screen (see `visible-bell` below). It also terminates any keyboard macro currently executing unless *dont-terminate* is non-`nil`.

beep &optional *dont-terminate*   Function
   This is a synonym for `ding`.

visible-bell   Variable
   This variable determines whether Emacs should flash the screen to represent a bell. Non-`nil` means yes, `nil` means no. This is effective under X windows, and on a character-only terminal provided the terminal's Termcap entry defines the visible bell capability ('vb').

35.16 Window Systems

Emacs works with several window systems, most notably the X Window System. Both Emacs and X use the term "window", but use it differently. An Emacs frame is a single window as far as X is concerned; the individual Emacs windows are not known to X at all.

window-system   Variable
   This variable tells Lisp programs what window system Emacs is running under. Its value should be a symbol such as `x` (if Emacs is running under X) or `nil` (if Emacs is running on an ordinary terminal).

window-setup-hook   Variable
   This variable is a normal hook which Emacs runs after loading your '`.emacs`' file and the default initialization file (if any), after loading terminal-specific Lisp code, and after running the hook `term-setup-hook`.

   This hook is used for internal purposes: setting up communication with the window system, and creating the initial window. Users should not interfere with it.

36 Customizing the Calendar and Diary

There are many customizations that you can use to make the calendar and diary suit your personal tastes.

36.1 Customizing the Calendar

If you set the variable `view-diary-entries-initially` to `t`, calling up the calendar automatically displays the diary entries for the current date as well. The diary dates appear only if the current date is visible. If you add both of the following lines to your '.emacs' file:

```
(setq view-diary-entries-initially t)
(calendar)
```

this displays both the calendar and diary windows whenever you start Emacs.

Similarly, if you set the variable `view-calendar-holidays-initially` to `t`, entering the calendar automatically displays a list of holidays for the current three-month period. The holiday list appears in a separate window.

You can set the variable `mark-diary-entries-in-calendar` to `t` in order to mark any dates with diary entries. This takes effect whenever the calendar window contents are recomputed. There are two ways of marking these dates: by changing the face (see Section 35.10 [Faces], page 288), if the display supports that, or by placing a plus sign ('+') beside the date otherwise.

Similarly, setting the variable `mark-holidays-in-calendar` to `t` marks holiday dates, either with a change of face or with an asterisk ('*').

The variable `calendar-holiday-marker` specifies how to mark a date as being a holiday. Its value may be a character to insert next to the date, or a face name to use for displaying the date. Likewise, the variable `diary-entry-marker` specifies how to mark a date that has diary entries. The calendar creates faces named `holiday-face` and `diary-face` for these purposes; those symbols are the default values of these variables, when Emacs supports multiple faces on your terminal.

The variable `calendar-load-hook` is a normal hook run when the calendar package is first loaded (before actually starting to display the calendar).

Starting the calendar runs the normal hook `initial-calendar-window-hook`. Recomputation of the calendar display does not run this hook. But if you leave the calendar with the `q` command and reenter it, the hook runs again.

The variable `today-visible-calendar-hook` is a normal hook run after the calendar buffer has been prepared with the calendar when the current date is visible in the window. One use of this hook is to replace today's date with asterisks; to do that, use the hook function `calendar-star-date`.

```
(add-hook 'today-visible-calendar-hook 'calendar-star-date)
```

Another standard hook function marks the current date, either by changing its face or by adding an asterisk. Here's how to use it:

```
(add-hook 'today-visible-calendar-hook 'calendar-mark-today)
```

The variable `calendar-today-marker` specifies how to mark today's date. Its value should be a character to insert next to the date or a face name to use for displaying the date. A face named `calendar-today-face` is provided for this purpose; that symbol is the default for this variable when Emacs supports multiple faces on your terminal.

A similar normal hook, `today-invisible-calendar-hook` is run if the current date is *not* visible in the window.

36.2 Customizing the Holidays

Emacs knows about holidays defined by entries on one of several lists. You can customize these lists of holidays to your own needs, adding or deleting holidays. The lists of holidays that Emacs uses are for general holidays (`general-holidays`), local holidays (`local-holidays`), Christian holidays (`christian-holidays`), Hebrew (Jewish) holidays (`hebrew-holidays`), Islamic (Moslem) holidays (`islamic-holidays`), and other holidays (`other-holidays`).

The general holidays are, by default, holidays common throughout the United States. To eliminate these holidays, set `general-holidays` to `nil`.

There are no default local holidays (but sites may supply some). You can set the variable `local-holidays` to any list of holidays, as described below.

By default, Emacs does not include all the holidays of the religions that it knows, only those commonly found in secular calendars. For a more extensive collection of religious holidays, you can set any (or all) of the variables `all-christian-calendar-holidays`, `all-hebrew-calendar-holidays`, or `all-islamic-calendar-holidays` to `t`. If you want to eliminate the religious holidays, set any or all of the corresponding variables `christian-holidays`, `hebrew-holidays`, and `islamic-holidays` to `nil`.

You can set the variable `other-holidays` to any list of holidays. This list, normally empty, is intended for individual use.

Each of the lists (`general-holidays`, `local-holidays`, `christian-holidays`, `hebrew-holidays`, `islamic-holidays`, and `other-holidays`) is a list of *holiday forms*, each holiday form describing a holiday (or sometimes a list of holidays).

Here is a table of the possible kinds of holiday form. Day numbers and month numbers count starting from 1, but "dayname" numbers count Sunday as 0. The element *string* is always the name of the holiday, as a string.

(holiday-fixed *month day string*)
> A fixed date on the Gregorian calendar.

(holiday-float *month dayname k string*)
> The *k*th *dayname* in *month* on the Gregorian calendar (*dayname*=0 for Sunday, and so on); negative *k* means count back from the end of the month.

(holiday-hebrew *month day string*)
> A fixed date on the Hebrew calendar.

(holiday-islamic *month day string*)
> A fixed date on the Islamic calendar.

(holiday-julian *month day string*)
> A fixed date on the Julian calendar.

(holiday-sexp *sexp string*)
> A date calculated by the Lisp expression *sexp*. The expression should use the variable `year` to compute and return the date of a holiday, or `nil` if the holiday doesn't happen this year. The value of *sexp* must represent the date as a list of the form (*month day year*).

(if *condition holiday-form*)
> A holiday that happens only if *condition* is true.

(*function* [*args*])
> A list of dates calculated by the function *function*, called with arguments *args*.

For example, suppose you want to add Bastille Day, celebrated in France on July 14. You can do this as follows:

```
(setq other-holidays '((holiday-fixed 7 14 "Bastille Day")))
```

The holiday form (`holiday-fixed 7 14 "Bastille Day"`) specifies the fourteenth day of the seventh month (July).

Many holidays occur on a specific day of the week, at a specific time of month. Here is a holiday form describing Hurricane Supplication Day, celebrated in the Virgin Islands on the fourth Monday in August:

```
(holiday-float 8 1 4 "Hurricane Supplication Day")
```

Here the 8 specifies August, the 1 specifies Monday (Sunday is 0, Tuesday is 2, and so on), and the 4 specifies the fourth occurrence in the month (1 specifies the first occurrence, 2 the second occurrence, −1 the last occurrence, −2 the second-to-last occurrence, and so on).

You can specify holidays that occur on fixed days of the Hebrew, Islamic, and Julian calendars too. For example,

```
(setq other-holidays
      '((holiday-hebrew 10 2 "Last day of Hanukkah")
```

```
(holiday-islamic 3 12 "Mohammed's Birthday")
(holiday-julian 4 2 "Jefferson's Birthday")))
```

adds the last day of Hanukkah (since the Hebrew months are numbered with 1 starting from Nisan), the Islamic feast celebrating Mohammed's birthday (since the Islamic months are numbered from 1 starting with Muharram), and Thomas Jefferson's birthday, which is 2 April 1743 on the Julian calendar.

To include a holiday conditionally, use either Emacs Lisp's `if` or the `holiday-sexp` form. For example, American presidential elections occur on the first Tuesday after the first Monday in November of years divisible by 4:

```
(holiday-sexp (if (= 0 (% year 4))
                  (calendar-gregorian-from-absolute
                   (1+ (calendar-dayname-on-or-before
                        1 (+ 6 (calendar-absolute-from-gregorian
                                (list 11 1 year)))))))
              "US Presidential Election"))
```

or

```
(if (= 0 (% displayed-year 4))
    (fixed 11
           (extract-calendar-day
            (calendar-gregorian-from-absolute
             (1+ (calendar-dayname-on-or-before
                  1 (+ 6 (calendar-absolute-from-gregorian
                          (list 11 1 displayed-year)))))))
           "US Presidential Election"))
```

Some holidays just don't fit into any of these forms because special calculations are involved in their determination. In such cases you must write a Lisp function to do the calculation. To include eclipses, for example, add `(eclipses)` to `other-holidays` and write an Emacs Lisp function `eclipses` that returns a (possibly empty) list of the relevant Gregorian dates among the range visible in the calendar window, with descriptive strings, like this:

```
(((6 27 1991) "Lunar Eclipse") ((7 11 1991) "Solar Eclipse") ... )
```

36.3 Date Display Format

You can customize the manner of displaying dates in the diary, in mode lines, and in messages by setting `calendar-date-display-form`. This variable holds a list of expressions that can involve the variables `month`, `day`, and `year`, which are all numbers in string form, and `monthname` and `dayname`, which are both alphabetic strings. In the American style, the default value of this list is as follows:

```
((if dayname (concat dayname ", ")) monthname " " day ", " year)
```

while in the European style this value is the default:

```
((if dayname (concat dayname ", ")) day " " monthname " " year)
```

The ISO standard date representation is this:

```
(year "-" month "-" day)
```

This specifies a typical American format:

```
(month "/" day "/" (substring year -2))
```

36.4 Time Display Format

The calendar and diary by default display times of day in the conventional American style with the hours from 1 through 12, minutes, and either 'am' or 'pm'. If you prefer the European style, also known in the US as military, in which the hours go from 00 to 23, you can alter the variable `calendar-time-display-form`. This variable is a list of expressions that can involve the variables `12-hours`, `24-hours`, and `minutes`, which are all numbers in string form, and `am-pm` and `time-zone`, which are both alphabetic strings. The default value of `calendar-time-display-form` is as follows:

```
(12-hours ":" minutes am-pm
          (if time-zone " (") time-zone (if time-zone ")"))
```

Here is a value that provides European style times:

```
(24-hours ":" minutes
          (if time-zone " (") time-zone (if time-zone ")"))
```

36.5 Daylight Savings Time

Emacs understands the difference between standard time and daylight savings time—the times given for sunrise, sunset, solstices, equinoxes, and the phases of the moon take that into account. The rules for daylight savings time vary from place to place and have also varied historically from year to year. To do the job properly, Emacs needs to know which rules to use.

Some operating systems keep track of the rules that apply to the place where you are; on these systems, Emacs gets the information it needs from the system automatically. If some or all of this information is missing, Emacs fills in the gaps with the rules currently used in Cambridge, Massachusetts, which is the center of GNU's world.

If the default choice of rules is not appropriate for your location, you can tell Emacs the rules to use by setting the variables `calendar-daylight-savings-starts` and `calendar-daylight-savings-ends`. Their values should be Lisp expressions that refer to the variable `year`, and evaluate to the Gregorian date on which daylight savings time starts or (respectively) ends, in the form of a list (*month day year*). The values should be `nil` if your area does not use daylight savings time.

Emacs uses these expressions to determine the start and end dates of daylight savings time as holidays and for correcting times of day in the solar and lunar calculations.

The values for Cambridge, Massachusetts are as follows:

```
(calendar-nth-named-day 1 0 4 year)
(calendar-nth-named-day -1 0 10 year)
```

i.e., the first 0th day (Sunday) of the fourth month (April) in the year specified by year, and the last Sunday of the tenth month (October) of that year. If daylight savings time were changed to start on October 1, you would set `calendar-daylight-savings-starts` to this:

```
(list 10 1 year)
```

For a more complex example, suppose daylight savings time begins on the first of Nisan on the Hebrew calendar. You should set `calendar-daylight-savings-starts` to this value:

```
(calendar-gregorian-from-absolute
  (calendar-absolute-from-hebrew
    (list 1 1 (+ year 3760))))
```

because Nisan is the first month in the Hebrew calendar and the Hebrew year differs from the Gregorian year by 3760 at Nisan.

If there is no daylight savings time at your location, or if you want all times in standard time, set `calendar-daylight-savings-starts` and `calendar-daylight-savings-ends` to `nil`.

The variable `calendar-daylight-time-offset` specifies the difference between daylight savings time and standard time, measured in minutes. The value for Cambridge is 60.

The variable `calendar-daylight-savings-starts-time` and the variable `calendar-daylight-savings-ends-time` specify the number of minutes after midnight local time when the transition to and from daylight savings time should occur. For Cambridge, both variables' values are 120.

36.6 Customizing the Diary

Ordinarily, the mode line of the diary buffer window indicates any holidays that fall on the date of the diary entries. The process of checking for holidays can take several seconds, so including holiday information delays the display of the diary buffer noticeably. If you'd prefer to have a faster display of the diary buffer but without the holiday information, set the variable `holidays-in-diary-buffer` to `nil`.

The variable `number-of-diary-entries` controls the number of days of diary entries to be displayed at one time. It affects the initial display when `view-diary-entries-initially` is `t`, as well as the command `M-x diary`. For example, the default value is 1, which says to display only the current day's diary entries. If the value is 2, both the current day's and the next day's entries are displayed. The value can also be a vector of seven elements:

for example, if the value is [0 2 2 2 2 4 1] then no diary entries appear on Sunday, the current date's and the next day's diary entries appear Monday through Thursday, Friday through Monday's entries appear on Friday, while on Saturday only that day's entries appear.

The variable `print-diary-entries-hook` is a normal hook run after preparation of a temporary buffer containing just the diary entries currently visible in the diary buffer. (The other, irrelevant diary entries are really absent from the temporary buffer; in the diary buffer, they are merely hidden.) The default value of this hook does the printing with the command `lpr-buffer`. If you want to use a different command to do the printing, just change the value of this hook. Other uses might include, for example, rearranging the lines into order by day and time.

You can customize the form of dates in your diary file, if neither the standard American nor European styles suits your needs, by setting the variable `diary-date-forms`. This variable is a list of patterns for recognizing a date. Each date pattern is a list whose elements may be regular expressions (see Section 30.2 [Regular Expressions], page 193) or the symbols `month`, `day`, `year`, `monthname`, and `dayname`. All these elements serve as patterns that match certain kinds of text in the diary file. In order for the date pattern, as a whole, to match, all of its elements must match consecutively.

A regular expression in a date pattern matches in its usual fashion, using the standard syntax table altered so that '`*`' is a word constituent.

The symbols `month`, `day`, `year`, `monthname`, and `dayname` match the month number, day number, year number, month name, and day name of the date being considered. The symbols that match numbers allow leading zeros; those that match names allow three-letter abbreviations and capitalization. All the symbols can match '`*`'; since '`*`' in a diary entry means "any day", "any month", and so on, it should match regardless of the date being considered.

The default value of `diary-date-forms` in the American style is this:

```
((month "/" day "[^/0-9]")
 (month "/" day "/" year "[^0-9]")
 (monthname " *" day "[^,0-9]")
 (monthname " *" day ", *" year "[^0-9]")
 (dayname "\\W"))
```

The date patterns in the list must be *mutually exclusive* and must not match any portion of the diary entry itself, just the date and one character of whitespace. If, to be mutually exclusive, the pattern must match a portion of the diary entry text—beyond the whitespace that ends the date—then the first element of the date pattern *must* be `backup`. This causes the date recognizer to back up to the beginning of the current word of the diary entry, after finishing the match. Even if you use `backup`, the date pattern must

absolutely not match more than a portion of the first word of the diary entry.
The default value of `diary-date-forms` in the European style is this list:

```
((day "/" month "[^/0-9]")
 (day "/" month "/" year "[^0-9]")
 (backup day " *" monthname "\\W+\\<[^*0-9]")
 (day " *" monthname " *" year "[^0-9]")
 (dayname "\\W"))
```

Notice the use of `backup` in the third pattern, because it needs to match part
of a word beyond the date itself to distinguish it from the fourth pattern.

36.7 Hebrew- and Islamic-Date Diary Entries

Your diary file can have entries based on Hebrew or Islamic dates, as
well as entries based on the world-standard Gregorian calendar. However,
because recognition of such entries is time-consuming and most people don't
use them, you must explicitly enable their use. If you want the diary to
recognize Hebrew-date diary entries, for example, you must do this:

```
(add-hook 'nongregorian-diary-listing-hook 'list-hebrew-diary-entries)
(add-hook 'nongregorian-diary-marking-hook 'mark-hebrew-diary-entries)
```

If you want Islamic-date entries, do this:

```
(add-hook 'nongregorian-diary-listing-hook 'list-islamic-diary-entries)
(add-hook 'nongregorian-diary-marking-hook 'mark-islamic-diary-entries)
```

Hebrew- and Islamic-date diary entries have the same formats as
Gregorian-date diary entries, except that 'H' precedes a Hebrew date and 'I'
precedes an Islamic date. Moreover, because the Hebrew and Islamic month
names are not uniquely specified by the first three letters, you may not
abbreviate them. For example, a diary entry for the Hebrew date Heshvan
25 could look like this:

```
HHeshvan 25 Happy Hebrew birthday!
```

and would appear in the diary for any date that corresponds to Heshvan 25
on the Hebrew calendar. And here is Islamic-date diary entry that matches
Dhu al-Qada 25:

```
IDhu al-Qada 25 Happy Islamic birthday!
```

As with Gregorian-date diary entries, Hebrew- and Islamic-date entries
are nonmarking if they are preceded with an ampersand ('&').

Here is a table of commands used in the calendar to create diary entries
that match the selected date and other dates that are similar in the Hebrew
or Islamic calendar:

i h d   Add a diary entry for the Hebrew date corresponding to the
           selected date (`insert-hebrew-diary-entry`).

i h m   Add a diary entry for the day of the Hebrew month corresponding to the selected date (`insert-monthly-hebrew-diary-entry`). This diary entry matches any date that has the same Hebrew day-within-month as the selected date.

i h y   Add a diary entry for the day of the Hebrew year corresponding to the selected date (`insert-yearly-hebrew-diary-entry`). This diary entry matches any date which has the same Hebrew month and day-within-month as the selected date.

i i d   Add a diary entry for the Islamic date corresponding to the selected date (`insert-islamic-diary-entry`).

i i m   Add a diary entry for the day of the Islamic month corresponding to the selected date (`insert-monthly-islamic-diary-entry`).

i i y   Add a diary entry for the day of the Islamic year corresponding to the selected date (`insert-yearly-islamic-diary-entry`).

These commands work much like the corresponding commands for ordinary diary entries: they apply to the date that point is on in the calendar window, and what they do is insert just the date portion of a diary entry at the end of your diary file. You must then insert the rest of the diary entry.

36.8 Fancy Diary Display

Diary display works by preparing the diary buffer and then running the hook `diary-display-hook`. The default value of this hook (`simple-diary-display`) hides the irrelevant diary entries and then displays the buffer. However, if you specify the hook as follows,

```
(add-hook 'diary-display-hook 'fancy-diary-display)
```

this enables fancy diary display. It displays diary entries and holidays by copying them into a special buffer that exists only for the sake of display. Copying to a separate buffer provides an opportunity to change the displayed text to make it prettier—for example, to sort the entries by the dates they apply to.

As with simple diary display, you can print a hard copy of the buffer with `print-diary-entries`. To print a hard copy of a day-by-day diary for a week by positioning point on Sunday of that week, type 7 d and then do M-x print-diary-entries. As usual, the inclusion of the holidays slows down the display slightly; you can speed things up by setting the variable `holidays-in-diary-buffer` to `nil`.

Ordinarily, the fancy diary buffer does not show days for which there are no diary entries, even if that day is a holiday. If you want such days to be shown in the fancy diary buffer, set the variable `diary-list-include-blanks` to `t`.

If you use the fancy diary display, you can use the normal hook `list-diary-entries-hook` to sort each day's diary entries by their time of day. Here's how

```
(add-hook 'list-diary-entries-hook 'sort-diary-entries t)
```

For each day, this sorts diary entries that begin with a recognizable time of day according to their times. Diary entries without times come first within each day.

Fancy diary display also has the ability to process included diary files. This permits a group of people to share a diary file for events that apply to all of them. Lines in the diary file of this form:

```
#include "filename"
```

includes the diary entries from the file *filename* in the fancy diary buffer. The include mechanism is recursive, so that included files can include other files, and so on; you must be careful not to have a cycle of inclusions, of course. Here is how to enable the include facility:

```
(add-hook 'list-diary-entries-hook 'include-other-diary-files)
(add-hook 'mark-diary-entries-hook 'mark-included-diary-files)
```

The include mechanism works only with the fancy diary display, because ordinary diary display shows the entries directly from your diary file.

36.9 Sexp Entries and the Fancy Diary Display

Sexp diary entries allow you to do more than just have complicated conditions under which a diary entry applies. If you use the fancy diary display, sexp entries can generate the text of the entry depending on the date itself. For example, an anniversary diary entry can insert the number of years since the anniversary date into the text of the diary entry. Thus the '%d' in this dairy entry:

```
%%(diary-anniversary 10 31 1948) Arthur's birthday (%d years old)
```

gets replaced by the age, so on October 31, 1990 the entry appears in the fancy diary buffer like this:

```
Arthur's birthday (42 years old)
```

If the diary file instead contains this entry:

```
%%(diary-anniversary 10 31 1948) Arthur's %d%s birthday
```

the entry in the fancy diary buffer for October 31, 1990 appears like this:

```
Arthur's 42nd birthday
```

Similarly, cyclic diary entries can interpolate the number of repetitions that have occurred:

```
%%(diary-cyclic 50 1 1 1990) Renew medication (%d%s time)
```

looks like this:

```
Renew medication (5th time)
```
in the fancy diary display on September 8, 1990.

The generality of sexp diary entries lets you specify any diary entry that you can describe algorithmically. A sexp diary entry contains an expression that computes whether the entry applies to any given date. If its value is non-nil, the entry applies to that date; otherwise, it does not. The expression can use the variable date to find the date being considered; its value is a list (*month day year*) that refers to the Gregorian calendar.

Suppose you get paid on the 21st of the month if it is a weekday, and on the Friday before if the 21st is on a weekend. Here is how to write a sexp diary entry that matches those dates:

```
&%%(let ((dayname (calendar-day-of-week date))
         (day (car (cdr date))))
     (or (and (= day 21) (memq dayname '(1 2 3 4 5)))
         (and (memq day '(19 20)) (= dayname 5)))
     ) Pay check deposited
```

The following sexp diary entries take advantage of the ability (in the fancy diary display) to concoct diary entries whose text varies based on the date:

%%(diary-sunrise-sunset)

> Make a diary entry for the local times of today's sunrise and sunset.

%%(diary-phases-of-moon)

> Make a diary entry for the phases (quarters) of the moon.

%%(diary-day-of-year)

> Make a diary entry with today's day number in the current year and the number of days remaining in the current year.

%%(diary-iso-date)

> Make a diary entry with today's equivalent ISO commercial date.

%%(diary-julian-date)

> Make a diary entry with today's equivalent date on the Julian calendar.

%%(diary-astro-day-number)

> Make a diary entry with today's equivalent astronomical (Julian) day number.

%%(diary-hebrew-date)

> Make a diary entry with today's equivalent date on the Hebrew calendar.

%%(diary-islamic-date)

> Make a diary entry with today's equivalent date on the Islamic calendar.

`%%(diary-french-date)`
> Make a diary entry with today's equivalent date on the French Revolutionary calendar.

`%%(diary-mayan-date)`
> Make a diary entry with today's equivalent date on the Mayan calendar.

Thus including the diary entry

    &%%(diary-hebrew-date)

causes every day's diary display to contain the equivalent date on the Hebrew calendar, if you are using the fancy diary display. (With simple diary display, the line '&%%(diary-hebrew-date)' appears in the diary for any date, but does nothing particularly useful.)

These functions can be used to construct sexp diary entries based on the Hebrew calendar in certain standard ways:

`%%(diary-rosh-hodesh)`
> Make a diary entry that tells the occurrence and ritual announcement of each new Hebrew month.

`%%(diary-parasha)`
> Make a Saturday diary entry that tells the weekly synagogue scripture reading.

`%%(diary-sabbath-candles)`
> Make a Friday diary entry that tells the *local time* of Sabbath candle lighting.

`%%(diary-omer)`
> Make a diary entry that gives the omer count, when appropriate.

`%%(diary-yahrzeit` *month day year*`)` *name*
> Make a diary entry marking the anniversary of a date of death. The date is the *Gregorian* (civil) date of death. The diary entry appears on the proper Hebrew calendar anniversary and on the day before. (In the European style, the order of the parameters is changed to *day, month, year*.)

36.10 Customizing Appointment Reminders

You can specify exactly how Emacs reminds you of an appointment, and how far in advance it begins doing so, by setting these variables:

`appt-message-warning-time`
> The time in minutes before an appointment that the reminder begins. The default is 10 minutes.

`appt-audible`

> If this is non-`nil`, Emacs rings the terminal bell for appointment reminders. The default is `t`.

`appt-visible`

> If this is non-`nil`, Emacs displays the appointment message in the echo area. The default is `t`.

`appt-display-mode-line`

> If this is non-`nil`, Emacs displays the number of minutes to the appointment on the mode line. The default is `t`.

`appt-msg-window`

> If this is non-`nil`, Emacs displays the appointment message in another window. The default is `t`.

`appt-disp-window-function`

> This variable holds a function to use to create the other window for the appointment message.

`appt-delete-window-function`

> This variable holds a function to use to get rid of the appointment message window, when its time is up.

`appt-display-duration`

> The number of seconds to display an appointment message. The default is 5 seconds.

Appendix A Tips and Standards

This chapter describes no additional features of Emacs Lisp. Instead it gives advice on making effective use of the features described in the previous chapters.

A.1 Writing Clean Lisp Programs

Here are some tips for avoiding common errors in writing Lisp code intended for widespread use:

- Since all global variables share the same name space, and all functions share another name space, you should choose a short word to distinguish your program from other Lisp programs. Then take care to begin the names of all global variables, constants, and functions with the chosen prefix. This helps avoid name conflicts.

  This recommendation applies even to names for traditional Lisp primitives that are not primitives in Emacs Lisp—even to `cadr`. Believe it or not, there is more than one plausible way to define `cadr`. Play it safe; append your name prefix to produce a name like `foo-cadr` or `mylib-cadr` instead.

  If you write a function that you think ought to be added to Emacs under a certain name, such as `twiddle-files`, don't call it by that name in your program. Call it `mylib-twiddle-files` in your program, and send mail to 'bug-gnu-emacs@prep.ai.mit.edu' suggesting we add it to Emacs. If and when we do, we can change the name easily enough.

  If one prefix is insufficient, your package may use two or three alternative common prefixes, so long as they make sense.

  Separate the prefix from the rest of the symbol name with a hyphen, '-'. This will be consistent with Emacs itself and with most Emacs Lisp programs.

- It is often useful to put a call to `provide` in each separate library program, at least if there is more than one entry point to the program.

- If a file requires certain other library programs to be loaded beforehand, then the comments at the beginning of the file should say so. Also, use `require` to make sure they are loaded.

- If one file *foo* uses a macro defined in another file *bar*, *foo* should contain this expression before the first use of the macro:

      (eval-when-compile (require 'bar))

  (And *bar* should contain (provide 'bar), to make the `require` work.) This will cause *bar* to be loaded when you byte-compile *foo*. Otherwise, you risk compiling *foo* without the necessary macro loaded, and that would produce compiled code that won't work right. See Section 12.3 [Compiling Macros], page 176, vol. 1.

Using `eval-when-compile` avoids loading *bar* when the compiled version of *foo* is *used.*

- If you define a major mode, make sure to run a hook variable using `run-hooks`, just as the existing major modes do. See Section 20.4 [Hooks], page 360, vol. 1.

- If the purpose of a function is to tell you whether a certain condition is true or false, give the function a name that ends in 'p'. If the name is one word, add just 'p'; if the name is multiple words, add '-p'. Examples are `framep` and `frame-live-p`.

- If a user option variable records a true-or-false condition, give it a name that ends in '-flag'.

- Please do not define C-c *letter* as a key in your major modes. These sequences are reserved for users; they are the **only** sequences reserved for users, so we cannot do without them.

  Instead, define sequences consisting of C-c followed by a non-letter. These sequences are reserved for major modes.

  Changing all the major modes in Emacs 18 so they would follow this convention was a lot of work. Abandoning this convention would make that work go to waste, and inconvenience users.

- Sequences consisting of C-c followed by {, }, <, >, : or ; are also reserved for major modes.

- Sequences consisting of C-c followed by any other punctuation character are allocated for minor modes. Using them in a major mode is not absolutely prohibited, but if you do that, the major mode binding may be shadowed from time to time by minor modes.

- You should not bind C-h following any prefix character (including C-c). If you don't bind C-h, it is automatically available as a help character for listing the subcommands of the prefix character.

- You should not bind a key sequence ending in ESC except following another ESC. (That is, it is ok to bind a sequence ending in ESC ESC.)

  The reason for this rule is that a non-prefix binding for ESC in any context prevents recognition of escape sequences as function keys in that context.

- Applications should not bind mouse events based on button 1 with the shift key held down. These events include S-mouse-1, M-S-mouse-1, C-S-mouse-1, and so on. They are reserved for users.

- Modes should redefine `mouse-2` as a command to follow some sort of reference in the text of a buffer, if users usually would not want to alter the text in that buffer by hand. Modes such as Dired, Info, Compilation, and Occur redefine it in this way.

- When a package provides a modification of ordinary Emacs behavior, it is good to include a command to enable and disable the feature, Provide a command named *whatever*-`mode` which turns the feature on or off, and make it autoload (see Section 13.2 [Autoload], page 185, vol. 1). Design the package so that simply loading it has no visible effect—that should not enable the feature. Users will request the feature by invoking the command.

- It is a bad idea to define aliases for the Emacs primitives. Use the standard names instead.

- Redefining an Emacs primitive is an even worse idea. It may do the right thing for a particular program, but there is no telling what other programs might break as a result.

- If a file does replace any of the functions or library programs of standard Emacs, prominent comments at the beginning of the file should say which functions are replaced, and how the behavior of the replacements differs from that of the originals.

- Please keep the names of your Emacs Lisp source files to 13 characters or less. This way, if the files are compiled, the compiled files' names will be 14 characters or less, which is short enough to fit on all kinds of Unix systems.

- Don't use `next-line` or `previous-line` in programs; nearly always, `forward-line` is more convenient as well as more predictable and robust. See Section 27.2.4 [Text Lines], page 122.

- Don't call functions that set the mark, unless setting the mark is one of the intended features of your program. The mark is a user-level feature, so it is incorrect to change the mark except to supply a value for the user's benefit. See Section 28.6 [The Mark], page 137.

  In particular, don't use these functions:

  - `beginning-of-buffer`, `end-of-buffer`
  - `replace-string`, `replace-regexp`

  If you just want to move point, or replace a certain string, without any of the other features intended for interactive users, you can replace these functions with one or two lines of simple Lisp code.

- Use lists rather than vectors, except when there is a particular reason to use a vector. Lisp has more facilities for manipulating lists than for vectors, and working with lists is usually more convenient.

  Vectors are advantageous for tables that are substantial in size and are accessed in random order (not searched front to back), provided there is no need to insert or delete elements (only lists allow that).

- The recommended way to print a message in the echo area is with the `message` function, not `princ`. See Section 35.4 [The Echo Area], page 277.

- When you encounter an error condition, call the function `error` (or
  `signal`). The function `error` does not return. See Section 9.5.3.1 [Sig-
  naling Errors], page 128, vol. 1.

  Do not use `message`, `throw`, `sleep-for`, or `beep` to report errors.

- An error message should start with a capital letter but should not end
  with a period.

- Try to avoid using recursive edits. Instead, do what the Rmail e command does: use a new local keymap that contains one command defined
  to switch back to the old local keymap. Or do what the `edit-options`
  command does: switch to another buffer and let the user switch back
  at will. See Section 18.10 [Recursive Editing], page 309, vol. 1.

- In some other systems there is a convention of choosing variable names
  that begin and end with '*'. We don't use that convention in Emacs
  Lisp, so please don't use it in your programs. (Emacs uses such names
  only for program-generated buffers.) The users will find Emacs more
  coherent if all libraries use the same conventions.

- Indent each function with C-M-q (`indent-sexp`) using the default indentation parameters.

- Don't make a habit of putting close-parentheses on lines by themselves;
  Lisp programmers find this disconcerting. Once in a while, when there
  is a sequence of many consecutive close-parentheses, it may make sense
  to split them in one or two significant places.

- Please put a copyright notice on the file if you give copies to anyone.
  Use the same lines that appear at the top of the Lisp files in Emacs
  itself. If you have not signed papers to assign the copyright to the
  Foundation, then place your name in the copyright notice in place of
  the Foundation's name.

A.2 Tips for Making Compiled Code Fast

Here are ways of improving the execution speed of byte-compiled Lisp
programs.

- Use the 'profile' library to profile your program. See the file
  'profile.el' for instructions.

- Use iteration rather than recursion whenever possible. Function calls
  are slow in Emacs Lisp even when a compiled function is calling another
  compiled function.

- Using the primitive list-searching functions `memq`, `member`, `assq`, or
  `assoc` is even faster than explicit iteration. It may be worth rearranging
  a data structure so that one of these primitive search functions can be
  used.

- Certain built-in functions are handled specially in byte-compiled code, avoiding the need for an ordinary function call. It is a good idea to use these functions rather than alternatives. To see whether a function is handled specially by the compiler, examine its `byte-compile` property. If the property is non-`nil`, then the function is handled specially.

  For example, the following input will show you that `aref` is compiled specially (see Section 6.3 [Array Functions], page 94, vol. 1) while `elt` is not (see Section 6.1 [Sequence Functions], page 91, vol. 1):

  ```
  (get 'aref 'byte-compile)
       ⇒ byte-compile-two-args
  ```

  ```
  (get 'elt 'byte-compile)
       ⇒ nil
  ```

- If calling a small function accounts for a substantial part of your program's running time, make the function inline. This eliminates the function call overhead. Since making a function inline reduces the flexibility of changing the program, don't do it unless it gives a noticeable speedup in something slow enough that users care about the speed. See Section 11.9 [Inline Functions], page 171, vol. 1.

A.3 Tips for Documentation Strings

Here are some tips for the writing of documentation strings.

- Every command, function, or variable intended for users to know about should have a documentation string.

- An internal variable or subroutine of a Lisp program might as well have a documentation string. In earlier Emacs versions, you could save space by using a comment instead of a documentation string, but that is no longer the case.

- The first line of the documentation string should consist of one or two complete sentences that stand on their own as a summary. `M-x apropos` displays just the first line, and if it doesn't stand on its own, the result looks bad. In particular, start the first line with a capital letter and end with a period.

  The documentation string can have additional lines that expand on the details of how to use the function or variable. The additional lines should be made up of complete sentences also, but they may be filled if that looks good.

- For consistency, phrase the verb in the first sentence of a documentation string as an infinitive with "to" omitted. For instance, use "Return the cons of A and B." in preference to "Returns the cons of A and B." Usually it looks good to do likewise for the rest of the first paragraph. Subsequent paragraphs usually look better if they have proper subjects.

- Write documentation strings in the active voice, not the passive, and in the present tense, not the future. For instance, use "Return a list containing A and B." instead of "A list containing A and B will be returned."

- Avoid using the word "cause" (or its equivalents) unnecessarily. Instead of, "Cause Emacs to display text in boldface," write just "Display text in boldface."

- Do not start or end a documentation string with whitespace.

- Format the documentation string so that it fits in an Emacs window on an 80-column screen. It is a good idea for most lines to be no wider than 60 characters. The first line can be wider if necessary to fit the information that ought to be there.

  However, rather than simply filling the entire documentation string, you can make it much more readable by choosing line breaks with care. Use blank lines between topics if the documentation string is long.

- **Do not** indent subsequent lines of a documentation string so that the text is lined up in the source code with the text of the first line. This looks nice in the source code, but looks bizarre when users view the documentation. Remember that the indentation before the starting double-quote is not part of the string!

- A variable's documentation string should start with '*' if the variable is one that users would often want to set interactively. If the value is a long list, or a function, or if the variable would be set only in init files, then don't start the documentation string with '*'. See Section 10.5 [Defining Variables], page 142, vol. 1.

- The documentation string for a variable that is a yes-or-no flag should start with words such as "Non-nil means...", to make it clear that all non-`nil` values are equivalent and indicate explicitly what `nil` and non-`nil` mean.

- When a function's documentation string mentions the value of an argument of the function, use the argument name in capital letters as if it were a name for that value. Thus, the documentation string of the function / refers to its second argument as '`DIVISOR`', because the actual argument name is `divisor`.

  Also use all caps for meta-syntactic variables, such as when you show the decomposition of a list or vector into subunits, some of which may vary.

- When a documentation string refers to a Lisp symbol, write it as it would be printed (which usually means in lower case), with single-quotes around it. For example: ``lambda''. There are two exceptions: write `t` and `nil` without single-quotes.

- Don't write key sequences directly in documentation strings. Instead, use the '\\[...]' construct to stand for them. For example, instead of writing 'C-f', write '\\[forward-char]'. When Emacs displays the documentation string, it substitutes whatever key is currently bound to forward-char. (This is normally 'C-f', but it may be some other character if the user has moved key bindings.) See Section 21.3 [Keys in Documentation], page 4.

- In documentation strings for a major mode, you will want to refer to the key bindings of that mode's local map, rather than global ones. Therefore, use the construct '\\<...>' once in the documentation string to specify which key map to use. Do this before the first use of '\\[...]'. The text inside the '\\<...>' should be the name of the variable containing the local keymap for the major mode.

It is not practical to use '\\[...]' very many times, because display of the documentation string will become slow. So use this to describe the most important commands in your major mode, and then use '\\{...}' to display the rest of the mode's keymap.

A.4 Tips on Writing Comments

We recommend these conventions for where to put comments and how to indent them:

';'   Comments that start with a single semicolon, ';', should all be aligned to the same column on the right of the source code. Such comments usually explain how the code on the same line does its job. In Lisp mode and related modes, the M-; (indent-for-comment) command automatically inserts such a ';' in the right place, or aligns such a comment if it is already present.

This and following examples are taken from the Emacs sources.

```
(setq base-version-list                 ; there was a base
      (assoc (substring fn 0 start-vn)   ; version to which
             file-version-assoc-list))   ; this looks like
                                         ; a subversion
```

';;'   Comments that start with two semicolons, ';;', should be aligned to the same level of indentation as the code. Such comments usually describe the purpose of the following lines or the state of the program at that point. For example:

```
(prog1 (setq auto-fill-function
          ...
          ...
   ;; update mode line
   (force-mode-line-update)))
```

Every function that has no documentation string (because it is use only internally within the package it belongs to), should have instead a two-semicolon comment right before the function, explaining what the function does and how to call it properly. Explain precisely what each argument means and how the function interprets its possible values.

';;;'   Comments that start with three semicolons, ';;;', should start at the left margin. Such comments are used outside function definitions to make general statements explaining the design principles of the program. For example:

```
;;; This Lisp code is run in Emacs
;;; when it is to operate as a server
;;; for other processes.
```

Another use for triple-semicolon comments is for commenting out lines within a function. We use triple-semicolons for this precisely so that they remain at the left margin.

```
(defun foo (a)
;;; This is no longer necessary.
;;;   (force-mode-line-update)
    (message "Finished with %s" a))
```

';;;;'   Comments that start with four semicolons, ';;;;', should be aligned to the left margin and are used for headings of major sections of a program. For example:

```
;;;; The kill ring
```

The indentation commands of the Lisp modes in Emacs, such as M-; (indent-for-comment) and TAB (lisp-indent-line) automatically indent comments according to these conventions, depending on the number of semicolons. See section "Manipulating Comments" in *The GNU Emacs Manual*.

A.5 Conventional Headers for Emacs Libraries

Emacs 19 has conventions for using special comments in Lisp libraries to divide them into sections and give information such as who wrote them. This section explains these conventions. First, an example:

```
;;; lisp-mnt.el --- minor mode for Emacs Lisp maintainers

;; Copyright (C) 1992 Free Software Foundation, Inc.

;; Author: Eric S. Raymond <esr@snark.thyrsus.com>
;; Maintainer: Eric S. Raymond <esr@snark.thyrsus.com>
;; Created: 14 Jul 1992
;; Version: 1.2
;; Keywords: docs

;; This file is part of GNU Emacs.
```
copying permissions...

The very first line should have this format:

```
;;; filename --- description
```
The description should be complete in one line.

After the copyright notice come several *header comment* lines, each beginning with ';; *header-name*:'. Here is a table of the conventional possibilities for *header-name*:

'`Author`'   This line states the name and net address of at least the principal author of the library.

If there are multiple authors, you can list them on continuation lines led by `;;` and a tab character, like this:

```
;; Author: Ashwin Ram <Ram-Ashwin@cs.yale.edu>
;;         Dave Sill <de5@ornl.gov>
;;         Dave Brennan <brennan@hal.com>
;;         Eric Raymond <esr@snark.thyrsus.com>
```

'`Maintainer`'
This line should contain a single name/address as in the Author line, or an address only, or the string '`FSF`'. If there is no maintainer line, the person(s) in the Author field are presumed to be the maintainers. The example above is mildly bogus because the maintainer line is redundant.

The idea behind the '`Author`' and '`Maintainer`' lines is to make possible a Lisp function to "send mail to the maintainer" without having to mine the name out by hand.

Be sure to surround the network address with '`<...>`' if you include the person's full name as well as the network address.

'`Created`'   This optional line gives the original creation date of the file. For historical interest only.

'`Version`'   If you wish to record version numbers for the individual Lisp program, put them in this line.

'`Adapted-By`'
In this header line, place the name of the person who adapted the library for installation (to make it fit the style conventions, for example).

'`Keywords`'
This line lists keywords for the `finder-by-keyword` help command. This field is important; it's how people will find your package when they're looking for things by topic area. To separate the keywords, you can use spaces, commas, or both.

Just about every Lisp library ought to have the '`Author`' and '`Keywords`' header comment lines. Use the others if they are appropriate. You can also put in header lines with other header names—they have no standard meanings, so they can't do any harm.

We use additional stylized comments to subdivide the contents of the library file. Here is a table of them:

`;;; Commentary:`
>   This begins introductory comments that explain how the library works. It should come right after the copying permissions.

`;;; Change log:`
>   This begins change log information stored in the library file (if you store the change history there). For most of the Lisp files distributed with Emacs, the change history is kept in the file `ChangeLog` and not in the source file at all; these files do not have a `;;; Change log:` line.

`;;; Code:`
>   This begins the actual code of the program.

`;;; filename ends here`
>   This is the *footer line*; it appears at the very end of the file. Its purpose is to enable people to detect truncated versions of the file from the lack of a footer line.

Appendix B   GNU Emacs Internals

This chapter describes how the runnable Emacs executable is dumped with the preloaded Lisp libraries in it, how storage is allocated, and some internal aspects of GNU Emacs that may be of interest to C programmers.

B.1   Building Emacs

This section explains the steps involved in building the Emacs executable. You don't have to know this material to build and install Emacs, since the makefiles do all these things automatically. This information is pertinent to Emacs maintenance.

Compilation of the C source files in the 'src' directory produces an executable file called 'temacs', also called a *bare impure Emacs*. It contains the Emacs Lisp interpreter and I/O routines, but not the editing commands.

The command 'temacs -l loadup' uses 'temacs' to create the real runnable Emacs executable. These arguments direct 'temacs' to evaluate the Lisp files specified in the file 'loadup.el'. These files set up the normal Emacs editing environment, resulting in an Emacs that is still impure but no longer bare.

It takes a substantial time to load the standard Lisp files. Luckily, you don't have to do this each time you run Emacs; 'temacs' can dump out an executable program called 'emacs' that has these files preloaded. 'emacs' starts more quickly because it does not need to load the files. This is the Emacs executable that is normally installed.

To create 'emacs', use the command 'temacs -batch -l loadup dump'. The purpose of '-batch' here is to prevent 'temacs' from trying to initialize any of its data on the terminal; this ensures that the tables of terminal information are empty in the dumped Emacs. The argument 'dump' tells 'loadup.el' to dump a new executable named 'emacs'.

Some operating systems don't support dumping. On those systems, you must start Emacs with the 'temacs -l loadup' command each time you use it. This takes a substantial time, but since you need to start Emacs once a day at most—or once a week if you never log out—the extra time is not too severe a problem.

You can specify additional files to preload by writing a library named 'site-load.el' that loads them. You may need to increase the value of PURESIZE, in 'src/puresize.h', to make room for the additional files. (Try adding increments of 20000 until it is big enough.) However, the advantage of preloading additional files decreases as machines get faster. On modern machines, it is usually not advisable.

You can specify other Lisp expressions to execute just before dumping by putting them in a library named 'site-init.el'. However, if they might alter the behavior that users expect from an ordinary unmodified Emacs, it is better to put them in 'default.el', so that users can override them if they wish. See Section 34.1.1 [Start-up Summary], page 249.

Before 'loadup.el' dumps the new executable, it finds the documentation strings for primitive and preloaded functions (and variables) in the file where they are stored, by calling `Snarf-documentation` (see Section 21.2 [Accessing Documentation], page 2). These strings were moved out of the 'emacs' executable to make it smaller. See Section 21.1 [Documentation Basics], page 1.

dump-emacs *to-file from-file*   Function
> This function dumps the current state of Emacs into an executable file *to-file*. It takes symbols from *from-file* (this is normally the executable file 'temacs').
>
> If you use this function in an Emacs that was already dumped, you must set `command-line-processed` to `nil` first for good results. See Section 34.1.4 [Command Line Arguments], page 252.

emacs-version   Command
> This function returns a string describing the version of Emacs that is running. It is useful to include this string in bug reports.
>
> ```
> (emacs-version)
>      ⇒ "GNU Emacs 19.29.1 (i386-debian-linux) \
>  of Tue Jun  6 1995 on balloon"
> ```
>
> Called interactively, the function prints the same information in the echo area.

emacs-build-time   Variable
> The value of this variable is the time at which Emacs was built at the local site.
>
> ```
> emacs-build-time
>      ⇒ "Tue Jun  6 14:55:57 1995"
> ```

emacs-version   Variable
> The value of this variable is the version of Emacs being run. It is a string such as "19.29.1".

The following two variables did not exist before Emacs version 19.23, which reduces their usefulness at present, but we hope they will be convenient in the future.

emacs-major-version   *Variable*
> The major version number of Emacs, as an integer. For Emacs version
> 19.29, the value is 19.

emacs-minor-version   *Variable*
> The minor version number of Emacs, as an integer. For Emacs version
> 19.29, the value is 29.

B.2 Pure Storage

Emacs Lisp uses two kinds of storage for user-created Lisp objects: *normal storage* and *pure storage*. Normal storage is where all the new data created during an Emacs session is kept; see the following section for information on normal storage. Pure storage is used for certain data in the preloaded standard Lisp files—data that should never change during actual use of Emacs.

Pure storage is allocated only while 'temacs' is loading the standard preloaded Lisp libraries. In the file 'emacs', it is marked as read-only (on operating systems that permit this), so that the memory space can be shared by all the Emacs jobs running on the machine at once. Pure storage is not expandable; a fixed amount is allocated when Emacs is compiled, and if that is not sufficient for the preloaded libraries, 'temacs' crashes. If that happens, you must increase the compilation parameter PURESIZE in the file 'src/puresize.h'. This normally won't happen unless you try to preload additional libraries or add features to the standard ones.

purecopy *object*   *Function*
> This function makes a copy of *object* in pure storage and returns it. It
> copies strings by simply making a new string with the same characters
> in pure storage. It recursively copies the contents of vectors and cons
> cells. It does not make copies of other objects such as symbols, but just
> returns them unchanged. It signals an error if asked to copy markers.
>
> This function is a no-op except while Emacs is being built and dumped;
> it is usually called only in the file 'emacs/lisp/loaddefs.el', but a
> few packages call it just in case you decide to preload them.

pure-bytes-used   *Variable*
> The value of this variable is the number of bytes of pure storage allocated so far. Typically, in a dumped Emacs, this number is very close
> to the total amount of pure storage available—if it were not, we would
> preallocate less.

purify-flag   *Variable*
> This variable determines whether `defun` should make a copy of the
> function definition in pure storage. If it is non-`nil`, then the function
> definition is copied into pure storage.
>
> This flag is `t` while loading all of the basic functions for building Emacs
> initially (allowing those functions to be sharable and non-collectible).
> Dumping Emacs as an executable always writes `nil` in this variable,
> regardless of the value it actually has before and after dumping.
>
> You should not change this flag in a running Emacs.

B.3 Garbage Collection

When a program creates a list or the user defines a new function (such
as by loading a library), that data is placed in normal storage. If normal
storage runs low, then Emacs asks the operating system to allocate more
memory in blocks of 1k bytes. Each block is used for one type of Lisp
object, so symbols, cons cells, markers, etc., are segregated in distinct blocks
in memory. (Vectors, long strings, buffers and certain other editing types,
which are fairly large, are allocated in individual blocks, one per object,
while small strings are packed into blocks of 8k bytes.)

It is quite common to use some storage for a while, then release it by (for
example) killing a buffer or deleting the last pointer to an object. Emacs
provides a *garbage collector* to reclaim this abandoned storage. (This name
is traditional, but "garbage recycler" might be a more intuitive metaphor
for this facility.)

The garbage collector operates by finding and marking all Lisp objects
that are still accessible to Lisp programs. To begin with, it assumes all
the symbols, their values and associated function definitions, and any data
presently on the stack, are accessible. Any objects that can be reached
indirectly through other accessible objects are also accessible.

When marking is finished, all objects still unmarked are garbage. No
matter what the Lisp program or the user does, it is impossible to refer to
them, since there is no longer a way to reach them. Their space might as
well be reused, since no one will miss them. The second ("sweep") phase of
the garbage collector arranges to reuse them.

The sweep phase puts unused cons cells onto a *free list* for future allo-
cation; likewise for symbols and markers. It compacts the accessible strings
so they occupy fewer 8k blocks; then it frees the other 8k blocks. Vectors,
buffers, windows, and other large objects are individually allocated and freed
using `malloc` and `free`.

> **Common Lisp note:** Unlike other Lisps, GNU Emacs Lisp does
> not call the garbage collector when the free list is empty. Instead,

it simply requests the operating system to allocate more storage, and processing continues until `gc-cons-threshold` bytes have been used.

This means that you can make sure that the garbage collector will not run during a certain portion of a Lisp program by calling the garbage collector explicitly just before it (provided that portion of the program does not use so much space as to force a second garbage collection).

garbage-collect   Command

This command runs a garbage collection, and returns information on the amount of space in use. (Garbage collection can also occur spontaneously if you use more than `gc-cons-threshold` bytes of Lisp data since the previous garbage collection.)

`garbage-collect` returns a list containing the following information:

```
((used-conses . free-conses)
 (used-syms . free-syms)
 (used-markers . free-markers)
 used-string-chars
 used-vector-slots
 (used-floats . free-floats))
```

```
(garbage-collect)
    ⇒ ((3435 . 2332) (1688 . 0)
       (57 . 417) 24510 3839 (4 . 1))
```

Here is a table explaining each element:

used-conses
> The number of cons cells in use.

free-conses
> The number of cons cells for which space has been obtained from the operating system, but that are not currently being used.

used-syms The number of symbols in use.

free-syms The number of symbols for which space has been obtained from the operating system, but that are not currently being used.

used-markers
> The number of markers in use.

free-markers
> The number of markers for which space has been obtained from the operating system, but that are not currently being used.

used-string-chars
> The total size of all strings, in characters.

used-vector-slots
> The total number of elements of existing vectors.

used-floats
> The number of floats in use.

free-floats The number of floats for which space has been obtained from the operating system, but that are not currently being used.

gc-cons-threshold   User Option
> The value of this variable is the number of bytes of storage that must be allocated for Lisp objects after one garbage collection in order to trigger another garbage collection. A cons cell counts as eight bytes, a string as one byte per character plus a few bytes of overhead, and so on; space allocated to the contents of buffers does not count. Note that the subsequent garbage collection does not happen immediately when the threshold is exhausted, but only the next time the Lisp evaluator is called.

> The initial threshold value is 300,000. If you specify a larger value, garbage collection will happen less often. This reduces the amount of time spent garbage collecting, but increases total memory use. You may want to do this when running a program that creates lots of Lisp data.

> You can make collections more frequent by specifying a smaller value, down to 10,000. A value less than 10,000 will remain in effect only until the subsequent garbage collection, at which time `garbage-collect` will set the threshold back to 10,000.

memory-limit   Function
> This function returns the address of the last byte Emacs has allocated, divided by 1024. We divide the value by 1024 to make sure it fits in a Lisp integer.

> You can use this to get a general idea of how your actions affect the memory usage.

B.4 Writing Emacs Primitives

Lisp primitives are Lisp functions implemented in C. The details of interfacing the C function so that Lisp can call it are handled by a few C macros. The only way to really understand how to write new C code is to read the source, but we can explain some things here.

An example of a special form is the definition of or, from 'eval.c'. (An ordinary function would have the same general appearance.)

```
DEFUN ("or", For, Sor, 0, UNEVALLED, 0,
   "Eval args until one of them yields non-nil, then return that value.\n\
The remaining args are not evalled at all.\n\
If all args return nil, return nil.")
   (args)
      Lisp_Object args;
{
   register Lisp_Object val;
   Lisp_Object args_left;
   struct gcpro gcpro1;

   if (NULL (args))
     return Qnil;

   args_left = args;
   GCPRO1 (args_left);

   do
     {
       val = Feval (Fcar (args_left));
       if (!NULL (val))
         break;
       args_left = Fcdr (args_left);
     }
   while (!NULL (args_left));

   UNGCPRO;
   return val;
}
```

Let's start with a precise explanation of the arguments to the DEFUN macro. Here is a template for them:

DEFUN (*lname, fname, sname, min, max, interactive, doc*)

lname This is the name of the Lisp symbol to define as the function name; in the example above, it is or.

fname This is the C function name for this function. This is the name that is used in C code for calling the function. The name is, by convention, 'F' prepended to the Lisp name, with all dashes ('-') in the Lisp name changed to underscores. Thus, to call this function from C code, call For. Remember that the arguments must be of type Lisp_Object; various macros and functions for creating values of type `Lisp_Object` are declared in the file `lisp.h`.

sname
: This is a C variable name to use for a structure that holds the data for the subr object that represents the function in Lisp. This structure conveys the Lisp symbol name to the initialization routine that will create the symbol and store the subr object as its definition. By convention, this name is always *fname* with 'F' replaced with 'S'.

min
: This is the minimum number of arguments that the function requires. The function `or` allows a minimum of zero arguments.

max
: This is the maximum number of arguments that the function accepts, if there is a fixed maximum. Alternatively, it can be `UNEVALLED`, indicating a special form that receives unevaluated arguments, or `MANY`, indicating an unlimited number of evaluated arguments (the equivalent of `&rest`). Both `UNEVALLED` and `MANY` are macros. If *max* is a number, it may not be less than *min* and it may not be greater than seven.

interactive
: This is an interactive specification, a string such as might be used as the argument of `interactive` in a Lisp function. In the case of `or`, it is 0 (a null pointer), indicating that `or` cannot be called interactively. A value of `""` indicates a function that should receive no arguments when called interactively.

doc
: This is the documentation string. It is written just like a documentation string for a function defined in Lisp, except you must write '`\n\`' at the end of each line. In particular, the first line should be a single sentence.

After the call to the `DEFUN` macro, you must write the argument name list that every C function must have, followed by ordinary C declarations for the arguments. For a function with a fixed maximum number of arguments, declare a C argument for each Lisp argument, and give them all type `Lisp_Object`. When a Lisp function has no upper limit on the number of arguments, its implementation in C actually receives exactly two arguments: the first is the number of Lisp arguments, and the second is the address of a block containing their values. They have types `int` and `Lisp_Object *`.

Within the function `For` itself, note the use of the macros `GCPRO1` and `UNGCPRO`. `GCPRO1` is used to "protect" a variable from garbage collection—to inform the garbage collector that it must look in that variable and regard its contents as an accessible object. This is necessary whenever you call `Feval` or anything that can directly or indirectly call `Feval`. At such a time, any Lisp object that you intend to refer to again must be protected somehow.

`UNGCPRO` cancels the protection of the variables that are protected in the current function. It is necessary to do this explicitly.

For most data types, it suffices to protect at least one pointer to the object; as long as the object is not recycled, all pointers to it remain valid. This is not so for strings, because the garbage collector can move them. When the garbage collector moves a string, it relocates all the pointers it knows about; any other pointers become invalid. Therefore, you must protect all pointers to strings across any point where garbage collection may be possible.

The macro `GCPRO1` protects just one local variable. If you want to protect two, use `GCPRO2` instead; repeating `GCPRO1` will not work. Macros `GCPRO3` and `GCPRO4` also exist.

These macros implicitly use local variables such as `gcpro1`; you must declare these explicitly, with type `struct gcpro`. Thus, if you use `GCPRO2`, you must declare `gcpro1` and `gcpro2`. Alas, we can't explain all the tricky details here.

You must not use C initializers for static or global variables unless they are never written once Emacs is dumped. These variables with initializers are allocated in an area of memory that becomes read-only (on certain operating systems) as a result of dumping Emacs. See Section B.2 [Pure Storage], page 325.

Do not use static variables within functions—place all static variables at top level in the file. This is necessary because Emacs on some operating systems defines the keyword `static` as a null macro. (This definition is used because those systems put all variables declared static in a place that becomes read-only after dumping, whether they have initializers or not.)

Defining the C function is not enough to make a Lisp primitive available; you must also create the Lisp symbol for the primitive and store a suitable subr object in its function cell. The code looks like this:

```
defsubr (&subr-structure-name);
```

Here *subr-structure-name* is the name you used as the third argument to `DEFUN`.

If you add a new primitive to a file that already has Lisp primitives defined in it, find the function (near the end of the file) named `syms_of_something`, and add the call to `defsubr` there. If the file doesn't have this function, or if you create a new file, add to it a `syms_of_filename` (e.g., `syms_of_myfile`). Then find the spot in 'emacs.c' where all of these functions are called, and add a call to `syms_of_filename` there.

The function `syms_of_filename` is also the place to define any C variables that are to be visible as Lisp variables. `DEFVAR_LISP` makes a C variable of type `Lisp_Object` visible in Lisp. `DEFVAR_INT` makes a C variable of type `int` visible in Lisp with a value that is always an integer. `DEFVAR_BOOL` makes a C variable of type `int` visible in Lisp with a value that is either `t` or `nil`.

Here is another example function, with more complicated arguments. This comes from the code for the X Window System, and it demonstrates the use of macros and functions to manipulate Lisp objects.

```
DEFUN ("coordinates-in-window-p", Fcoordinates_in_window_p,
  Scoordinates_in_window_p, 2, 2,
  "xSpecify coordinate pair: \nXExpression which evals to window: ",
  "Return non-nil if POSITIONS is in WINDOW.\n\
\(POSITIONS is a list, (SCREEN-X SCREEN-Y)\)\n\
Returned value is list of positions expressed\n\
relative to window upper left corner.")
(coordinate, window)
     register Lisp_Object coordinate, window;
{
  register Lisp_Object xcoord, ycoord;

  if (!CONSP (coordinate)) wrong_type_argument (Qlistp, coordinate);
  CHECK_WINDOW (window, 2);
  xcoord = Fcar (coordinate);
  ycoord = Fcar (Fcdr (coordinate));
  CHECK_NUMBER (xcoord, 0);
  CHECK_NUMBER (ycoord, 1);
  if ((XINT (xcoord) < XINT (XWINDOW (window)->left))
      || (XINT (xcoord) >= (XINT (XWINDOW (window)->left)
                              + XINT (XWINDOW (window)->width))))
    return Qnil;
  XFASTINT (xcoord) -= XFASTINT (XWINDOW (window)->left);
  if (XINT (ycoord) == (screen_height - 1))
    return Qnil;
  if ((XINT (ycoord) < XINT (XWINDOW (window)->top))
      || (XINT (ycoord) >= (XINT (XWINDOW (window)->top)
                              + XINT (XWINDOW (window)->height)) - 1))
    return Qnil;
  XFASTINT (ycoord) -= XFASTINT (XWINDOW (window)->top);
  return (Fcons (xcoord, Fcons (ycoord, Qnil)));
}
```

Note that C code cannot call functions by name unless they are defined in C. The way to call a function written in Lisp is to use `Ffuncall`, which embodies the Lisp function `funcall`. Since the Lisp function `funcall` accepts an unlimited number of arguments, in C it takes two: the number of Lisp-level arguments, and a one-dimensional array containing their values. The first Lisp-level argument is the Lisp function to call, and the rest are the arguments to pass to it. Since `Ffuncall` can call the evaluator, you must protect pointers from garbage collection around the call to `Ffuncall`.

The C functions `call0`, `call1`, `call2`, and so on, provide handy ways to call a Lisp function conveniently with a fixed number of arguments. They work by calling `Ffuncall`.

'eval.c' is a very good file to look through for examples; 'lisp.h' contains the definitions for some important macros and functions.

B.5 Object Internals

GNU Emacs Lisp manipulates many different types of data. The actual data are stored in a heap and the only access that programs have to it is through pointers. Pointers are thirty-two bits wide in most implementations. Depending on the operating system and type of machine for which you compile Emacs, twenty-four to twenty-six bits are used to address the object, and the remaining six to eight bits are used for a tag that identifies the object's type.

Because Lisp objects are represented as tagged pointers, it is always possible to determine the Lisp data type of any object. The C data type `Lisp_Object` can hold any Lisp object of any data type. Ordinary variables have type `Lisp_Object`, which means they can hold any type of Lisp value; you can determine the actual data type only at run time. The same is true for function arguments; if you want a function to accept only a certain type of argument, you must check the type explicitly using a suitable predicate (see Section 2.5 [Type Predicates], page 35, vol. 1).

B.5.1 Buffer Internals

Buffers contain fields not directly accessible by the Lisp programmer. We describe them here, naming them by the names used in the C code. Many are accessible indirectly in Lisp programs via Lisp primitives.

name   The buffer name is a string that names the buffer. It is guaranteed to be unique. See Section 24.3 [Buffer Names], page 57.

save_modified
              This field contains the time when the buffer was last saved, as an integer. See Section 24.5 [Buffer Modification], page 61.

modtime   This field contains the modification time of the visited file. It is set when the file is written or read. Every time the buffer is written to the file, this field is compared to the modification time of the file. See Section 24.5 [Buffer Modification], page 61.

auto_save_modified
              This field contains the time when the buffer was last auto-saved.

last_window_start
              This field contains the window-start position in the buffer as of the last time the buffer was displayed in a window.

undo_list
> This field points to the buffer's undo list. See Section 29.9 [Undo], page 157.

syntax_table_v
> This field contains the syntax table for the buffer. See Chapter 31 [Syntax Tables], page 211.

downcase_table
> This field contains the conversion table for converting text to lower case. See Section 4.8 [Case Table], page 68, vol. 1.

upcase_table
> This field contains the conversion table for converting text to upper case. See Section 4.8 [Case Table], page 68, vol. 1.

case_canon_table
> This field contains the conversion table for canonicalizing text for case-folding search. See Section 4.8 [Case Table], page 68, vol. 1.

case_eqv_table
> This field contains the equivalence table for case-folding search. See Section 4.8 [Case Table], page 68, vol. 1.

display_table
> This field contains the buffer's display table, or nil if it doesn't have one. See Section 35.14 [Display Tables], page 294.

markers This field contains the chain of all markers that currently point into the buffer. Deletion of text in the buffer, and motion of the buffer's gap, must check each of these markers and perhaps update it. See Chapter 28 [Markers], page 133.

backed_up
> This field is a flag that tells whether a backup file has been made for the visited file of this buffer.

mark This field contains the mark for the buffer. The mark is a marker, hence it is also included on the list **markers**. See Section 28.6 [The Mark], page 137.

mark_active
> This field is non-nil if the buffer's mark is active.

local_var_alist
> This field contains the association list describing the variables local in this buffer, and their values, with the exception of local variables that have special slots in the buffer object. (Those slots are omitted from this table.) See Section 10.9 [Buffer-Local Variables], page 151, vol. 1.

base_buffer
> This field holds the buffer's base buffer (if it is an indirect buffer), or nil.

keymap
> This field holds the buffer's local keymap. See Chapter 19 [Keymaps], page 315, vol. 1.

overlay_center
> This field holds the current overlay center position. See Section 35.9 [Overlays], page 284.

overlays_before
> This field holds a list of the overlays in this buffer that end at or before the current overlay center position. They are sorted in order of decreasing end position.

overlays_after
> This field holds a list of the overlays in this buffer that end after the current overlay center position. They are sorted in order of increasing beginning position.

B.5.2 Window Internals

Windows have the following accessible fields:

frame
> The frame that this window is on.

mini_p
> Non-nil if this window is a minibuffer window.

buffer
> The buffer that the window is displaying. This may change often during the life of the window.

dedicated
> Non-nil if this window is dedicated to its buffer.

pointm
> This is the value of point in the current buffer when this window is selected; when it is not selected, it retains its previous value.

start
> The position in the buffer that is the first character to be displayed in the window.

force_start
> If this flag is non-nil, it says that the window has been scrolled explicitly by the Lisp program. This affects what the next redisplay does if point is off the screen: instead of scrolling the window to show the text around point, it moves point to a location that is on the screen.

last_modified
> The modified field of the window's buffer, as of the last time a redisplay completed in this window.

`last_point`
: The buffer's value of point, as of the last time a redisplay completed in this window.

`left`
: This is the left-hand edge of the window, measured in columns. (The leftmost column on the screen is column 0.)

`top`
: This is the top edge of the window, measured in lines. (The top line on the screen is line 0.)

`height`
: The height of the window, measured in lines.

`width`
: The width of the window, measured in columns.

`next`
: This is the window that is the next in the chain of siblings. It is `nil` in a window that is the rightmost or bottommost of a group of siblings.

`prev`
: This is the window that is the previous in the chain of siblings. It is `nil` in a window that is the leftmost or topmost of a group of siblings.

`parent`
: Internally, Emacs arranges windows in a tree; each group of siblings has a parent window whose area includes all the siblings. This field points to a window's parent.

    Parent windows do not display buffers, and play little role in display except to shape their child windows. Emacs Lisp programs usually have no access to the parent windows; they operate on the windows at the leaves of the tree, which actually display buffers.

`hscroll`
: This is the number of columns that the display in the window is scrolled horizontally to the left. Normally, this is 0.

`use_time`
: This is the last time that the window was selected. The function `get-lru-window` uses this field.

`display_table`
: The window's display table, or `nil` if none is specified for it.

`update_mode_line`
: Non-`nil` means this window's mode line needs to be updated.

`base_line_number`
: The line number of a certain position in the buffer, or `nil`. This is used for displaying the line number of point in the mode line.

`base_line_pos`
: The position in the buffer for which the line number is known, or `nil` meaning none is known.

`region_showing`
> If the region (or part of it) is highlighted in this window, this field holds the mark position that made one end of that region. Otherwise, this field is `nil`.

B.5.3 Process Internals

The fields of a process are:

`name`   A string, the name of the process.

`command`   A list containing the command arguments that were used to start this process.

`filter`   A function used to accept output from the process instead of a buffer, or `nil`.

`sentinel` A function called whenever the process receives a signal, or `nil`.

`buffer`   The associated buffer of the process.

`pid`   An integer, the Unix process ID.

`childp`   A flag, non-`nil` if this is really a child process. It is `nil` for a network connection.

`mark`   A marker indicating the position of the end of the last output from this process inserted into the buffer. This is often but not always the end of the buffer.

`kill_without_query`
> If this is non-`nil`, killing Emacs while this process is still running does not ask for confirmation about killing the process.

`raw_status_low`
`raw_status_high`
> These two fields record 16 bits each of the process status returned by the `wait` system call.

`status`   The process status, as `process-status` should return it.

`tick`
`update_tick`
> If these two fields are not equal, a change in the status of the process needs to be reported, either by running the sentinel or by inserting a message in the process buffer.

`pty_flag` Non-`nil` if communication with the subprocess uses a PTY; `nil` if it uses a pipe.

`infd`   The file descriptor for input from the process.

outfd   The file descriptor for output to the process.

subtty   The file descriptor for the terminal that the subprocess is using. (On some systems, there is no need to record this, so the value is nil.)

tty_name   The name of the terminal that the subprocess is using, or nil if it is using pipes.

Appendix C Standard Errors

Here is the complete list of the error symbols in standard Emacs, grouped by concept. The list includes each symbol's message (on the `error-message` property of the symbol) and a cross reference to a description of how the error can occur.

Each error symbol has an `error-conditions` property that is a list of symbols. Normally this list includes the error symbol itself and the symbol `error`. Occasionally it includes additional symbols, which are intermediate classifications, narrower than `error` but broader than a single error symbol. For example, all the errors in accessing files have the condition `file-error`.

As a special exception, the error symbol `quit` does not have the condition `error`, because quitting is not considered an error.

See Section 9.5.3 [Errors], page 128, vol. 1, for an explanation of how errors are generated and handled.

symbol   *string; reference.*

error   "error"
               See Section 9.5.3 [Errors], page 128, vol. 1.

quit   "Quit"
               See Section 18.8 [Quitting], page 305, vol. 1.

args-out-of-range
               "Args out of range"
               See Chapter 6 [Sequences Arrays Vectors], page 91, vol. 1.

arith-error
               "Arithmetic error"
               See / and % in Chapter 3 [Numbers], page 41, vol. 1.

beginning-of-buffer
               "Beginning of buffer"
               See Section 27.2 [Motion], page 120.

buffer-read-only
               "Buffer is read-only"
               See Section 24.7 [Read Only Buffers], page 63.

cyclic-function-indirection
               "Symbol's chain of function indirections contains a loop"

               See Section 8.2.4 [Function Indirection], page 114, vol. 1.

end-of-buffer
               "End of buffer"
               See Section 27.2 [Motion], page 120.

end-of-file
            "End of file during parsing"
            This is not a file-error.
            See Section 16.3 [Input Functions], page 244, vol. 1.

file-error
            This error and its subcategories do not have error-strings, be-
            cause the error message is constructed from the data items alone
            when the error condition file-error is present.
            See Chapter 22 [Files], page 11.

file-locked
            This is a file-error.
            See Section 22.5 [File Locks], page 19.

file-already-exists
            This is a file-error.
            See Section 22.4 [Writing to Files], page 18.

file-supersession
            This is a file-error.
            See Section 24.6 [Modification Time], page 61.

invalid-function
            "Invalid function"
            See Section 8.2.3 [Classifying Lists], page 113, vol. 1.

invalid-read-syntax
            "Invalid read syntax"
            See Section 16.3 [Input Functions], page 244, vol. 1.

invalid-regexp
            "Invalid regexp"
            See Section 30.2 [Regular Expressions], page 193.

no-catch   "No catch for tag"
            See Section 9.5.1 [Catch and Throw], page 125, vol. 1.

search-failed
            "Search failed"
            See Chapter 30 [Searching and Matching], page 191.

setting-constant
            "Attempt to set a constant symbol"
            The values of the symbols nil and t may not be changed.
            See Section 10.2 [Variables that Never Change], page 138, vol. 1.

undefined-color
            "Undefined color"
            See Section 26.19 [Color Names], page 116.

`void-function`
> "Symbol's function definition is void"
> See Section 11.8 [Function Cells], page 169, vol. 1.

`void-variable`
> "Symbol's value as variable is void"
> See Section 10.6 [Accessing Variables], page 145, vol. 1.

`wrong-number-of-arguments`
> "Wrong number of arguments"
> See Section 8.2.3 [Classifying Lists], page 113, vol. 1.

`wrong-type-argument`
> "Wrong type argument"
> See Section 2.5 [Type Predicates], page 35, vol. 1.

These error types, which are all classified as special cases of `arith-error`, can occur on certain systems for invalid use of mathematical functions.

`domain-error`
> "Arithmetic domain error"
> See Section 3.9 [Math Functions], page 53, vol. 1.

`overflow-error`
> "Arithmetic overflow error"
> See Section 3.9 [Math Functions], page 53, vol. 1.

`range-error`
> "Arithmetic range error"
> See Section 3.9 [Math Functions], page 53, vol. 1.

`singularity-error`
> "Arithmetic singularity error"
> See Section 3.9 [Math Functions], page 53, vol. 1.

`underflow-error`
> "Arithmetic underflow error"
> See Section 3.9 [Math Functions], page 53, vol. 1.

Appendix D Buffer-Local Variables

The table below lists the general-purpose Emacs variables that are automatically local (when set) in each buffer. Many Lisp packages define such variables for their internal use; we don't list them here.

`abbrev-mode`
> see Chapter 32 [Abbrevs], page 223

`auto-fill-function`
> see Section 29.13 [Auto Filling], page 164

`buffer-auto-save-file-name`
> see Section 23.2 [Auto-Saving], page 50

`buffer-backed-up`
> see Section 23.1 [Backup Files], page 45

`buffer-display-table`
> see Section 35.14 [Display Tables], page 294

`buffer-file-format`
> see Section 22.12 [Format Conversion], page 40

`buffer-file-name`
> see Section 24.4 [Buffer File Name], page 59

`buffer-file-number`
> see Section 24.4 [Buffer File Name], page 59

`buffer-file-truename`
> see Section 24.4 [Buffer File Name], page 59

`buffer-file-type`
> see Section 22.13 [Files and MS-DOS], page 42

`buffer-invisibility-spec`
> see Section 35.5 [Invisible Text], page 279

`buffer-offer-save`
> see Section 22.2 [Saving Buffers], page 14

`buffer-read-only`
> see Section 24.7 [Read Only Buffers], page 63

`buffer-saved-size`
> see Section 27.1 [Point], page 119

`buffer-undo-list`
> see Section 29.9 [Undo], page 157

`cache-long-line-scans`
> see Section 27.2.4 [Text Lines], page 122

mode-name
         see Section 20.3.2 [Mode Line Variables], page 356, vol. 1

overwrite-mode
         see Section 29.4 [Insertion], page 146

paragraph-separate
         see Section 30.8 [Standard Regexps], page 209

paragraph-start
         see Section 30.8 [Standard Regexps], page 209

point-before-scroll
         Used for communication between mouse commands and scroll-
         bar commands.

require-final-newline
         see Section 29.4 [Insertion], page 146

selective-display
         see Section 35.6 [Selective Display], page 280

selective-display-ellipses
         see Section 35.6 [Selective Display], page 280

tab-width
         see Section 35.13 [Usual Display], page 293

truncate-lines
         see Section 35.3 [Truncation], page 276

vc-mode   see Section 20.3.2 [Mode Line Variables], page 356, vol. 1

Appendix E Standard Keymaps

The following symbols are used as the names for various keymaps. Some of these exist when Emacs is first started, others are loaded only when their respective mode is used. This is not an exhaustive list.

Almost all of these maps are used as local maps. Indeed, of the modes that presently exist, only Vip mode and Terminal mode ever change the global keymap.

Buffer-menu-mode-map

A full keymap used by Buffer Menu mode.

c-mode-map

A sparse keymap used by C mode.

command-history-map

A full keymap used by Command History mode.

ctl-x-4-map

A sparse keymap for subcommands of the prefix C-x 4.

ctl-x-5-map

A sparse keymap for subcommands of the prefix C-x 5.

ctl-x-map

A full keymap for C-x commands.

debugger-mode-map

A full keymap used by Debugger mode.

dired-mode-map

A full keymap for dired-mode buffers.

edit-abbrevs-map

A sparse keymap used in edit-abbrevs.

edit-tab-stops-map

A sparse keymap used in edit-tab-stops.

electric-buffer-menu-mode-map

A full keymap used by Electric Buffer Menu mode.

electric-history-map

A full keymap used by Electric Command History mode.

emacs-lisp-mode-map

A sparse keymap used by Emacs Lisp mode.

facemenu-menu

The keymap that displays the Text Properties menu.

`facemenu-background-menu`

> The keymap that displays the Background Color submenu of the
> Text Properties menu.

`facemenu-face-menu`

> The keymap that displays the Face submenu of the Text Prop-
> erties menu.

`facemenu-foreground-menu`

> The keymap that displays the Foreground Color submenu of the
> Text Properties menu.

`facemenu-indentation-menu`

> The keymap that displays the Indentation submenu of the Text
> Properties menu.

`facemenu-justification-menu`

> The keymap that displays the Justification submenu of the Text
> Properties menu.

`facemenu-special-menu`

> The keymap that displays the Special Props submenu of the
> Text Properties menu.

`function-key-map`

> The keymap for translating keypad and function keys.
> If there are none, then it contains an empty sparse keymap.

`fundamental-mode-map`

> The local keymap for Fundamental mode.
> It is empty and should not be changed.

`Helper-help-map`

> A full keymap used by the help utility package.
> It has the same keymap in its value cell and in its function cell.

`Info-edit-map`

> A sparse keymap used by the e command of Info.

`Info-mode-map`

> A sparse keymap containing Info commands.

`isearch-mode-map`

> A keymap that defines the characters you can type within in-
> cremental search.

`key-translation-map`

> A keymap for translating keys. This one overrides ordinary key
> bindings, unlike `function-key-map`.

`lisp-interaction-mode-map`

> A sparse keymap used by Lisp mode.

`lisp-mode-map`

> A sparse keymap used by Lisp mode.

`menu-bar-edit-menu`

> The keymap which displays the Edit menu in the menu bar.

`menu-bar-files-menu`

> The keymap which displays the Files menu in the menu bar.

`menu-bar-help-menu`

> The keymap which displays the Help menu in the menu bar.

`menu-bar-search-menu`

> The keymap which displays the Search menu in the menu bar.

`menu-bar-tools-menu`

> The keymap which displays the Tools menu in the menu bar.

`mode-specific-map`

> The keymap for characters following `C-c`. Note, this is in the global map. This map is not actually mode specific: its name was chosen to be informative for the user in `C-h b` (display-bindings), where it describes the main use of the `C-c` prefix key.

`occur-mode-map`

> A local keymap used by Occur mode.

`query-replace-map`

> A local keymap used for responses in `query-replace` and related commands; also for `y-or-n-p` and `map-y-or-n-p`. The functions that use this map do not support prefix keys; they look up one event at a time.

`text-mode-map`

> A sparse keymap used by Text mode.

`view-mode-map`

> A full keymap used by View mode.

Appendix F Standard Hooks

The following is a list of hook variables that let you provide functions to be called from within Emacs on suitable occasions.

Most of these variables have names ending with '-hook'. They are *normal hooks*, run by means of `run-hooks`. The value of such a hook is a list of functions. The recommended way to put a new function on such a hook is to call `add-hook`. See Section 20.4 [Hooks], page 360, vol. 1, for more information about using hooks.

The variables whose names end in '-function' have single functions as their values. Usually there is a specific reason why the variable is not a normal hook, such as the need to pass arguments to the function. (In older Emacs versions, some of these variables had names ending in '-hook' even though they were not normal hooks.)

The variables whose names end in '-hooks' or '-functions' have lists of functions as their values, but these functions are called in a special way (they are passed arguments, or else their values are used).

```
activate-mark-hook
after-change-function
after-change-functions
after-init-hook
after-insert-file-functions
after-make-frame-hook
auto-fill-function
auto-save-hook
before-change-function
before-change-functions
before-init-hook
before-make-frame-hook
blink-paren-function
c-mode-hook
calendar-load-hook
command-history-hook
comment-indent-function
deactivate-mark-hook
diary-display-hook
diary-hook
dired-mode-hook
```

```
disabled-command-hook
edit-picture-hook
electric-buffer-menu-mode-hook
electric-command-history-hook
electric-help-mode-hook
emacs-lisp-mode-hook
find-file-hooks
find-file-not-found-hooks
first-change-hook
fortran-comment-hook
fortran-mode-hook
ftp-setup-write-file-hooks
ftp-write-file-hook
indent-mim-hook
initial-calendar-window-hook
kill-buffer-query-functions
kill-emacs-query-functions
LaTeX-mode-hook
ledit-mode-hook
lisp-indent-function
lisp-interaction-mode-hook
lisp-mode-hook
list-diary-entries-hook
m2-mode-hook
mail-mode-hook
mail-setup-hook
mark-diary-entries-hook
medit-mode-hook
mh-compose-letter-hook
mh-folder-mode-hook
mh-letter-mode-hook
mim-mode-hook
minibuffer-setup-hook
minibuffer-exit-hook
news-mode-hook
news-reply-mode-hook
```

```
news-setup-hook
nongregorian-diary-listing-hook
nongregorian-diary-marking-hook
nroff-mode-hook
outline-mode-hook
plain-TeX-mode-hook
post-command-hook
pre-abbrev-expand-hook
pre-command-hook
print-diary-entries-hook
prolog-mode-hook
protect-innocence-hook
rmail-edit-mode-hook
rmail-mode-hook
rmail-summary-mode-hook
scheme-indent-hook
scheme-mode-hook
scribe-mode-hook
shell-mode-hook
shell-set-directory-error-hook
suspend-hook
suspend-resume-hook
temp-buffer-show-function
term-setup-hook
terminal-mode-hook
terminal-mode-break-hook
TeX-mode-hook
text-mode-hook
today-visible-calendar-hook
today-invisible-calendar-hook
vi-mode-hook
view-hook
window-setup-hook
write-contents-hooks
write-file-hooks
write-region-annotate-functions
```

Index

All variables, functions, keys, programs, files, and concepts are in this one index. A Roman numeral I before a page number indicates that the reference is to that page in the first volume.

D

M

O

P

S